Alex

Building a Life

● ● ● ● ● ● ● ● ● ● ●

Alex
Building a Life

**The Story of an American Who Fell Defending Israel
Told in His Letters, Journals and Drawings**

Foreword by Sir Martin Gilbert

gefen publishing house
בית הוצאה לאור גפן

Design: AURAS Design

ISBN 965-229-160-9

Edition 9 8 7 6 5 4 3 2 1

Gefen Publishing House Ltd.   Gefen Books
POB 6056, Jerusalem   12 New St.
91060 Israel   Hewlett, N.Y. 11557 U.S.A.

Printed in the United States of America

Send for our free catalogue

Contents

Door to the Sinagoga Del Transito

21 · III · 83

Foreword

●●

I never met Alex Singer. But I feel, as every reader of this book will surely feel, very close to him. He was killed in battle on his twenty-fifth birthday. But through his thoughtful and evocative journal, his letters and his drawings, his character and ideas live on.

In 1983, during the last days of February and the first few days of March, I spent a week visiting refusenik families in their homes in Leningrad. It was a freezing, disagreeable few days, and the refuseniks were in a bad mood, unable to see how they would ever be allowed to leave the Soviet Union. I remember how, late on the Friday evening, when I visited the ebullient young Yevgenia Utevskaya and her friends, she had just been entertaining at Shabbat supper another visitor from abroad. He was a young man whom I must have passed on the dark, crumbling, stinking stairway. Given the nervous conditions which then attached to all such refusenik visits, however, we avoided both gaze and greeting as we shuffled past each other.

Yevgenia Utevskaya, a leader of the young religious refuseniks, had several times been warned by the KGB not to receive visitors from abroad. She told me, with great excitement, that a year earlier this same young man had heard her father, Lev Utevksii, give a talk in the United States about the refusenik problem. Her father was fighting not only for his daughter's emigration, but for the teaching of Jewish history to Soviet Jewish children, something that the Soviet authorities had made an illegal activity. The refuseniks had been so pleased that the young man had brought them kosher wine and matza, and had read the Friday evening service with them.

Somewhat to my amazement, the same young man who had been visiting Yevgenia Utevskaya for Shabbat supper—when he, like I an hour later, had twice seen a rat in the kitchen—had also just been at the home of Yevgeni and Irina Lein, and their son Alex, when I called on them very late the following night. I knew that the visitor's name was Alex, because the Leins were tremendously excited to have found someone with the same name as their son, and who was holding out to them the hand of contact and concern. Alex had impressed them by his warm character, his Jewish soul, and his love of Israel, the country they aspired to live in, and where they are now.

In one of his letters, Alex Singer describes the lecture that he heard Lev Utevskii give in February 1982. In another he describes the Shabbat supper (and the rats) at Yevgenia's apartment, and his evening meeting with Yevgeni Lein. The next morning he left Leningrad for London. His mission had brought great joy, as well as essential gifts, to the refuseniks. Today, in their homes in Israel, they remember him with affection.

Alex Singer's drawings, with which this book is illustrated, are a delight. They evoke places which many of us know well, including the London School of Economics, through whose portals students still flow; the Nada Bakery in Jerusalem, whose breads and cakes so many of us still devour; and even the cafe doorway near the Nevsky Prospekt where visitors to the refuseniks watched Russians eating their dishes of vanilla ice cream, in deepest midwinter.

Last week, when I attended the shloshim (memorial on the thirtieth day after death) for Yitzhak Rabin on Mount Herzl, I went to look at Alex's grave there, to say a prayer, and to place a stone. In seeing this book through to publication, Suzanne and Max Singer have created a lasting and poignant memorial to their remarkable son.

Sir Martin Gilbert
12 December 1995

Preface and Acknowledgments

. . . .

Alexander Learned Singer was born in White Plains, N.Y. on September 15, 1962. On the last day of 1984, having graduated from college at Cornell, he moved to Israel. In 1987, while serving in the Israeli army, he was killed in a battle with terrorists in Southern Lebanon on his 25th birthday.

Alex left three journals written while he was in the Israeli army, hundreds of letters and scores of drawings. They bring to life the period that began when he was a sophmore at Cornell University, getting ready to spend his junior year at the London School of Economics, and they end at a border outpost in southern Lebanon.

In this book Alex speaks through his letters and journals and drawings. Other than minor corrections in spelling and punctuation, and the regularization of words and names in Hebrew and Arabic, his writing has not been changed or "prettied up." The few words added for clarification are shown in brackets, but we have not used ellipses to show the many words that have been cut. Information about people, places, and events mentioned—and explanations of Hebrew and Arabic phrases—can be found in the Glossary on p. 259.

The necessary facts about Alex's life before 1982 can be summarized quickly. He lived with us, his older brother Saul, and his younger brothers Daniel and Benjy, in Croton-on-Hudson, N.Y., through the sixth grade, when we went to Israel to spend what we thought would be a year. Alex and his brothers attended public schools in Jerusalem, and our stay extended to four years, during the last of which Alex and Saul lived on Kibbutz Kissufim and went to the local kibbutz high school. In 1977 we returned to the States, moving to the Washington, D.C. area. Alex spent the next two years at Bethesda–Chevy Chase High School and then went on to college at Cornell.

The idea for this book came in the first weeks after Alex's death, but its accomplishment was spread over eight years, with the devoted help of many people.

The first task was gathering Alex's handwritten letters, most of which had been saved by those who received them, and were sent to us when we asked. Then the letters and journals had to be copied into a computer. Volunteers appeared, some whom we had not known before. For their help, as well as for the consolation they gave, we thank: Wendy Senor (who later married our son Saul), Stuart Rosenthal and Judy Katzoff (now married), Claire Landers and Steve Falk (now married), Sara Averick, Ellen Epstein, Miriam Cohen, Rochelle Thorman, Cindy Beres, Maryl Levine and Toby Dershowitz, and any other volunteers whose names we may have neglected to record.

After we had made a preliminary selection and editing of the hundreds of pages of Alex's writings, we were very grateful when novelist Mark Helprin carefully read the text and led us to editor Tom Johnson. Mark's determination to see Alex's writings published helped us in many ways, not least by his confidence when the task seemed formidable. Tom Johnson immersed himself in Alex's world, a world unfamiliar to him, but one which he became part of, and understood. He was able to use his writer's skill to cut away that which interfered with the flow of Alex's story—without omitting anything of significance. The carefully edited text that Tom Johnson produced is the basis of this book.

For his impatience to see Alex's book in the backpacks of young Jews and for his certainty that we could produce it ourselves, we thank our longtime friend and Sue's colleague, Hershel Shanks. He gave us his experienced judgment as editor of three magazines and as author of a number of books, including *The Art and Craft of Judging,* a collection of the opinions of Judge Learned Hand, after whom Alex received his middle name. Hershel goaded us to move ahead and infected us with the contagion of his energy to make things happen. Like Alex, whom he knew and remembers, Hershel compresses the time between ideas and action.

The design of this book is the work of Robert Sugar of Auras Design in Washington, D.C. Since Alex died, our friend Rob helped us many times with design work needed by the Alex Singer Project. In this book he was a partner who gave form to our partly defined thoughts. Production details were ably carried out by Mark Colliton, Terry Cohen and David Fox.

Cheryl McGowan and Eva Greene carefully typed and copyedited the book in its latest stages when we were pushing for quality and speed.

Susan Laden offered to find the printer who could do this book as we wished. Her generous and skilled assistance saved us wasteful floundering and mistakes.

The many contributors to the Alex Singer Project gave us the financial resources to prepare this book and to put it into the hands of those for whom Alex's life can be an inspiration. We are determined to let no one be without the book because they cannot afford to buy it. The Alex Singer Project contributors continue to make that possible.

One of Alex's great gifts to our family was his ability to draw us together through his love and concern for us and his three brothers. It has fallen to us to do most of the work needed for this book, as our sons are in Israel, busy with their growing families. But throughout we had the counsel and encouragement of Saul and Wendy, Daniel and Anat, and Benjy and Dafi. And all along we have turned to Jeanne, Max's mother, for her sensitive eye and keenly literate ear.

From the time Alex died we knew we were not interested in making monuments. The purpose of the Alex Singer Project is to continue Alex's work and his determination to improve the world and to demonstrate through his example how Judaism can enrich and beautify a fully modern life. This book allows Alex to speak to those who never knew him. It has been our loving responsibility to make it available to those who did not have the good fortune to cross his path.

The book is not the story of a life cut short; it is the full and joyful voice of a maturing mind and a questioning soul.

Suzanne and Max Singer
December 31, 1995
Alex Singer Project
5400 Greystone St.
Chevy Chase, MD 20815

Drawings and Photographs

"Let [young people] remember that there is meaning beyond absurdity.

Let them be sure that every deed counts, that every word has power.

...And, above all, let them remember to build a life as if it were a work of art."

—Rabbi Abraham Joshua Heschel,
television interview, 1972

1.
Jewish Footsteps in Europe

"The more I travel,
the more I love
letting things flow."

Cornell Blues

Jan. 28, 1982
[Ithaca, NY]

Dear Mom and Dad and Daniel and Benjy (and Dune),*

Cornell is like the blues. It's beautiful, full of friends, interesting things, and many good people...but it's still Cornell.... I watched the last few minutes of the Superbowl.... See you at Pesach.

L'hitraot [Hebrew, colloquially:
I'll be seeing you].
Love,
Alex

Conservative But No Idiot

Feb. 2 & 3, 1982
[Ithaca, NY]

Dear Family,

I went to a lecture by Lev Utevskii. It was impressive how much he says the Soviets oppose the teaching of history. They oppose teaching of Jewish history less than Christian underground education because the Jewish groups oppose the Soviet system by trying to leave the country but the Christian groups, without a homeland to leave to (a Christian Israel), oppose the system with proposals for reform and freedom—proposals which many Jews avoid making in order to protect their chances of being allowed out.

One thing that's made me very pleased about school is how well I've been received. I get the feeling that some of these profs think I'm a bit misguided in my "conservatism" but that I'm no idiot.

I'm going to bed now. I just listened to Josh White sing the blues and now Bob Marley is singing about how evil white people are. I still like the music.

L'hitraot,
Alex

*A glossary of terms and names mentioned in these letters is on page 259. "Alex's Family" is on page 267.

Empty and Beautiful Land

During the summer of 1982, Alex attended the Brandeis-Bardin Camp Institute (BCI), today called the Brandeis-Bardin Collegiate Institute, which provides an intensive immersion in Judaism for young adults. The experience had a lasting effect on him. Here he writes to Dolores O'Higgins, an Irish friend at Cornell.

August 1982

[Brandeis, CA]

Dear Dolores [O'Higgins],

I'm writing to you from Brandeis, California. The institute I'm attending is fascinating. It replaces the uncommitted lectures of Cornell with the highest level of intellectual discussion I have ever encountered. We are looking into questions I haven't ever thought about.

I was sorry to hear about you being worn to a shadow of your former self. If this goes on you'll be nothing more than a smile with an Irish accent—at least you'll be able to catch a Frisbee with your teeth.

It's really beautiful here in Southern CA. I'm in the mountains in a "camp" which could be a kibbutz in the Northern Galilee. All the land around is empty and beautiful.

Love,

Alex

Questions I Had Never Thought About

August 2, 1982

[Brandeis, CA]

Dear Grandma Jeanne,

.... BCI is totally isolated from the rest of the U.S. in hills which could easily be in the Northern Galilee around Almagor. Every day was full of the most stimulating activities I could ask for—the lectures dealt brilliantly with the questions which I have never really bothered to think about:

—Is there a God (logically)?

—What are the implications of the belief that man is good by nature?

—Is morality likely to continue to exist in a society that is secular?

Brandeis   Alex Singer 1982

Torah ark at BCI.

I never thought I would enjoy sitting every day for two weeks with an orthodox rabbi in a seminar studying the Talmud's discussion of Jewish law of war and killing. But I did. Brandeis also got me back to drawing. I did quite a few sketches which I'll show you.

Love,
Alex

On To London

In the fall of 1982, Alex began his junior year abroad at the London School of Economics.

September 1982
London

Dear Grandma, Grandpa, and Mu,

London is a very warm city in some ways. It doesn't pound you the way NYC does. The pubs are mellow and friendly, unlike American bars which have lots of noise and drunk people.

I'm reading a lot of morbid books now about suffering and death (and how they relate to faith and God) because I am very mixed up about those things—especially after BCI. It seems hard to have faith in a God who allowed the Holocaust to occur, but it is also hard to have any faith in anything other than something super-human after the Holocaust. If BCI did anything for me, it mixed me up sufficiently to start me reading about the different answers to the "big questions."

Be happy and busy. *Shana Tovah!* [Happy New Year!]

Love,
Alex

Happy But Lonely

Sept. 22, 1982
[London]

Dear Saul,

You should read Viktor Frankl's *Man's Search for Meaning....* London is very good but I miss the family.

Went to services at an orthodox shul [synagogue] in Central London. The rabbi couldn't get very good notes from the shofar and the black guy (with his own shofar) sitting next to us said that this meant that the coming years would be very bad for the enemies of the Jews....

We did a lot of talking, Mel and I. He's right. I do have to suspect my own correctness more often. I just assumed I was right in my fights with Cornell. I'm too damn over-confident.

All in all I'm happy but lonely.

> Love,
> Alex

Swordracks and Silk Hats

> Sept. 29, 1982
> [London]

Dear Mom and Dad,

Some random thoughts:

Yom Kippur: Two armed guards (unusual) outside the synagogue, candlelight inside, all new tunes, beautiful shofar—the sound was the perfect call to God that we're ready for a new year and to the people that Yom Kippur had meant something.

Today was my first day of being psyched for LSE. Now I'm looking forward to classes.

The "Burghers of Calais" by Rodin, in bronze, life size, is outside Parliament in a garden I'll go through every day on the way to LSE.

St. Paul's is quite incredible—both in its beauty and size, and the fact it wasn't destroyed in World War II. Bevis Marks Synagogue, also untouched, was built in 1701, has swordracks upstairs, no less than 15 Torah scrolls, original benches, bimah, chandeliers, and men in silk hats.

> Love,
> Alex

An Old Synagogue in London

October 4, 1982
[London]

Dear Mom and Dad,

I'm writing to y'all from a library in LSE with oriental carpets, chandeliers, and classical music playing. It's very nice.

Mom, you asked me about the Bevis Marks Synagogue. It is almost identical in structure to the genizah synagogue in Cairo—a second-story women's section, a bimah downstairs, and an ark for the torahs on the end wall. Brass chandeliers hang from the ceiling and illuminate the room with candles. The men almost all wear silk hats, and the atmosphere is friendly and neither affected nor ostentatious. I liked it. Some of the service was in Portuguese and I didn't know any of the tunes. That was the only bummer. There's a choir of about ten men and boys which sits on the bimah behind the Rabbi and which is so unprofessional, laidback, and unskilled as to be quite nice to listen to and sing with.

Love,
Alex

Hebrew on the Way to Windsor

Oct. 10, 1982
[London]

Dear Saul,

Today, I went to Windsor castle. I decided that I needed to get out of London so I took a shuttle bus to Waterloo Station, got a no-smoking car and started to read *Terrorism* by Walter Laqueur. A head came through a window of the car spewing Hebrew. I said, *"Me'eyfoh atem?"* [Where are you from?] She said, *"Me'israel kamuvan!"* [From Israel, of course!] These people, with their sixteen-year-old son, turned out to be from Arad. We sat together and talked the whole trip in Hebrew. (I've also found the *Reshet Bet* [Israeli radio] on my shortwave for news in Hebrew.)

The castle is very impressive—it's not too fortress-like and has beautiful views over the countryside that looks just like the picture you have in your mind of "English country side"—a winding small river, playing fields of Eton and forests, a small town.

A Gate at Windsor Castle   10 October, 1982 Alex Singer

I did two drawings on this outing—one of the castle's tower and another, from inside the "King's Drawing Room," of the countryside through a window. I'm really quite good at drawing (he said modestly).

When I got home I went up to Penny and Stanley's flat and had dinner with them and with a "Yager Lager"...(cheap beer). They're a nice couple—he's a black Zambian and she's a white English girl (23 and 19).... After dinner I went down to my flat and, listening to Radio Luxembourg, wrote a letter that went like this: "Dear Saul, Today I went to Windsor. I decided that I needed...."

> Love,
> Alex

Adjusting to LSE

> October 20, 1982
> [London]

Dear Mom, and Dad, and Daniel, and Benjy (in order of increasing height),

Things are changing very fast here. Since my visit to Oxford with Neil and Daniel Taub.... I've changed my outlook on LSE. I'm just going to attend the lectures I like and concentrate on Philip Windsor's seminar on strategic studies. I'll try to write at least one essay a week too which I'll discuss with my tutor. Windsor is incredibly highly recommended by Neil. I met with him yesterday and he said I could attend his seminar. I also showed him a short piece I wrote on Lebanon, which he agrees with except for one point which I changed. I've sent it off to *Commentary* and would be interested to see if they print it. I didn't tell NP [Norman Podhoretz] that I'm your son and since the letter is from London maybe he'll never know—don't tell him unless he asks.

Last night was wonderful. I decided to walk home from LSE even though it was late. It was so nice and dark out I decided to walk home on the other side of the river. I walked along the wide riverside path called (I think) the Queensway. I looked across the river at Parliament, Kings College, the Tate and most of London's other "finest." Everything was lit beautifully—Westminster Bridge was lit green. London is beautiful at night but rather dreary during days which are full of rain.

> Love,
> Alex

A Church with a Mikveh

October 27, 1982

[London]

Dear Ellen [Epstein],

LSE is an interesting place—it has an atmosphere very different from the University of London or Oxford or any other school. It is very casual, its teachers are all outspoken (though often conservative), and its students are so international that they seem to form a community very different (older too) from all others. I like it but I would also like to spend time in an Oxford-like setting for a year or so some day.

On my way to LSE, via a new route, I stopped—it was a beautiful day—at St. Mary's Church at Lambeth Palace. I did a drawing, in the cemetery (which turned out poorly) and while I was drawing an elderly lady opened the church. I went inside and the place had been turned into a shop, tea parlor, and the museum of the Tradescant Trust (named after John Tradescant who was a gardener to Charles I). The namesake of the trust is buried in the garden next to Captain Bligh. Inside is a full immersion bath (one of only two in Anglican churches in England) that is just like a *Mikveh* [Jewish ritual bath].

The nice thing about the miserable weather here is that it makes you appreciate the sunny days.

Love,

Alex

First Thoughts About Signing Up

October 29, 1982

[London]

Dear *Imma* and *Abba* [Hebrew: Mother and Father],

My biggest (possibly only) problem now relates to reading. I don't read fast enough, I remember little of what I read, and I'm not sure what to read from the huge list of things I was given.

I'm going to write one two-to-four-page paper every week. So far I've done a paper on the role of guerrilla warfare and one on military intervention. Michael Banks has seen the former and liked it a lot, told me it deserved a "high second or

The L.S.E.

June 13, 1983

London School of Economics.

maybe a low first" (B+ or A-), and gave good comments as to what could make it better. Each paper is a response to a question from earlier exams in my International Relations course; I try to answer it as I would on an exam. I think Banks is impressed with my work; he mentioned something about it being similar to that done by the fellow who was declared "General Course Student of the Year" last year (a wonderful thing to be declared since it is a key to other places—Oxford).

I feel that I should have a military experience in my life but the U.S. military is out (unless I'm drafted) and I'd feel funny joining the Israeli army as a college grad. I'll send you Amos Perlmutter's "Letter from Lebanon" which is in this month's *Encounter* magazine. It shows an *esprit de corps* which it would be a privilege to be part of. Don't take this letter too seriously; it's late and I'm in a state of shock because I did laundry tonight.

Love,

Alex

Alone in the Mist

November 3, 1982

Election Day

[London]

Dear Mom and Dad,

On Thursday was my lecture on Southern Asia which was not well delivered but so full of new info that I'll probably stick with it. Friday was the best lecture of the week on *International Communism* with Geoffrey Stein who always wears clothes that clash (purple jacket, green shirt, violet tie). Excellent lectures on Marxist theory, its problems, the realities which the ideals have to be measured against. GOOD STUFF.

I saw *Romeo and Juliet* tonight (alone—bummer) and then walked home. There was a very thick mist all around Whitehall and Westminster making the places mysterious.

L'hitraot,

Alex

Writing Something Good

November 3, 1982
[London]

Dear Saul,

First I'll be newsy then I'll give some advice. I saw the Queen, Di, and Chas today. I stopped at Westminster on the way to my one class and watched the parade which is the first stage of the Queen's opening of Parliament. The whole business struck me as sort of comical. The streets were lined with fur-hatted guards.

After the first set of carriages carrying officials (the Lord Mayor etc.) the royal pooper-scooper cart went by to make sure the Queen didn't have to see or (God forbid) ride over that which queens should not see.

It's 2:30 or so now and I'm sitting at a table looking out the bay window of my flat over St. George's Square with the Thames on my left. It's very quiet and I'm drinking tea.

I'm finding that I feel most satisfied with myself when I write something good. When all I do is go to lectures and read, I feel that I'm falling behind and get very depressed about my lousy memory, snail-like reading speed, inability to spel [sic], ten wpm typing. But when I write, I feel like I've just bitten into a York Peppermint Patty. So, I'm trying to write a short essay every week.

This week I've been having a lot of trouble with the question "What factors tend to limit wars? Are all wars limited?" I've written the damn thing three times but haven't been able to write what I'm trying to say. I like the LSE system of no exams during the year so far, but I might learn to hate it when exam-time comes around in June.

"The Lone Drainer...and pronto": an ad from the subway for the English equivalent of Roto Rooter.

I only hope that you're not as suicidal as your letter makes you sound—just keep remembering that things tend to work out well for people who have something to offer the world. (If I wasn't clear enough, you *do* have something to offer the world.)

Love,
Alex, a Learned singer

Depression Relieved by Drawing and Cheesecake

November 7, 1982

[London]

Dear Saul,

I went to Canterbury today. I sat in the front seat of the bus and talked to the driver. He was in the Navy for 24 years [and] he said he'd seen a lot of places. I asked if he had been to the Falkland Islands and he had, just before World War II. I asked where he was during the war. He was a P.O.W. in Japan! He said that when he and his other shipmates (on shore in Singapore) realized they wouldn't get out (their ship had left them) before the Japanese arrived, they went to a bar and were sloshed when they were taken prisoner.

The cathedral is very beautiful but the day was dreary and cold and wet and windy enough to make me slightly depressed. I did two drawings and did manage to find a good piece of cheesecake.

Love,

Alex

(your brother who is going into deep depression—suicidal almost—due to the lack of letters from home)

P.S. "But soft. What light through yonder window breaks. It is the east and Juliet is the sun...." (An ad for Juliet Light Beer—which doesn't exist but should.)

Pleased to Be Without a Camera

November 18, 1982

[London]

Dear Grandma Jeanne,

....I just returned from school and am sitting in my flat listening to BBC World Service on my shortwave radio. The news is not good but it's nowhere near as bad as I've heard since I arrived here.

LSE is still very good. I've cut down the number of lectures I am attending so that I have more reading time. Yesterday I read two books on the Israeli raid on the Osirak reactor in Iraq. One was very thrilling—verging on the "cheap novel" style, but very informative.... It's called *Two Minutes over Baghdad*.... I'm still draw-

February 22, 1983   My Flat

ing wherever I go—I did a couple of sketches at Canterbury, one at Cambridge, two at Hampton Court Palace, one on the Thames near my school.... I'm using watercolors on some of them on top of the ink. I'm still pleased I didn't bring a camera, but I don't know if I'll be able to draw fast enough when I start touring. (It's also hard to draw when it's very cold outside.)...

Love,

Alex

Encounter On a Train to Oxford

November 27, 1982

[London]

Dear Maternal and Paternal Parental Units,

Thanksgiving was very nice. I went up to Oxford on one of the modern fast trains which is very pleasant since it's perfectly smooth at 125 mph. I met some interesting people on the train but I don't feel like telling you about the seventeen-year-old girl who'd been kicked out of her house with $50 and whose mother married her ex-boyfriend, and who spent six months living in Italy with a man who owned a ranch, gave her a horse, diamonds and anything else until she got tired of it and hitchhiked home—to England—in 72 hours without sleep. I also don't want to tell you about the old guy who said that English beer hasn't been the same since it stopped coming in oak barrels.

I made chicken tonight which turned out wonderfully!

Love,

Alex

Sampling the Continent

December 19, 1982

[London]

Dear Deb[orah Wilburn],

Thanks for your letter. I just got back last night from a week of skiing in Val d'Isere in France. The Alps are beautiful. Ninety per cent of the skiing is far above the treeline and on the two sunny days we had we could see for miles (and miles and miles...oh yeah). I didn't ski very well since I had never really "done" powder before but I did have quite a few excellent runs. During the last day of skiing Josh and I had lunch at the restaurant at the top of one of the lifts and started the drinking for the day early (usually we waited until the 13 of us—who had rented two chalets—had gotten off the mountain). Skiing drunk is faster and more fun than any other way. That night we had a party in our chalet and people who we had met all through the day came. Unfortunately, I passed out rather early and woke up the next AM still drunk which made the bus ride out of town rather uncomfortable.

Now about me and London: the news is 1) I had a letter published in this month's *Commentary* magazine! 2) My courses are going incredibly well since I've done lots of writing and even a little thinking. 3) London is still wonderful but the weather here is miserable (cold and wet and windy and grey and dark and yeach). I live eight minutes' walk from the Tate Gallery, which has a beautiful exhibit now of the work of Jennifer Bartlett...the nicest paintings I've seen by a young artist in years. We have a bay window that looks out on a quiet, tree-lined square (St. George's) and a "gasfire" to keep the place warm. When I walk to school I go right along the river past Parliament and Big Ben.

In any case I remain an optimist and miss you. It would be nice to wander around Europe with you because I think we like to see the same kinds of things.

Love,

Alex

P.S. I recommend being rather deterministic about life—not planning too much—and remembering that you'll always find something. The key is the balance between living each day as if it were the last day of your life and living each as if you were to live forever. From the Talmud (I think).

Psyched for Visits

December 19, 1982

[London]

Dear Dolores [O'Higgins],

Thanks for your card. I will almost definitely be back in Cornell next year. My parental units (maternal and paternal) and Saul (my fraternal unit #1) are coming to visit this week; I'm psyched. Now it's Thursday night and Saul arrives tomorrow

Near the path to Lamorna   22 December 1982

AM.... Realizing that my family wouldn't be here for a few days, I decided to take a small trip in England. Cornwall sounded nice so I took the train to Plymouth (in Devon) and stayed there Tuesday night in a bed and breakfast. (I had the worst meal I've ever had that night in an Indian restaurant—painfully hot and lousy taste.) The next day I hitched to Penzance.... I ate in the Turk's Head Pub which was delicious but rather odd since the place was full of people on their way to a costume party.

After a nice night in a room with a view of the harbor, I went for one of the nicest walks I've ever had from Penzance to Lamorna. The walk was along a coastal path—there was no one else around and the sun kept popping out. The path went through a beautiful forest of old pines and along the moors.... I got to Lamorna and stopped in the...only pub—The Wink.... Then I hitched to Land's End so that I could say "I've been to Land's End." ...Merry Christmas.

Love,
Alex

Giving People Enthusiasm

January 10, 1983
[London]

Dear Janice and Dennis [Prager],

I received your letter last week. I liked what you said in the BCI News piece, especially your point about the press favoring neutrality over truth. People make accusations like "you can't be objective about Israel because you lived there." People feel that anyone with a link to an issue is automatically corrupted whether they are election experts looking at elections in El Salvador or Jews speaking about anti-semitism.

Saul and I are very interested in returning to BCI. Saul would make an excellent advisor and is very good about getting people excited about (Jewish) ideas by making them seem simple and important at the same time. As for myself, I'm not sure that it's right to become an advisor while feeling that I will gain more from participating in the program and hearing the ideas again than I have to offer. But I'm sure I could at least give people some enthusiasm with the optimism I'm always accused of having too much of.

Yours sincerely,
Alex

Sketching in hills near Jerusalem, 1974.

Bar Mitzvah at the Western Wall in Jerusalem, October 1975.

*A drawing of tractors at
Kibbutz Kissufim, 1977.
The only drawing Alex ever sold.*

*Receiving his paratrooper's
red beret at the end of the
55-mile march to the Western
Wall in Jerusalem, July 1985.*

With Daniel (left and Benjy at the completion of Sergeant's School April 1986.

With Daniel at the ceremony at the end of Alex officer course, October 1986.

At home in Chevy Chase, MD,
for his last visit, spring 1987.

Sketching in the City of David,
Jerusalem, May 1987.

Brotherly Advice

January 22, 1983

[London]

Dear Doobs [Daniel],

I've broken my 11th commandment and have not answered your letter on the same day I received it. Tough.

Thank you for the invitation to your graduation. I wish I could be there because finishing high school does mark a major turning point in your life. You cease to be a student and become...a student. The difference is that from now on you're one by choice and, given the freedom to choose, you can now appreciate learning more than ever before.

Saul left for Tufts this morning. We had a good visit and didn't fight too much. Yesterday we went up to Oxford and had a nice visit with Daniel Taub (from BCI) and a wonderful Shabbat.... It was the first time I'd ever heard the blessing over the candles done by more than one woman—this time it was one woman and two daughters all with nice (but high) voices. I love good food.

On the tube from the train station to my neighborhood we met an interesting dude. He was from Connecticut, used to work at Yale, is now an associate fellow at New College-Oxford, was working in London as a consultant on an educational movie, and had held the Dead Sea Scrolls in his hand. The guy's name was Hal (or something) Cohen and he had bigger feet than Saul's!

Love,

Alex

Chicken Soup and Proliferation

January 22, 1983

[London]

Dear *Imma* and *Abba*,

I had to write to you now because I'm in a good mood, am trying to put off doing an economics problem that was due two weeks ago—and because I made the best chicken soup I've ever had and am sitting listening to music, drinking [the soup] in front of my "gasfire."

Saul left yesterday. We had a good week together of classes. Friday and Thursday were especially good with an excellent seminar on "nucular" (Jimmy Carter) proliferation and an even better class with just eight students and Windsor on Clausewitz's *On War*—which gave me a wonderful understanding of what [Clausewitz] was trying to say. Dad, if you haven't read *On War* I think you'll like it. Saul was impressed too because Windsor wasn't at all superficial about Clausewitz's concepts and showed what is behind the oft-misquoted dictum of "war is nothing more than the continuation of politics by other means." Good stuff.

I got a very impressive letter from Benjy this week.

Love,

Alex

The Pain of Death

February 1, 1983

[London]

Dear Mom and Dad, Benj and the graduate,

I was very depressed today because my International Economics class isn't going well and I'm having trouble writing well and thinking efficiently.

I wrote to Grandpa last week and maybe I'll call too, but I don't know. I hope everything works out. I'm not sure death is something I fear at all. It is only bad for two reasons—the pain caused to your friends and relatives and the things you didn't get a chance to do. So, death after a long, full life leaves only the pain, and if people can see that death is just the last part of life even the pain should be lessened.

Love,

Alex

Jewish Law in a Wine Bar

February 9, 1983

[London]

Dear Grandma Jeanne,

Last night was quite wonderful. I went to dinner, a play, and a wine bar with a nice girl (since she's a feminist she'd say "woman" and there's no intermediate term in English like there is in Hebrew). Dinner was nice and the play was one of the best I've ever seen—it was called "Messiah" starring Maureen Lipman as a Jewish woman who survived the Chmielnicki pogroms of the Cossacks in the 1600s. She made the show and may well be the best actress I have ever seen. In the show she becomes a (reluctant at first) follower of one of Judaism's few false messiahs—Shabtai Zvi—who, along with Jesus of Nazareth 1600 years earlier, convinced many Jews that the messianic age was due.

After the play Lisa and I talked for a long time in a wine bar about Jewish law—a topic I hadn't discussed much at all since [BCI] this summer.

Love,
Alex

Shabbat in Oxford

Alex also talks about a trip he is planning to Russia.

February 11, 1983
[London]

Dear Mom and Dad and Benjy,

It's 1:20 a.m. now. I got back half an hour ago from a nice Shabbat in Oxford with Daniel Taub. The Jewish community in Oxford is very special and has a nice friendly feeling to it. I went to evening services and Shabbat dinner at the Oxford Jewish Center. The food was terrible but easily made up for by the people.

Daniel [Taub] gave me the name of someone to talk to here about what to do in Russia for the Jews. He says they generally speak very good Hebrew and have Russian accents. Maybe I'll teach some of them calligraphy with simple, hand-made pens. I'm looking forward to the trip and will be careful not to get myself kicked out. I assume that if the Soviets feel I'm seeing too many Jews they'll try to set me up.

Love,
Alex

Happy Anniversary, Whenever It Was

February 19, 1983
[London]

Dear Mom and Dad,

Happy anniversary! I wasn't sure when it was (I still am not sure) so I asked Benj to find out and tell me but I haven't got the word yet. What year were you married?

I had a great class with Windsor on Soviet strategic thought—really excellent explanation of why what's done is done, and how the thinking in the Soviet Union goes. I'm in the stage of my work now where I have a lot of ideas (on terrorism) but have yet to put down one of them. All is well in general.

I'M SORRY I DIDN'T CALL ON YOUR ANNIVERSARY (whenever it was).

Love,
Alex

Leaving for Leningrad

February 27, 1983
[London]

Dear Mom and Dad and Benj,

I leave tomorrow (actually later this morning as it is 1:30 a.m.) for Leningrad. I think this coming week will be one of the most interesting of my life and I'm psyched about it.

I will be careful but will also see to it that the things I'm taking in get to their destinations if at all possible. One of my best missions is legal. I'm delivering two books to the Director of the Hermitage Museum with instructions to hand them over personally.

What a world we live in—and what a world they live in.

Be well.

Don't worry.

Love,
Alex

Searching for Refuseniks in Leningrad

Until shortly before the breakup of the Soviet Union, Soviet citizens were generally for-bidden to leave. Judaism was of course oppressed, because communism denied God and suppressed all religions. Because of U.S. pressure, some Jews received visas to leave the country, but Jews who applied for visas to leave automatically lost their jobs and liveli-hood during what could be years of waiting. Jews in the United States and Israel tried to provide comfort and support. The number of Jews let out often varied widely from year to year, depending on relations between the superpowers.

This was the situation when Alex visited Leningrad to talk to "Refuseniks," Jews who had been refused visas or who were waiting and hoping for visas. In the years follow-ing the breakup of the Soviet Union, when Jews were freely allowed to leave, over 500,000 Jews emigrated to Israel. More than 100,000 came to the United States and Canada.

March 9, 1983

London

Dear Everyone,

On Sunday I returned from the most intensely different week I've ever expe-rienced. The previous Sunday I arrived in Leningrad on an Aeroflot flight with a group of eight Londoners.

Leningrad is a beautiful city. Its central area is little changed from the days of Peter the Great and if you took away the few cars, many busses and trams, and the neon signs which are on so many of the stores, you would see the same avenues, and frozen rivers and canals, and fur-hatted Russians that were there a hundred years ago. I went with the group to many of the city's treasures—the Hermitage with the best collection of Impressionist paintings I've ever seen (not to mention the icons), St. Isaak's Cathedral. The problem is there is more to Leningrad than just Petersburg.

The city seems to be crumbling everywhere—even at the Hermitage the plas-ter is falling off the outside of the building just as it is off the outside of almost every other building in the city. In my tourist hotel, tiles are falling off the walls in the bathrooms, the water comes out of the tap tasting like chlorine and looking like thin soup, and the construction of the building leaves many rooms very drafty.

As soon as you get away from buildings made for outsiders, the crumbling

St. Isaak's Cathedral   March 3, 1983

A Cafe doorway near Nevsky Prospect   March 2, 1983

comes closer to the surface. Toilet seats (when they are to be found at all) in public places are often made of plywood. The women shovelling the patched streets use primitive plywood shovels. Broken windows of shops seem never to be repaired as long as one pane is still intact. In fact it often seems that buildings and bridges have not been painted or patched since the "glorious revolution" of 1917.

The Soviets have added their own style of ugliness to the natural crumbling which might have occurred without them. This new contribution is mostly of drabness and uniformity. Shops look the same regardless of whether they are selling food, clothing, books, or furniture. The few cars (so few, in fact, that the city has barely any traffic lights and no traffic lane lines on the streets—they're simply not needed) all look like they came from a 1965 showroom of Fiat sedans which had been rejected for being too dull. In the shops the clothes look similarly dull, the covers of the books look like they were designed by the same "artist" and the furniture and fabric and baby carriages and everything else have the same cheapness and unoriginality to them.

The uniformity of products is complemented by uniformity over time. My visit was in below-zero February but the share of stores devoted to bathing suits and sandals was as large as that selling sweaters and boots. Ice cream sandwiches were being sold on the street. Although I never saw the large groups of people crowded around the ice cream sellers which I saw around the people selling hot meat-filled pastries, some people were actually eating them. In fact, when I popped into a cafe one night to get warm when it was so cold my eyes were hurting, all the tables were full of people eating dishes of vanilla ice cream. The oddities of the "System" in which the Russians live are only a background to the much more interesting oddities of the people themselves. I don't speak Russian and our guide would have been the only Russian I met at length had it not been for the list of names of English-speaking and Hebrew-speaking "refuseniks" which I smuggled in with me.

Refuseniks make up only a minority of the Jews in Russia and they really don't represent the "average" Russian. Of these "average" Russians, those who are smart, or unscrupulous, or Machiavellian enough to be corrupt can lead lives that are materially quite adequate. They supplement their meager Soviet incomes with earnings from a wide variety of illegal activities—usually related to black marketeering. They are very materialistic and are willing to pay exorbitant sums in order to look western and wealthy.

The names of the refuseniks I had came from two organizations in London which work for Soviet Jews. After several days of unsuccessful attempts to contact any of them, I went to the apartment of one (Leonid) where his Russian mother-in-law managed to get through on the phone to him at his work. I spoke to him in Hebrew and we arranged to meet that evening near the statue of Lenin at one of the Metro stops near his home.

When I arrived at the Metro station I was very worried because I saw that it had two exits and I didn't know which one to use. I picked one of them and when I reached the street I was very amused that I had worried at all because the statue of Lenin was huge and impossible to miss from either of the exits. Leonid and I went back down into the Metro and travelled to the neighborhood where he was to teach a Hebrew lesson. He teaches first grade Hebrew to seven people once a week while studying a third grade lesson himself. We met two of Leonid's students on the way to the apartment where the lesson was to be held but didn't walk with them to avoid attracting attention. I was the first guest lecturer they ever had.

The two and a half hours of the lesson went by very quickly. I spoke to them in slow Hebrew about Israel and the West in general and they tried to ask questions in Hebrew about me and my world. Often the questions became more important than the Hebrew and they reverted to Russian which Leonid translated for me. They wanted to know about Jerusalem, the kibbutz I used to live on, about how hard it was to travel in the West (they were very impressed at how easy I said it was to go from the U.S. to England and Israel), and they wanted to know why no one in the West had managed to get them out of Russia.

Like all refuseniks, Leonid doesn't have the chance to be corrupt so he has to live on 110 rubles a month, his salary as a neurologist in a hospital. He told me that in his hospital there aren't enough stretchers or beds or medicine, that people die every day in operations for lack of drugs, and that there are dead bodies all over. Apparently, there is only one good and stocked hospital in the city and that is reserved for the elite. He told me that the KGB doesn't always wait for an excuse to hassle refuseniks and that a friend of his had recently been pushed in a subway station, told he had assaulted the man who pushed him, and thrown into jail for fifteen days. He also said that the same week police and KGB had stopped three different attempts to do the traditional Purim acting out of Megillat Esther. They had blocked the entrances to the flats and kept

A bridge over a Leningrad Canal   March 5, 1983

Jews from going in (taking down the names of people who came).

Locating individual apartments in the USSR can be very difficult. After managing to find the right building on Morscoii Prospect where I was to meet the other refuseniks I had to walk completely around it before I could find the entrance (one of about ten) which I needed. The stairwells inside each entrance are usually filthy and this one, smelling awful, was no exception. Inside the apartment, where a refusenik named Jenia lives with her six-year-old son and an old woman (it is a communal flat), there were four other Jews: Michail, Mordechai, a man whose name I didn't catch, and a young woman named Sasha (Nehama is what she calls herself now). While Leonid is not a religious Jew, all of the people in Jenia's flat (except the old woman who I saw only for a moment) were religious. While Sasha and Jenia worked on dinner, the rest of us read through the Friday evening service in old prayer books while Moshe read a storybook in Russian. The woman in London who had given me the tapedeck for Leonid had also given me Jewish books to give to Sasha which I gave her with some kosher wine and matza which I brought from London. Since no kosher things are available in Leningrad, she was very happy to get my little care-package because Passover without wine and matzo is doubly difficult.

Partly because kosher food is unavailable and partly because they are so poor, Shabbat dinner in Leningrad consisted of potato salad, red cabbage salad, and sardines (I think) with pickles. The Shabbat splurging was evident in the main part of the meal only in the few limp scallions and rubbery carrots which had been cut into the food. Dessert was more lavish with lots of different cakes and cookies, chocolate which had been sent by Jenia's father from Israel and Israeli coffee from the same care-package.

Twice during the evening a rat showed itself in the kitchen and all attempts to lure it into a trap were unsuccessful. But the rat didn't really spoil the evening at all which was made a bit more festive with some vodka and a bottle of kosher liquor which Michail had brought up from Moscow. None of the refuseniks I met drink vodka the way most Russians do. While many of the people you see in the Metro at night are in vodka stupors or at least have vodka on their breath, refuseniks don't drink the same excessive way, if they drink at all.

Michail, who is nineteen but looks about thirty with his big beard, has not had a job since his short stint in the army which he spent shovelling. Jews have a difficult choice when it comes to the Soviet army—they can refuse to serve and go to jail for an average of two years or they can accept the draft if it comes and try to do some sort of work (like shovelling) in the army that is less likely to be used later to keep them in the country when they apply for exit visas. The problem is the authorities rarely differentiate between shovelling and sensitive work in the services and refuse ex-soldiers visas on the grounds they know "military secrets" for up to ten years. At dinner Sasha gave me a message from Leonid that he wanted to see me before I left and, after calling him at work the next day (Saturday), we arranged to meet at another Metro stop at nine o'clock that evening. I spent Saturday morning at the Dostoevsky Museum with the group. Afterwards I walked to what turned out to be Leningrad's only remaining working synagogue for a service I heard would start at noon. When I finally found the place about quarter-to-one the building was silent and all the doors were locked. I went up a staircase in an adjacent building also within the synagogue's courtyard. At the top of the second flight of the restroom-smelling stairs was a door to a small shul behind which an old man was sitting at a desk. He turned out to be the *shamash*, and in very Ashkenazi Hebrew told me the service had started at ten and had long since finished. He seemed very sorry that I had come all that way and had missed the service, so after showing me around the main synagogue building (easily the most beautiful synagogue I've seen), he pulled a bottle of vodka and some honey bread out of a little room next to the shul and we had a kiddush. The shamash was a wonderful old man reading out of a prayer-book that looked almost as old as his eighty years and the synagogue's ninety. He had lots of stories and customs to tell me from not downing the vodka in one gulp to splitting each piece of bread in half before eating it. When he heard that I was a Levite he gave me a big kiss and said that because he was a Cohen he could give me a priestly blessing (which I think was special for Levites). I only wish I could have understood a bit more of what he was saying.

At nine I met Leonid and we tried to find a cafe where we could sit and talk. All the cafes closed at nine so when we walked past a big tourist hotel I suggested that we sit in the lobby. Leonid was worried that they wouldn't let him in, as Russians are generally not allowed into hotels without a pass. I told him that I could play "dumb American" and we had no trouble getting in. The things Leonid was most interested in having me try to get him were quality clothes for his two- and five-year-old sons, vitamins, and books on neurology so that he can keep up with his field. In many ways he is lucky he is working as a neurologist now. Most refuseniks have trouble finding work at all and when they do, it is often totally unrelated to their

Statue of Pushkin with Russian Museum behind   March 2, 1983

skills. The man I met next that night [Yevgeny] has a doctorate in mathematics and is a computer specialist—he now works as an apprentice to a coal stoker for 65 rubles a month.

Yevgeny had started in early 1981 to organize a course on Jewish history and culture. After being turned down when he tried to reserve a lecture hall, the lectures began in various apartments. I think that he said that the police and the KGB prevented one lecture the same way they stopped the performance of the megillah this year—by blocking the entrance to the flat where the lecture was to take place. In any case, on May 10, 1981, 20 security men entered his apartment while 70 people were there for a lecture. They started to take names and photographs of the participants and, when they began to rough up some people and Yevgeny moved towards them, they took him and (I think) some others and threw them into prison.

The prison cell was seven square meters in area and had in it four beds and seven or eight other prisoners who were not dissidents but real criminals. Yevgeny slept on the floor. He was there for two months without seeing a lawyer or even the prosecutor. Only then was he told that he had kicked a KGB [agent] and would stand trial. Half a month later the trial began. Yevgeny had met the state-provided lawyer for the first time only two days before. The lawyer was remarkably frank and said that, as Yevgeny's case was a political one (despite the fact that he was to be tried as a criminal), there was little he could do to help him and that he would be likely to get off more easily if he pleaded guilty. He was innocent and decided to defend himself in court.

Yevgeny gave a long testimony which stressed how his constitutional guarantees had been denied him again and again, but when the proceedings of the trials were printed, his testimony had been reduced to one paragraph. The maximum penalty for Yevgeny's "crime" is five years (the minimum is one year) so he considered it quite a victory when he heard he had only gotten two years in exile as punishment. He felt that only because his testimony was so overwhelmingly convincing [he had] not gotten a longer term of the harsher (prison) type of punishment.

The rail trip to Siberia was divided into two three-day and one one-day legs with stops in intermediate prisons along the way. The railcar he was in looked normal from the outside, but inside was divided into cells. Yevgeny's was six square meters and had three layers of two cots each. There were sixteen criminals in his cell and they had to sit on top of each other in order to fit. He didn't eat during the train travel because the only food that was given them was salted fish and since no water was given he preferred to stay hungry.

Yevgeny arrived in his town of exile in November, six and a half months after being thrown into jail. When he arrived, it was twenty-five degrees below zero and he was still wearing the clothes he had been arrested in in May. Irina soon joined her husband in Siberia and brought with her money, warm clothing and the Soviet legal code.

The exile town, being an exile for criminals more often than dissidents, was not a safe place. Along with the problems of having no running water or toilet inside (and negative temperatures more common than not) there was thus the danger of unlit streets. Yevgeny told me that people were killed there every day. He spent little time in the street, working in a factory and writing an appeal when he was home. The appeal ran along the same lines as his testimony in court, stating the various articles of the constitution and legal code at the top of each paragraph with how each had been violated in his case below.

The appeal, combined with lots of international pressure on his behalf, led to Yevgeny's release after six and a half months in Siberia. He showed me a letter from a mathematical society in the U.S. which had made him an honorary member and he said he thought it had been very important in securing his release. From the time of his arrest to his release were thirteen months. He told me that when he landed in Leningrad he was put into a black car on the runway and he thought he was being arrested again. It turned out that there had been a lot of people waiting to greet him at the airport and the Soviets didn't want a scene so they drove him and Irina to their flat.

After the celebration of his return, Yevgeny tried for six months to find a job— a period which ended with him stoking coal. His problems came from the Catch-22 nature of the Soviet employment system. Yevgeny was told he could not work in the sensitive area of computers (his specialty), but when he applied for unskilled work he was told that he was overqualified. His current job stoking pays him only fifteen rubles a month more than his rent. He is lucky enough to be able to earn money on the side legally by tutoring math. Without his stoking job, which he only keeps to insure himself against being arrested as a parasite, he would probably have been in prison again by now. As the two of them walked me back to the Metro station at half past midnight Yevgeny pointed to a spot near his building where Sasha had been attacked a few months earlier by two men. After being refused visas themselves five years ago their daughter lost her job and place in university. Attacks like the one she experienced have happened to four (I think) other refuseniks. It was clear that Sasha's attackers were government agents because after her father and another man, hearing screams, had jumped the two men and caught one, the man they caught was released immediately after they brought him to the police. Sasha, then, had nothing to lose by applying for a visa (which she did) as her life had already been made intolerable by her parents' application to leave.

The train I caught back to my hotel was the last one of the night and as I rode the escalator out of the Metro at one-fifteen the lights were turned out in the escalator tube. I had none of the trouble the next morning getting through customs that I've heard some people who have visited refuseniks have encountered.

Go to the Soviet Union because it is almost impossible to conceive of how different it is without seeing it (even if only for a short time); and see if there is anything you can do for Soviet Jews from wherever you are because, while visits are the most important gifts they can have, gifts short of visits do make a big difference in their lives even if the gifts are no more than a bottle of vitamins or a pair of long underwear.

Shalom,

Alex

Bopping Through Europe Alone

March 10, 1983

London

Dear Saul,

My break starts on the 18th of March. I'm going to buy a rail pass and bop down to Spain for a week or so. Then Italy, where I'll meet Jill (from Cornell) in Florence. Then probably through Yugoslavia and by ship to Greece. I want to see Istanbul too but don't know if that'll work out. Whew. I'm psyched, but a little worried as I'll be travelling alone. I'll do one shitload of drawings and try to do serious "Jew-hopping"—visiting Jewish communities to see old shuls and old Jews. It should be interesting. Now I'm drinking sherry from an Aeroflot glass which I borrowed from the flight back to London.

In the public cafeteria we ate with aluminum silverware but in the tourist hotel we had caviar. Talk about classless societies.

L'hitraot,
Alex

P.S. I'm tired of being a student!

I'm tired of being a jackass!

I'm tired of being self-pitying!

I'm tired of being a hypocritical mixed-up advice-giver. Self-determination is not as easy as it sounds.

Surprise from Spacey Russophile

March 10, 1983

London

Dear Mommy and Daddy,

I just won L3.20 in the fruit machine at my pub but I'm still depressed.

Before I unfold my depression I'll answer your questions. Mom, my group included the American, Calvinist, non-leftist strategic studies student Peter, who told me about the trip [originally]. Annee—the French woman (about 40) who seemed to be a spacey Russophile interested only in Leningrad's beauties...until the last day when I found out that she had spent much of her time with refuseniks too, and the Russophilism was—beyond her love of the culture—a bit of an act. Liz (about 35)—a wonderful English woman who knew Russia and was both a culture lover and a Soviet hater (I think) while at the same time very radical looking smoking Russian cigarettes. Roberta—a Russophile (through and through I think) from Canada originally. Alice and Tony, two English students who came together and were the only ones...who neither knew any Russian nor had any people to visit—she an airhead and a nudnik, he a quiet sufferer. Roger—a tall thin English radical student who said toward the end of the trip that the week made him rethink some long and strongly held beliefs (leftist ones). The young and beautiful Jenny, who was in the same lonely position of Tony and Alice but nicer and better in general.

I got to know Roger and Liz quite well and liked them both. They neither interrogated me nor I them on political questions. We talked a lot about art and life in the USSR today—prices, jobs, entertainment, trivial in London but interesting in Leningrad.

Aeroflot was OK but slightly Soviet—the plane was clearly easily convertible into a military vehicle because the carpets kept sliding around and the seats, bolted to the floor in tracks, had not been evenly spaced so that on the way to Russia I had no leg room and on the way home I had more than a Western first-class seat (Aeroflot is classless).

I didn't go to Moscow. The trip was only to Leningrad. I stayed in a tourist hotel—the Gavan—which is on a large island of the city near a neighborhood "Palace of Culture" (community center), a movie theater and a train depot. The typical huge blocks of flats were all around too. The hotel was comfortable but shoddy—the beds were sofas with sheets, lots of pillows, blankets, sharp soap, ragged towels that looked like they came from the hotel's restaurant. All the meals in the hotel (except for one night with chicken Kiev) were very dull—like poor cafeteria food except for the beer and caviar which we had with dinner. The group had its own table in the hotel restaurant and the menu was "pre-ordained."

Love,

Alex

P.S. The depression was my usual pissed-offedness at not being able to express myself in class the way I want to be understood. At least I can write.

Dangers and Commitments

During the spring of Alex's year at the London School of Economics, Daniel, three years younger than Alex, was living on an Israeli kibbutz as part of his senior year at the Charles E. Smith Jewish Day School, in Washington. Alex decided to visit Daniel during spring break.

After finishing high school, Daniel moved to Israel, became a citizen and was drafted into the Israeli army in October 1983. In this letter, Alex is already considering joining the Israeli army. Eventually, after completing college, Alex followed his younger brother's path.

March 12, 1983
London

Dear Doobs [Daniel],

As far as the Israeli army is concerned I am reluctant to give advice in this letter but I am an excellent advice-giver after a long talk, so let's talk! How's late March or early or mid-April sound? My five-week spring break begins on Friday and I'll be getting (somehow) to Israel in April. As you may have heard, I was just in Leningrad for a week.

Had I gone to the IDF out of BCC [Bethesda Chevy Chase High School], I probably wouldn't have gone to Cornell—mainly because it is harder (but not necessarily worse) to enter university when you're 21 or 22 than 18. This doesn't mean that university is necessary—most people waste their school times. Right now, I'd probably say that in your position I'd be very likely to join the army rather than do more school, but that is by no means definite. You do also have to think about the dangers involved and the commitments joining now will mean later (reserve duty) and whether other thoughts about your future would be hurt by those commitments.

L'hitraot,
Alex

P.S. Don't bother to answer this letter as I'll see you before I'd get a letter.
P.P.S. In trying to weigh any advice that I give you, remember that it is coming from a very mixed up dude hence might be hypocritical.
P.P.P.S. Write down your thoughts as you have them so that you don't forget—even if you put them on scraps of paper all over the place—writing them down will help.
P4.s. I've never written a P4.s.

"Spain Is Perfect (Almost)"

March 23, 1983
Seville, Spain

Dear Saul,

I'm writing from a telephone office in Seville, Spain. In about one half hour they'll put a collect call to the U.S. through for me. Seville has the third-largest cathedral in the world, huge gardens, small alleys, and very funny people. They all smoke like chimneys and seem to consider it ridiculous that anyone should tell them when to smoke (hence the smoke-filled no-smoking cars in trains). They also litter as a hobby, but they do so in a funny way at times. While in the trains they don't hesitate to throw bottles, cigarette packs, papers etc. out the window. When they litter inside they're more discreet. In the bars they drop napkins (not bottles) on the floor very quietly—sort of letting their hand (with the paper) fall to their side and bringing it up empty. They litter so much in fact that there is a sign in the cathedral (!) saying not to drop paper on the floor.

But, aside from that, Spain is perfect (almost). Wine costs 75 cents a bottle, beer has 13% alcohol and is almost as cheap, and the Spanish idiosyncracies like littering and smoking are the only negative of a wonderful type of people—really. I've been speaking lots of Spanish (although I have an odd mental block which has made me forget how to say the number "9"), except for my short stints of Hebrew. I was on a train for a good three hours with two Israelis who worked for IBM, and today in the cathedral I hooked onto a group of Israelis.

I had a little trouble with the second group because I kept using Spanish for all the little words like "and," "if," "yes"...I do the same with Hebrew when I'm speaking Spanish.

Before I forget to put it down for posterity. The train to Burgos (Spain) stopped in between stations and lots of us got out along the tracks because we knew we weren't about to start again soon, because we saw the train staff running away from the train along the tracks we had just covered. It turned out that we had run over a 53-year-old man who had committed suicide by throwing himself under the train. I didn't see him or feel the thump and the odd thing is that it really didn't affect me or make me think about life or anything—whew!

Now I'm in my room in a "pension" right near the old quarter and the cathedral—only $4.00 for a nice room. I'm sharing it platonically with an American woman student I met on the train. She (Sue) is a student in Madrid for one term.

Love,

Alex

The Alhambra

March 25, 1983

Spain

Dear Mom and Dad and Benj,

I'm on the train from Granada to Cordoba. The hills here are like the Alhambra—rough and gray on the outside but bright soil below the crust. In the case of the Alhambra, this brightness is beautiful tiled Arabesque rooms inside a beautiful—but not ornate—building. All is well.... *Hasta la vista mis buenos parentes y hermano.* [Goodbye to my good parents and brother.]

Love,

Alex

P.S. The olive trees going by are wonderful.

"I'm Drawing Non-stop"

March 26, 1983

Babadilla, Spain

Dear Deb,

I'm standing outside a train station in a dinky town in southern Spain (Babadilla). It's so small that a flock of goats just walked by, and there's only one *panaderia* [bakery]. I'm on my way to Italy. Spain is beautiful and very different. I went past a butcher shop with little whole pigs in the window—one was dressed up with glasses and a hat. Hotels cost about $3 a night and beer is 25 cents a glass. I'm drawing non-stop. Here's one of the public toilets of Babadilla—probably the first time they've ever been drawn.

Be well.

Love,

Alex

A Drunk Anti-Semite in Cordoba

March 28, 1983

train, Italy

Dear Mom, Dad, Benj and Dune,

Just a few things before the train starts up again. I'm in Ventimiglia (Italy) just past Monaco and Nice on the Mediterranean coast. I've been in the compartment with two Italian couples all night—very nice. They have a five-language *dizzionario* which, combined with Spanish, allows us to communicate. They gave me a cup of *cafe*—not coffee (*very* strong stuff).

I had a whole day to spend in Barcelona before my 7:00 p.m. train. I wandered to Antonio Gaudi's Church of the Sacred Family with one of the girls from my compartment, did a drawing, fought my way through thousands of people attending an outdoor Palm Sunday mass outside the church to get back to the Metro, and left this girl to wander some more and draw on my own. I managed to get into the cathedral (old—not Gaudi) despite the throngs there and did my first drawing with live people—also of a mass.

I'm in a great mood and can look back at my anti-semitic experience without being at all pissed—only amazed. I met a dude (American) in a bar in Cordoba who came up to me and asked if I'd finished my drawing of Maimonides. He'd seen me doing it earlier. I ran into him again that night after visiting the Mosque. He turned out to be an English teacher who had been in Cordoba four years. He already had a bit to drink and I joined him, but for some reason I didn't get at all intoxicated despite having one drink after another as we talked. He kept getting drunker, but he had offered to let me stay on his floor if I was going to stay in Cordoba.... I was thinking that Cordoba is like Ithaca [N.Y.]—very relaxing and friendly (despite signs I had seen on the walls that not everyone was friendly—swastikas...and "kill the Jews" in Spanish—especially odd since there are no Jews in Cordoba). Then he said, "I've just raised my price 500 pesetas" (for sleeping on his floor). I said, "Why?" And he said, "I don't like your religion"—in all seriousness. I left Cordoba that night and still don't understand if this anti-semitism was a characteristic of his all the time or whether he was a generally tolerant person whose bigotry emerged in special cases. The evening was odd because I kept getting soberer as I drank and he got drunk. Maybe I sensed hostility and was protecting myself against it.

All is well, very well, and my Cordoba experience was interesting more than frightening.

Pesach is tonight. *Chag Samayach* [Happy Holiday].

Love,

Alex

Maimonedes in Plaza de Tiberias, Cordoba   25·II·83

Discovering A Walk on the Wall

April 7, 1983

Rodos, Greece

Dear Dad,

I'm writing in a Greek coffee-bar which you'd love. It's in an old, old, vaulted ceiling building with a pebble floor and a bare bulb—next to an old chandelier made of brass without candles or bulbs. The walls are lined with rickety tables and chairs filled with Greek men playing backgammon and drinking coffee—I'm the only traveler here.

Lindos is a postcard town of whitewashed houses nestled next to the sea and below its own acropolis—very touristy but still beautiful. After seeing what there was to see I started walking north and after a short ride in a Greek's pickup and four km or so of walking, I was picked up by a very nice German couple who helped me in my never-ending battle against my ever-increasing anti-German prejudice which I've had since my German Sinai trip [as a boy, with German tourists]. They're both money people—he an auditor, she a tax something-or-other. They're wealthy and were on Rhodes for a few days to get their yacht ready for summer. I went with them, sitting in the back of the jeep all the way back to Rodos on a beautiful roundabout route through the mountains of the island. Perfect pine-forests, dirt roads, no people around, a great afternoon (if a little windy).

I went to the one place in Rodos where it's possible to climb onto a wall of the city without going into someone's yard. (My route goes up a staircase, over a low wall, onto a roof and up a ten-foot climb onto the wall itself.) I walked left towards the harbor, which took me through high weeds getting me soaked for the second time that day—still, a beautiful walk.

This morning Solomon (of Connecticut), who had shown me the wonderful Rosa Lisa (where I am now) when I arrived, thanked me for telling him about the "high point of his visit to Rhodes"—the route onto the wall. I had found the route the day before yesterday and had, on my first time up, walked to the right, away from the harbor. Of course there is no one up there—even the Greeks don't know how or don't care to go up. From the wall (a wide, grassy walkway broken by occasional cisterns, and towers, with the crenellation on one side) you can see all of the old city and the huge, otherwise unnoticed, moat which is next to the wall. The walls were built by the Crusaders and are in essentially perfect shape. I walked for about

View from one of the towers in the wall of Rodos   6-IV-83

two miles (half-way around the city) before I could go no farther due to a locked gate. "The wall" is a beautiful walk in a beautiful city.

You'll also love the "Rosa Lisa"—eight little tables, a waiter—who sits at one table talking with friends and drinking retsina—and delicious, cheap food; Greek music on the jukebox which looks like a spaceship and is much older than I am. There is no rush here. I can come in at 7:30 and stay until 11:00 without ever feeling pressure to leave because it takes that long for food to come. The trick to enjoying travelling is putting yourself in the time-frame and speed of wherever you are. (The cat just jumped off my lap.)

I arrived in Rhodes—choosing it because it's on the boat route to Israel—after three hectic days of travel from Florence. From Florence I took a train to Venice where I checked my (your) backpack, donned my (your) raincoat, and in my (your) worn tennis shoes, set out to case the joint for a few hours before going to sleep on the floor of the train station. I've been in the Rosa Lisa for an hour or so now and my French fries still haven't come—and I'm one of three customers. (The others came after me but already have gotten theirs; I guess the waiter feels I'm in no hurry since I'm sitting in the corner writing this letter.)

I loved Venice for a few hours because the city is beautiful (unbelievably so) and my first hours there were in the evening when everything was closed and I wandered empty streets after going to a service (Friday evening) in the shul in the Ghetto. But after a night on the noisy floor and a day (until my 16:55 train) among the throngs of tourists (mostly German) I couldn't wait to leave.

The 16:55 train is the Venice–Athens "Express" stopping only in every other city in Yugoslavia. I had no trouble at the border, but while we sat on the Yugoslavian side, the Yugoslav police "raided" the train, tapping on walls and floors, and finding vast amounts of coffee (not drugs or guns). One stash was under the floor of the train near my compartment (where I spent an afternoon with two Yugoslavs, two Japanese, and one American girl).

Well, if you've been able to follow this letter up to now I'm impressed. The more I travel, the more I love "letting things flow," not planning or relying on my amazing luck to introduce me to interesting people and places. It's 22:30 now and my food came and was delicious. (I had Greek meatballs with my fries.) I'm going to bed now.

Leila Tov,

Alex

With Daniel In Israel

April 17, 1983
Israel

Dear Dad,

I'm sitting now in Daniel's room at [Kibbutz] Ein Tsurim, and have been having a wonderful visit both here and in Jerusalem where I stayed with Shlomo. It looks very much like you'll have two sons in the IDF in just over a year as my thinking about joining has suddenly solidified. Being here has made me feel very tired of being out of Israel. I've also realized you should be here too and that *aliyah* is best not put off forever. I don't feel like writing about that here, but I'll talk with you in June.

Love,
Alex

Following Daniel

As this short letter and the following one reflect, Alex was considerably affected by his trip to Israel to visit Daniel and Kibbutz Kissufim, where he had lived when he was 13, during his last year in Israel. At Kissufim Alex saw Israeli classmates who had fought in Lebanon when Israel attacked the PLO there. When Israel withdrew from Lebanon in 1985, it retained a military presence in an 8-mile strip of southern Lebanon known as the security zone. It was here that Alex was to die.

By the time of Alex's visit Daniel had decided to move to Israel after graduation from high school, where he would serve in the army like other Israelis.

April 23, 1983
London

Dear Grandma and Grandpa,

It's been a while since my last letter. I'm just getting back into the flow of things here in London again after my long wandering through Europe to Israel.
I dropped in on Daniel straight away after getting off the plane from Greece. He was surprised to see me (to say the least).

Mom looked fine too when she arrived a few days later. I also had a wonderful visit to my old kibbutz where I saw a lot of old classmates of mine who have all fought in Lebanon since the last time I saw them. I really felt like I should have been there too, and there's a good chance that I'll follow in Daniel's footsteps after I finish up at Cornell.

Good night. Be well.

Love,
Alex

Thinking About the Army and About Death

April 24, 1983
[London]

Dear Saul, Dad, and Benj,

I have a lot on my mind which a letter will help organize. Now I'm having trouble thinking about Israel, about the army, about timing and money. I'm very impatient to get back to Israel and until that impatience disappears I'll continue to have trouble appreciating LSE now and Cornell next year.

I have the feeling that I could get into the type of IDF unit I'm interested in, and that in such a unit things would be interesting and exciting for me and helpful to Israel. Since the security clearance might be hindered by your presence in the U.S., I might only get in through *protectzia*, if at all. If I couldn't get into such a unit I'm sure the less special units would be interesting, too, although I'd be willing to serve a little longer if the work was significantly better.

Saul, the kibbutz (Kissufim) was awesome. I took a bus down from Jerusalem on Tuesday afternoon and spent the afternoon and night down there. Mani, from the orchard, picked me up as I hitched from the Tel Gemma intersection, and I said to him that I remembered his face, and as a hint to who I was, I told him, "I'm Saul's brother." He said, "Oh, Alex?" He told me where I could find Beni's room so I went up and surprised him a little.

Beni is an excellent dude. He still works in *masgeria* (welding) and he got out of the army only a few months ago. Of course he was in Lebanon in the elite unit of the Golani. He was pissed most at the conduct of the war. He felt we didn't need to take Beaufort Castle because the war could have gone around it, and taking it cost too much (six lives). His unit took it. He was on alert while I was there, since Kissufim still is a "border kibbutz" and there are always people on alert. So he had a Kalachnikov by his bed. He sends greetings and says you should write to him.

The saddest thing on the kibbutz, which otherwise still has a good "feeling" to it, is that Yossi Levi's son Shai has leukemia. He was 12 or so when we left, and although he's in remission now (I saw him in the dining hall) his chances of living much longer are small. Death in war is both more glorious and less painful—in general easier—than death from disease.

Kissufim didn't lose anyone in Lebanon but Bet Sefer Nisui [The Experimental School] did—Yaron (Dad probably told you).

I've got to go to bed so instead of doing the usual and keeping this letter around for a week before I finish it, I'll send it now. PLEASE WRITE RIGHT AWAY with your plans for this summer. I still haven't heard from BCI about my "advisorship." They told me I was being considered but I had to say that I could only make the second session. I hope they ask me. I'd love to do it both for me and for them. I have done a lot of thinking on our issues (blah, blah, blah) even if I haven't become religious myself.

> *L'hitraot,*
> Alex

"I Feel Myself Almost Totally Invulnerable"

> April 27, 1983
> [London]

Dear Dad,

I started working on my terrorism paper yesterday, reading a book called *PLO—Strategy and Tactics* which is good on PLO history and PLO–Arab politics, but it barely touches on terrorism. My understanding is working out to be a patchwork of the various sources I have next to my bed now. I hope to start writing in a day or so.

Another thing on my mind is you. Since the middle of my visit in Israel I've felt it important for you and Mom to make aliyah. I understand that you don't feel that's possible now, with Benj in school, your business starting, and (maybe) reluctance on your part to move to a country where you don't know the language too well. But, I think that if aliyah was in the back of your mind you should think about shifting it forward. I'd love it if you could write to me about your thoughts about aliyah, how much Hebrew is a problem, whether you think there's work for you in Israel, whether kibbutz life has any attraction to you (although I suspect that kibbutzim won't usually take 53-year-olds.)

I know you like to hear your sons' opinions and I'm sorry this son isn't more coherent with his, but you know I've never planned too far ahead, and seeing you working hard on The Potomac Organization now, without money coming back yet, is a foreign experience to me—I've always been paid in cash for my work.

But for the first time I am now planning ahead and I like the feeling of thinking that I'll be in *Tzahal* in a little over a year (less than two years). I'm waiting with bated breath for the letter which Mat (Lt. Col.) promised me on how long I must serve and what the chances are of getting into what I called (in my letter to him) an "interesting unit," possibly in active intelligence.

The prospect of going into the army makes me happy in more ways than one. I like the idea of getting away from the hypocrisy of Cornell profs who teach "X" without ever having done "X." I also like the idea of being "in" at the same time that Daniel is, the idea of being in the best Armed Forces for the best country in the world, the shape I could get into, and a zillion other unmentionable reasons. (It's not "cool" to say you like the idea of going in the IDF because you want to kill people who are trying to destroy your country and your people—even your family.) I said to my friend Beni on Kissufim that it is much easier to die ("die" doesn't mean to be killed) in a war than of a disease like leukemia. But I'm not planning on dying soon. Now that I'm on the subject, an interesting thing about me (maybe lots of people) is that I feel myself almost totally invulnerable, while I tend to worry about other people even if they're doing things about which I wouldn't have second thoughts. And I am not reckless.

It was good to see *Imma* in Jerusalem and Doobs [Daniel], too. We're finally friends after all of these years of being just brothers.

Love,

Alex

Early Death

May 9, 1983
[London]

Dear Saul,

It was good to talk to you tonight.

I've actually been doing a lot of thinking about death recently—I think as a result of seeing the kid in the kibbutz who's going to die in a year (more or less) of leukemia. All the arguments about death as a beautiful conclusion to life don't jibe too well with unglorious early deaths like his. I'm really a priest—giving advice which, good or bad, comes from someone with little experience, knowledge, or "spiritual oneness."

Love,
Alex

Struggling with Death

May 10, 1983
[London]

Dear Saul,

I got your letter today....

Did you see the small notice that was in the London *Times* about the man who sacrificed his six-year-old son (by stabbing him to death) in the precinct of a temple in India? The boy was an offering to the temple deity. (It is 1983.) My roommate Bill asked what the difference was between the Isaac and Abraham story and the Indian one. I told him that the point of Abraham and Isaac is that Abe stopped because human life is not to be sacrificed. He said that he didn't see why Abe was a hero then for being willing to do it, and why God ordered Abe to do it in the first place. Interesting.

The year is passing quickly along (38 more days until my last exam), and the comet is passing slowly overhead (but it is cloudy).

Goodnight.

Love,
Alex

P.S. Deathwise. Same questions about Shai Levi (leukemia kid in Kissufim).

—While death is a beautiful end to a full life, what about a short one?

—Short vs. full distinction?

—How do you talk to Yossi Levi? (Shai's father?)

—Early death reaffirms the view that God is on vacation but other things point otherwise.

—If mourning is a time of solitude and separation from the world (at first), then how do families mourn?

—How can we, not believing in original sin, honestly say "*rofeh holim*" ["healer of the sick"] prayers? If He doesn't, why thank Him for it or ask.

Decision Time

May 11, 1983

[London]

Dear Mom and Dad,

I received long letters from both of you yesterday and this morning. Thank you. First of all, about reasons for going to the army: The things I wrote were more a stream of things that hit me when I think about *Tzahal* than the reasons for going. I will go because it's right for me and for Israel (in that order—for if it were the other order and I changed my mind I'd have to fool myself with rationalizations as to why I shouldn't go). The fitness attracts me but is not a reason—it's a bonus which it doesn't make sense to deny. The killing intrigues me but I don't think attracts me in any way. Killing "the enemy" doesn't mean killing its soldiers, it means destroying that which implements hatred—whether it is an organization, a person, a faction, an idea. Don't worry about my valuation of life. (Note: that letter is between the two of you only, please, as I don't mind giving you flow of consciousness, but I don't want my often odd thought patterns to be public.)

I haven't yet heard from the Lt. Col. who said he would send me info about my case.

Aliyah-wise, (sorry Dad) both of your thoughts sound good to me and are in many ways similar to mine as I too can't picture myself spending all my time in Israel after the army.

Mom, the Jewish Theological Seminary program in Jerusalem sounds interesting but I think the time has come for me to make some decisions, rather than only doing what's interesting all the time (if you know what I mean).

Keep those cards and letters coming.

Love,

Alex

A London Play

May 17, 1983

[London]

Israel = end of inferiority complex

Dear Deb,

I don't think your letters embarrass yourself. My wonderful grandmother [Jeanne] is here on a visit from NY. She started to paint in the mid-1970s after a life as a public-relations person with the U.S. delegation to the UN. Last night we went to see G.B. Shaw's *Heartbreak House* with Rex Harrison and Diana Rigg. It was no less than awesome—hilarious, confusing, perfectly acted, meaningful (but I don't know how). Harrison's character, Captain Shotover, says something like: man's concern for the world is just the overflow of his concern for himself; when he is a young man and his vessel is overflowing he cares about the world; when he is an old man and his vessel has dried up he is like a child again with no concerns greater than his own desires.*(Not the exact quote but you get the gist.) I hope it's not true.

Love,

Alex

Struggling with a Virus

At the end of the London winter, Alex caught a virus that dogged him for months, eventually turning into pneumonia. He refers to his health in this and later letters.

---

*At the end of this speech (in the second act of the play *Heartbreak House*,) Captain Shotover says to a young friend of his daughter: "At your age I looked for hardship, danger, horror, and death, that I might feel the life in me more intensely. I did not let the fear of death govern my life; and my reward was, I had my life."

May 19, 1983
[London]

Dear Dad, Mom, and Benj,

It has rained for the past 32 days in a row. (Typical weather report: "Rain, with scattered showers.")

Grandma is taking good care of me. I'm spending less time thinking about death nowadays, you'll be happy to hear. I went to the best gallery I've ever seen, on the fifth floor of a University of London building.

My paper is not going too well but it'll be okay. I sort of think this paper won't be up to my expectations or ability but I've learned a large amount writing it, both about how to write and terrorism, the Soviet Union, the KGB, and intellectual honesty or the lack of it.

I just had yogurt with apples as part of my Marxian diet. (The yogurt was communistic with Bulgarian cultures—not a contradiction in terms.)...

Love,
Me

May 21st

P.S. Now my little cold is a big fever—I'd guess around 102 or so. Grandma is taking wonderful care of me and I'll go to the doc on Monday. I've been sick off and on for three months and I'm sick of it!

Don't worry.

Girlwise, Sicknesswise, Examwise and Paperwise

May 31, 1983

Dear Saul,

.... Girlwise, while I seem much more open and etc. than you, I'm still a wimp at heart. Last year was my year for a zillion little relationships which shouldn't be called more than flirtations. So this year I decided to be a recluse and haven't even had one. In fact, the woman I've gotten closest to this year [Deborah Wilburn] I haven't even seen since August. She graduated Cornell last year and we've been in touch by mail since. The odd thing is that I think we're much closer now. The long-distance discussions haven't led our friendship to peter off. It's too bad Deb lives in Cedarville, Ohio, isn't Jewish, and won't be at school next year. She's one of those people who are perfect. She used to be a life-member of the NRA...but she gave it up.

Sicknesswise I've lost ten pounds (the positive part of my pneumonia), so that now I'm a trim (almost) 182 lbs. I'm feeling OK now, but my lung isn't finished coughing up scum. Just think, if I'd gotten this fifteen years ago, it could have killed me. With antibiotics its gone in a week!

Shit, Saul. I'm depressed, psyched, sick (the doc said I can't swim for a couple of weeks! oioi oioi). I just shaved for the first time in two weeks or so.

I'm worried about my week-away exam which I haven't even started studying for yet, and about the other exam that's even further off. I'm not a good student.

I've got lots of good, no, brilliant ideas for my terrorism stuff, but now I won't even get to finish the paper until I get home. What a bummer. Mega, even.

Write to me.

> Love,
> Alex

A Host of Inabilities

> June 2, 1983
> [London]

Dear Mom, Dad, Saul, Benj, Dan,

Some thoughts: I feel unmotivated. I want to do well on my exams but I can't get myself to engage in the inane activity of cramming information into my head so as to be able to spew it back in a painful three-hour spasm of conversations. It is almost impossible to answer four questions in three hours. Forty minutes each to organize an idea and an answer, organize the answer itself, outline it, and put it down with a neat conclusion to show that you understand what you've written. So much for exams.

I'm unmotivated to study, to write, to work. The things I'm looking forward to are travelling in Scotland, drawing, the flight home, onto which I intend to bring cheese and bread and a bottle of wine. I'd also like to start swimming again—not because I'm a superjock who enjoys swimming lengths but because it was getting me into very good shape and I liked the post-swim feeling of strength.

But I won't be swimming for two weeks. I've just started a whole new course of antibiotics. My right lung is beginning to hurt when I cough (which isn't a bad sign but isn't pleasant either). I have—on the positive side—done lots of reading since I got sick.

Hello. It's tomorrow now and I'm a bit less depressed. Not, mind you, because I've been able to work—rather because I went for a little walk and saw some of London that was new to me near Oxford Circus. But now I'm beat, wiped out, drained, etc.

Back to my *in*abilities. I am really bothered by being unable to convince people of the truth. I need to learn technique. I think I've learned some but what I've learned (that it is better to *seem* like you're not sure, like you're still weighing the arguments yourself... "what do you think?", etc.) bothers me for its slimy duplicitousness.

Today I went to Kings Road to watch the Punks. They are the epitome of all I despise—self-centered, hedonistic, masochistic, lecherous bums living on the welfare checks which others work hard to supply. My thoughts about the welfare state in general are not clear but what the punks are allowed clearly seems wrong because they don't work. I don't think society needs to support those who decide not to work, only those who can't work. Anyway, they are irritating.

I hope this hasn't left y'all too depressed.

G'night. Love,

Alex

Bouncing Back

June 6, 1983

Dear Benj, Daniel, Saul, Mom and Dad,

It's nice to be able to write to more than two or three of you at a time. [Everyone was back in Washington—except Alex. *–Ed.*] I just got back from the doctor who said my chest is sounding much better. I'll be fine soon. I'm sorry about that last depressing letter of mine. I'm fine now because I've made some decisions that solve the problems of the last letter.

I've decided not to take my Foreign Policy exam on the 17th. I will take Strategic Studies tomorrow (I think) but as I haven't studied for it I won't do overly well on it.

So, all is very well now. I'm getting better. I'll be swimming in two weeks or less (I hope). I'm psyched for Scotland. My rapidograph [drawing pen] is ready to go. I've gotten lots of reading done. I've lost weight. It's nice out and I'm not depressed.

Bye, Love,
Alex

Sick of Being Sick

June 13, 1983
[London]

Dear Shuls [Saul],

Your work sounds cool. I'm very angry about Soviet Jewry now, both at the system which created their problems and at our system for not working to help them more. But I'm a hypocritical SOB.

I'm tired of not being 100% well. I've been sick on and off for three and a half months, which is far too long.

I'm tired of owning things. I wish I had fewer possessions; but I guess too much is better than too little.

L'hitraot,
Alex

Broken Propaganda Machine

June 13, 1983
[London]

Dear Mom,

I realize that most of my letters have been directed toward Dad on El Salvador, etc. I guess that's because I no longer ask you as many questions as I used to, because as I become more independent I feel more reluctant to have others solving my "living problems." Dad just happens to be doing and thinking so much about those things which intrigue me the most, I end up writing more to him. In many ways this is odd because you've always been the parent I talked to most—both when I was at Cornell and during my summers at home—since you were at home.

But, don't worry. I can still talk to you. The problem is "what about," if my letters are to be anything more than reports of my activities.

I could write to you about my feelings and less political thoughts, but they tend to be rather depressing quite often. But since I know that you love to hear about my being depressed, here goes: The children of Soviet Jews make me saddest when I think of what they'll go through if they don't get out. I'm angry because their plight looks so hopeless because the VOA reported that the "Soviet Anti-Zionist Committee" said that there are essentially no longer Jews in the Soviet Union who still want to leave—based on the fact that the flow of visa applications has dropped to next to nothing. VOA didn't say anything else—they broadcast their Soviet propaganda straight-off, without mentioning that the decreased number of visa applications reflects hopelessness and fear more than contentment. And VOA is supposed to be OUR propaganda machine. OY!

Don't worry. I'm not as neurotic as I sound and I'm really not depressed. I'll be going to Scotland soon alone.

Love,

Alex

"I Love Desolate"

June 22, 1983

[London]

Dear Deb,

I wish you'd stop bumping your head on things. As for me: pneumonia—and promptly, stupidly, ran off to Scotland where within four days had worn myself down, in my antibiotic-induced-post-sickness-vulnerability-to-germs, into a nice fever and a bitching (pardon) case of the "runs." I decided it would be best for all concerned (myself—as I was traveling alone) to return to the city of my youth for, (as Samuel Johnson said), "if you are tired of London you are tired of life."

Anyway, I'm sitting on the balcony of a "flat" in my house which is empty as no one can afford to rent it and I have the key. It's nice out here.

Scotland was really quite beautiful. It's so far north that it doesn't get completely dark during the night at all. It's harder to describe beautiful things than ridiculous ones so I'll stop writing about Scotland now.

As far as my thoughts are concerned I sometimes think I'm going nuts. I'm sure this is largely due to the fact that I've spent so much time recently sick, doing nothing. I HATE doing nothing. I'm depressed about no longer feeling enthusiastic about what I do at school. I sense a futility in studying international relations (IR), government, economics. I'm not the one to be giving advice about the world if I have IR degrees. The only people who have that right are those with insight, and insight comes not from reading other's insights alone, but from doing. I'm a lousy student and a very, very good doer, yet I'm about to go to school for another year.

So it seems I could solve my problems by constantly telling myself that in a year the charade will be over and I'll be able to begin to do. The problem is that there are problems in the world I can help solve—not necessarily by originating solutions. But, while I feel I could do "world-helping" work, I'm neither a good convincer nor explainer and that pisses me off.

By the way, in response to your question about my finding beauty everyplace—the answer is yes especially if "everyplace" is desolate. I love desolate—you could even say that I have a desolate-fetish. Urban sprawl is a bit more difficult but not impossible.

Be well.

Love,

Alex

Interior of Firenze Synagogue   31-XII-83

Old City rooftops, Jerusalem   8-29-84   Alex Singer

2.
Cornell, Jerusalem and Jordan

....

*"I'm not worried
about the future,
only intrigued."*

Dad Won't Drive You to the Border

In the summer of 1983, Alex returned to Brandeis-Bardin Camp Institute for a month as an advisor. Here he reports on that experience after returning to Cornell for his senior year.

September 5, 1983
Ithaca, N.Y.

Dear Daniel,

I'm sitting in the periodical room of the Olin Library at Cornell. BCI was excellent.... I learned a lot from hearing the ideas a second time around and also from having to explain them to others. I've increased my observance level to include a more elevated Shabbat and much more *kashrut*. But I don't know how long I'll keep them up. I'll do my best.

I also got more emotionally shaken than I ever remember being—thanks to you. I was watching a play by BCIers about *akedat Yitzchak* in modern times, in which a father is driving his son off to the front to fight in Lebanon. It was only then that it hit me that you're gone...because I realize that Dad won't have the chance to drive his son to the border and you won't have the chance to be driven by your father.

I'll write again soon.

Love,
Alex

Sticking Around to Repair the World

September 17, 1983
Yom Kippur
[Cornell]

Dear Daniel,

I'm writing to you on Yom Kippur. I don't consider it a form of *malacha* [work, which is forbidden on the Sabbath].

The Kol Nidre service was nice, so was the service this morning, but it's not the same as Ein Tsurim [Daniel's kibbutz in Israel], or even the rest of Israel. When I was walking home some frat-boys saw me in my nice clothes and kipah [skullcap] and yelled, "Where's your calculator, your little beard?" as they drove by in their white Lincoln.

Dennis [Prager] sees anti-semitism as a result of Judaism the religion—not the "race" (which doesn't exist), and not the political situation of homelessness. Dennis's interpretation of anti-semitism means that he thinks assimilation could end the Jews's problems, but only if they cease being Jews (convert). So, since he wants Jews to stick around and *tikun olam* [repair the world], he wants to solve anti-semitism by working towards that very goal. When the rest of the world accepts the ethics which we follow, we'll be safe.

Gamar Chatimah Tova! [May you be inscribed for a good year!]

Love,

Alex

[Alex wrote on the back of the envelope:]

Daniel,

Congratulations on your Oct. 31 draft date [to enter the IDF].

"His Atheism is Thought Out"

September 1983

[Cornell]

Shalom David [Weiss],

I was sorry to miss you when you left BCI this summer, but I'm very grateful to have gotten to know you as much as I did. There is an interesting professor here at Cornell named William Provine. He is a teacher of the history of biology and an atheist who believes that there *can* be a godless morality, and that you can't "believe" in science (evolution) and God at the same time. Of course, you immediately came to mind, and I gave him your papers on determinism and evolution. I haven't gotten a reaction yet, but I think he'll be impressed.

The reason I say he's interesting and not foolish is because I feel that, even though his views about religion (at least Judaism) are wrong, his atheism is thought out. He's also very well read and can support his views with interesting cases. I know I can't convince him to believe in God, but I feel I can show him a bit more to respect about the intellect (at least) of those who believe that science and religion are compatible.

L'hitraot b'karov,

Alex

Tying It All Together

The project that was to become Alex's senior thesis at Cornell, Letters from the Diaspora, *included a series of "letters" based on actual letters he had written during his year in London; drawings from London, from his trip to the Soviet Union, and from his travels through Western Europe; and essays about the history of the dispersion and persecution of Jews, especially in England, Spain, and the Soviet Union.*

September 21, 1983
[Cornell]

Dear Deb,

I hope this project works out. I really can't get started until I figure out how to tie all of the work together—that will be the hardest thing to do. One possibility is to consider the year a modern pilgrimage—not to a place but to a readiness to move on to the place—Israel. My wanderings took me in the end to Israel but...the year was not directed towards Israel as a whole. The trip to Russia was the biggest factor in bringing my thinking back toward Jewish issues. When I heard my brother Daniel had decided to join the Israeli army it came even closer.

Love,
Alex

Judaism Is a Fitness Program

September 22, 1983
[Cornell]

Dear Saul,

Some interesting ideas:

If humans are muscles, then Judaism is a fitness program whose goal is to bring the individual muscles to their fullest potential—both as individuals and as part of a larger whole.

From Herzl: Zionism is a cure for anti-semitism.

Me: Anti-semitism is a, if not the, major reason for Zionism. The disappearance of anti-semitism does not, however, make Israel superfluous—just as peace does not make the strength that led to that peace obsolete.

I'm getting quite observant in my old age. "And you shall bind them...."*

Write to me.

Alyosha Meshulamovich

A Rationalist Confronts the Commandments

September 26, 1983

[Cornell]

Dear Daniel,

I got your first letter today. Thanks.

I had an interesting talk with Elissa, a friend of mine who's also a senior here and also worked at BCI this summer. The topic was *mitzvot*—I've had a lot of trouble figuring out whether all mitzvot are equally important. It seems that there is a hierarchy; the mitzvot related to the treatment of others are more immediately necessary than those relating to elevating or otherwise perfecting yourself. The problem is that as soon as you start saying some are more important than others, and that there has to be a reason, beyond God's say-so, behind your following of any mitzvah, you open yourself up to the accusation that you are not the one to decide which of God's commandments He really meant, and which are there for show or something. Anyway, realizing that dilemma I accept that I should try to follow all the mitzvot. The problem becomes convincing myself, a superrationalist, to do things like wrap leather strips around my arms [*tefillin*] (which I do), and to not wear clothing which has both wool and linen woven together [*shatnes*] (which I don't worry about).

Elissa has a devout Christian roommate who has helped Elissa reach an understanding of mitzvot which is both very similar to some Christian notions, and totally compatible with *halacha*. Christianity also seeks to make people better, but unlike Judaism—which uses the Torah as a guide to betterness, it simply says that the acceptance of Christ's love will lead you to do good. I've always thought that was

*From Deuteronomy 6:5-8: "Bind them as a sign on your hand and let them serve as frontlets between your eyes." Jews are commanded to wear *tefillin*—small leather boxes containing the four brief verses from the Torah in which *tefillin* are commanded—strapped to arm and forehead while saying morning prayers.

unreliable at best (even though it does work for some), but Elissa's point was that by trying to discover God's (not Jesus') love we gain a reason for doing mitzvot which would be difficult on a purely rational level. The view that once we recognize that we are loved, and once we try to return that love, we suddenly will want to do things out of love, can be a useful boost to Jews as long as no one tries to use it to replace the Torah. Acting out of love is at times easier than out of rationality, but it is not a sufficient push to goodness to justify annulling commandments. People are not always in loving moods.

If the preceding was a bit heavy for a letter, I'm sorry. While I'm convinced that Elissa's idea can be useful, I have not yet crossed the rationality threshold, and my observance remains guided by my understanding, in balance with my acceptance of the implications of saying that some mitzvot are more desired by God than others. *Tefillin* was a big step for me and I'm not sure how long it will last.

I don't have time to write about it now, but I think that my College Scholar project of putting my drawings and letters from last year together into a book has a lot of potential. I'm trying to figure out a way to link it all together. Briefly my favorite idea so far is to treat the year as a sort of a pilgrimage to Israel, where instead of going to Israel the country, the year's thoughts and experiences led me to Israel, the third part of Judaism's God, Torah, Israel. Like the early Zionists, spending time in Christian Europe led to my realization of the importance of Israel as a haven, and the weakness of the Jews without it. Send me any ideas you have about the subject.

Be well. I miss you.

Love,

Alex

A Letter a Week to Help Soviet Jews

October 11, 1983
[Cornell]

Dear Mom and Dad,

I had a great idea for Soviet Jews. I want to try to convince the Student Society for Soviet Jewry (SSSJ) to finance a project that will put addressed envelopes (to Jews, and American and Russian leaders) on the seats of every synagogue each week. I want letter writing to become a weekly habit for Jews, either after *havdalah*, or on Shabbat for the less observant [who write on Shabbat].

I think I'll try to get a "sermon-slot" at one of the local synagogues to test out the idea. I could end the talk by asking everyone to give $100 less each year to *tzedaka* [charity]—and use that money to send a registered letter a week to the Soviet Union. There might even be a way to get a Jewish-owned list-seller to put the addresses on the labels for the project. What do you think?

I've got to go now.

L'hitraot,

Alex

"I'll need a lot of practice"

November 19, 1983

[Cornell]

Dennis, Janice and David Dov [Prager],

Last night I gave a short talk after Friday night services here at Cornell. The talk was the beginning of what I hope will be a large campaign to help Soviet Jews.

The question was how to make people write weekly. I think one answer is to convince them to make that writing—i.e., their solidarity with their Soviet brothers—part of their observance of Judaism. To convince them of this was the goal of the talk.

I divided the talk in my mind into three parts. The first, using anecdotes from my trip to the USSR, describes how it is to try to live as a Jew in that country; the second deals with how letter writing can help refuseniks (if not helping them to get out, then at least giving them the strength—by telling them that they're not alone—to continue to fight); and finally, I spoke about how to write. "How" meaning two things: the technical how, and the mental how. The former dealing with postage, content, form, etc., and the latter presenting a way to insert writing into observance.

The talk went well but not excessively so. If I'm to become a good public speaker I'll need a lot of practice. But I think that I did affect some people enough to write weekly, and everyone there enough to write once. (That I'm quite sure of because—this was the idea that got everything started—I had the Cornell SSSJ address envelopes to SJ's which I put in each of the *siddurim* [prayer books] before services. Ideally this would be done every week, but that takes more time and effort than I have). What do you think?

Dennis, I really can't thank you enough for giving BCI what it gave me—both as a participant and last summer as an advisor. Your and BCI's effect on my life and way of thinking are treasures I will always be grateful for. I only wish I had gotten a chance to get to know you well enough not to be intimidated by you. But, it takes me longer to feel at ease with some people than with others, and that difficulty lies less in you than in my own, rarely but occasionally irrational, mind. Oh well.

In friendship, love,

Alex

A Chance for Good Argumentation

December 4, 1983
[Cornell]

Dear David,

.... About the [History of Science] seminar: I was the next to last to speak and I told everyone how surprised I was to find that of twenty people there was only one who felt comfortable with his religion, that it had no conflict with science, that free will and determinism could be compatible (your work, David). I was especially bothered when some of the "lapsed" students said they saw a lot of evil in the world which they attributed to religions. I should have brought up Mao, Hitler and Stalin, Pol Pot and Castro...oh well, I didn't.

Anyway, the course looks like it will offer a chance for good arguments.

In friendship,

Alex

To Daniel in the Army

February 16, 1984
[Cornell]

Dear Daniel,

I just heard you were chosen to be communications man in your unit. Good work. I wish my Hebrew were better but I guess it will improve when I am next in Israel. .... The US is all screwed up and has been about Lebanon. We kept Israel from making their type of peace, and refused to give our forces the power to make theirs. All that was left with the power and freedom to act was Syria, and they were smart enough to take advantage of the vacuum by filling it. It's especially sad because the U.S. blew two chances to see a healthier Lebanon—one through Israeli force and the other through American pressure.... Bummer....

Love,

Alex

A Movie in Hebrew

March 1, 1984

[Cornell]

Dear Daniel,

I'm still not ready to send you my thesis but I will at some point. I'm learning more writing this thesis than in three years in Cornell and LSE....

I saw an excellent movie called "Stigma" in English (I don't know what the Hebrew title was because I missed the first 15 minutes. It's about a dude in Tzanhanim [paratroops] who goes nuts (not because of the war), and about the comfort he finds in the *hevra* [friendship] in his unit, away from his troubles at home. It would have really been depressing had I not been so happy to see a movie in Hebrew filmed in Israel. Beautiful scenes along the border in Lebanon, and very Israeli characters acted excellently. Don't see it if you don't like depressing movies.

Love,

Alex

Getting Past the Israeli Censor

March 13, 1984

[Cornell]

Dear Daniel,

I got your letter today—the one you wrote in a neck brace. It's amazing how long it took for it to get here. You shouldn't write about breaking all those rules in your letters because the military censor opens them. The envelope had been opened and resealed with a sticker [that said]..."*tsenura tsvait* [military censor]." But they probably don't care about eating on duty as much as exposing where Israel hides its nuclear weapons.

I really have nothing new to add since my last letter. I'm still working on the section of my thesis about the history of the Jews in England. I hope to finish it by the end of the week but I may not. It's actually quite fascinating. The Jews were readmitted to England, 366 years after being expelled, mostly because of a historical aberration: philo-semitism, or "love of Jews." In Oliver Cromwell's time there was a new interest among Christians in Hebrew, the Old Testament, and bringing about the "Second Coming." Readmission of the Jews was seen to fit all of these goals. Oddest was the last motive. Many Christians read the prophecy from the Book of Daniel, that the End would only come when the destruction of the holy people (us) was complete. So readmission of the Jews would make the world ready for the Second Coming. Well, Jews shouldn't spend too much time questioning people's motives.

Love,

Alex

Wasting Time on Myself

The Last Day of Winter, 1984

[Cornell]

Dear Benjy,

I haven't been a very good correspondent so it's good that you're having a birthday to give me an excuse to write. HAPPY BIRTHDAY!

I can't even picture working as many hours as you do in school, or working as hard as Daniel does in the paratroops. If you decide to do something new, the key is to make your activity something that you are NOT doing for yourself—to find something that you can do for OTHERS. This sounds very, very odd but it is true. I know that Daniel would say that was true about defending Israel; Saul would say it was true about the political work he is doing at Tufts from which only future students (long after Saul has moved on) will benefit.

Anyway, I'm sorry for preaching. But I don't want you to kick yourself when you're 21, like I am kicking myself, for having wasted so much time when I was younger on myself.

Love,

Alex

To Go or Not to Go

April 6, 1984

Dear Daniel,

I'm off to Rochester in half an hour where there is an Aliyah Conference, where I'm told I'll be able to find people who can tell me about the different options for next year.

On Monday I found out that I am an Israeli citizen and have no rights*—not even those of a returning child—because I was over age fourteen when we left Israel. I think I'll be able to get some of them back through appeals but not all.... What it boils down to is this: I'm afraid that if I don't go to Israel soon I'll put it off indefinitely. But I also feel that if my commitment to aliyah is so weak that it can be broken by staying here for an extra year then maybe I shouldn't come. Actually this doesn't convince me, and I'm not really that afraid of losing my commitment. We'll see....

Love,

Alex

Putting Arabic to Work in Jordan

After graduating from Cornell, Alex went to Jerusalem to study Arabic at Hebrew University. Immediately after the intense summer course, he decided to get a firsthand look at Arab society and culture and traveled to Jordan, via Cyprus, under his American passport. (Anything that identified him with Israel would have made this journey impossible at that time.)

Hitchhiking to Cyprus

September 8, 1984

Polis, Cyprus

Dear Benjy,

I'm in a little town called Polis on the western edge of Cyprus. You'd like my hotel. It's $5/night and has a restaurant downstairs with an outdoor area for eating which is

---

*Immigrants to Israel are granted special rights to make their transition easier—including rent subsidies, tax abatements, etc., and the right to import appliances and a car without the normal high tariffs.

completely covered by a grapevine, with bunches of grapes the size of basketballs hanging from it. I made my own dinner upstairs, so all I'm having now is a Cyprus beer (KEO) and a bunch of grapes which the waitress/cook gave me. The floor is made of dirt; there are cats around, and Greek music in the background. Very mellow.

When I was done spending three days helping an archeologist friend of Mom's on his dig, I came here. It took two days to get here, and as you might expect it was an interesting two days. Five minutes after I started hitching, a car—a black, new Mercedes with "United Arab Emirates" plates—pulled over. The driver was a guy (William) from Egypt who had lived for 15 years in the UAE until his father died and he had to leave. The car had been his Dad's and was the nicest I've ever been in. William turned out to be more interesting than his car, because of what he said about the Arabs. He's an Egyptian, but a Copt—a Christian. (There are 15 million Copts in Egypt.) He doesn't want to go home because it is not good to be under Moslems. He hates Moslems. But he hates Palestinians even more. He says they're ruining Cyprus (the PLO has an office here and works to stir up tension between Palestinians and Christians).

About *tefillin*: I lay *tefillin* for a while at Cornell but stopped. I found that they helped me create a time of day devoted to improving my "relations" with God. This relationship is an important part of Judaism—one which I feel I haven't developed. The key is to remember that it is not the only relationship which Judaism wants Jews to think about. Our relationships with other people, with animals, and with the land are also important, and can also benefit from observance of *halacha*.

I now have my ticket to Jordan and will fly there tomorrow. Wish me luck.

Love,

Alex

Report from Jordan: Kind and Dangerous

September 22, 1984
[Jerusalem]

Dear Everyone,

I returned yesterday from a three-week trip to Jordan (via Cyprus). I had wanted to see an Arab country, and because Egypt isn't really Arab, and the other Arab countries are either too unstable or too dangerous for a lone Jew to visit, Jordan was left.

The easiest way to get from Israel to Jordan without a visa is to travel through

Cyprus. After a smooth night on the deck of the *Sol Phyrne* from Haifa, I spent a week and a half in Cyprus trying to find a flight to Amman, hearing from a Greek Cypriot how he had cut off the noses of thirty-two Turks during the war in 1974, sorting ancient gaming stones, pounders, grinders, querns, and pecking stones with an archeologist in Episcopi (a small village off the island's southern coast), and enjoying a mouth-watering meal of swordfish-kebab in another town (Paphos).

I arrived on an Air Alia flight at the Queen Alia International Airport towards the end of Tuesday afternoon. The airport is a showcase of the modern wealth of Jordan and is quite handsome. It is far from Amman but I managed to avoid the whopping taxi fares to the city by getting on a bus for 500 fils ($1.25).

I walked from the bus station downhill along one of the valleys which, together with seven Jebels (mountains), form Amman. It was already dark, and when I reached the city center I felt almost like I was in Times Square in New York, with thousands of flashing lights and signs and storefronts. Down an alley with two hummos restaurants was the Bader Hotel, where I found a room entered from a balcony, with a perfect view of the city, for less than six dollars a night. Muhammad, the Egyptian at the desk, knew very little English, but was very friendly. We were talking about Egypt and he told me that Ghaddafi is known to everyone in Egypt as "Al Magnun"—the crazy one. I liked his example of why: he said that Ghaddafi claims to own the entire U.S. because its present rulers stole it from red Indians, and the red Indians were really Libyans who only he—Ghaddafi—could represent. Later I sat on the balcony and watched the city's traffic die down as its shops closed and signs dimmed.

I devoted my first full day in Amman to my bureaucratic needs. I walked to the "third circle" and the departments of Tourism and Antiquities for maps and advice.... Next came the Ministry of the Interior where I filled out an application form to cross into the West Bank.

Back on the balcony I talked a long time with Fallah Bader from Hebron (the brother of the hotel's owner). But, when I started to ask him a question about the West Bank, he stopped me and said that I could talk to him about any subject, that he would be happy to help me in Jordan (and I believe he was sincere) with anything at all, but that I shouldn't talk politics. What he said next was sad and true. He said that politics was like a circle. We could talk about controversial issues all we wanted to—proposing solutions and complaining about situations—but, since our talk itself would not solve any problems, why suffer with its consequences. Bader asked hypothetically about the

Amman at night with the back of the "فيليپيّن" sign from BADER hotel   12 Sept, 1984

point of saying something bad about the King [Hussein] if it couldn't change anything and it could land him in jail. This hypothetical question was the closest thing I had heard in Jordan to resentment of Hussein. Everyplace I went, including the Bader Hotel, had a picture of Hussein, sometimes as a young man, sometimes with a beard, at times in uniform, or with Queen Nur. He is on all the money and stamps as well.

When I said I wanted to go to the hummos restaurant downstairs in the alley, Bader insisted that one of the two Egyptians who worked in the hotel bring up dinner for me instead. So, I had the usual felafel etc. on the balcony as we continued to talk and watch Amman dim.

On Thursday night I saw Amman's sights. Both of them. The Roman theater in the city center, ten minutes on foot from the hotel, is truly impressive for its size and for its mint condition. Next I climbed up to the ruins of "The Citadel" near the theater. Amman's hills and wadis are so steep that the climb was very tiring, but the view from the ruins was worth the effort. On the way down the hill I spoke to a guy about my age. He was on his way to study in Italy and as most people with whom I'd spoken had done, he asked me where I learned Arabic (usually conversations started with my asking directions and then turn to the topic of Arabic). Then he asked me if I knew Hebrew. "Only 'Shalom,'" I said.

At 6:30 in the morning I found a service to the bus station and found that the "Arabella" bus would leave for Jerash for even less money than the "service." An hour and a half later I was in Jerash. For the first time since I arrived, I met some people who were not Arabs. It was a group of students (on their way to Jerusalem) from the Eastern Mennonite University in Virginia. I took a picture of the whole group on the steps of one of the site's temples with each of their cameras, rode on their bus into the town of Jerash, bought cookies and bread, and walked off to hitch to Ajlun. I waited for a ride for close to an hour as the cars with no room went by without stopping. Then a pickup truck pulled over. Within a minute I regretted getting in. The driver, a young Palestinian, asked me to take off my hat. I thought, "Arab custom—no hats in cars." Then he said, "You very beautiful." Shit. After about 20 minutes which seemed much longer of his telling me in Arabic, "you know what I want," and my answering that I "know but don't want" as I arranged my things so that I could jump out of the truck fast. I convinced him to stop, got out, and felt very relieved.

I had gotten out in the middle of nowhere and was not optimistic about getting a ride, but within five minutes an ancient Mercedes taxi full of children pulled over. All the children in the back (seven of them) moved over and made room for me. The driver was a nice man from Haifa who had come here after the Six-Day War [1967] as a refugee. In the front seat with him were his wife and eight children (there was one more at home). She turned out to be the mother of all of them (age 1 to 14). They helped to balance out the experience of my previous ride which, rightly or wrongly, would have made me feel very bad about Palestinians in general.

I walked almost all the way to the ruins of Qalat Rabadh castle, but got a ride for the last mile. The view from the ramparts of the largely intact castle (built by a cousin of Salah a'Din, in response to the Crusaders' construction of Belvoir across the Jordan Valley) was beautiful and I could have seen Beit Shean had it not been for the haze. I sat for a long time on the wall with the view to the west, eating (and spilling peach marmalade all over my backpack and pants) and talking to Jordanian kids who were at the castle with their families. I was the only Western tourist at the site but the parking lot was full of Jordanians out for the day. It was nice to see that they get out and see their country.

I sketched one of the towers and started on my way back down the mountain. A Saudi family picked me up, asked me where I wanted to go, and drove me all the way to Irbid (to a restaurant I'd heard had good pizza) even though it was many miles out of their way. The driver asked about my religion. I said I had none. He said it was important to have a religion which realizes that there is one God. I said I agreed. They recommended Islam and I said I'd look into it when I got home. After pizza I caught the last bus to the small town of Um Qeis where I'd heard there was an unexcavated Roman basalt Roman theater. I arrived just as the sun was going down, and was shown to the theater (past people drawing water by hand from a well). The view was even more breathtaking than in Ajlun and I could see the whole Sea of Galilee and the Golan Heights. I put my sleeping bag on one of the wide seats of the theater and watched the lights flicker on in Tiberias and the southern Galilee kibbutzim. A good way to spend the last evening of my twenty-first year.

For a while I tried to sleep but had trouble because the step I was on tilted slightly towards the stage and I felt as if I would roll off. When the moon came up (almost full) I moved to a bench near the top of the theater which was flat and slept until first light.

Until well after dark I'd heard voices and vehicles from the Jordanian army encampment across a small valley on the plateau which lay between the theater and the Jordan Valley. In the morning I walked onto the plateau after a local resident

Sept. 14, 1984 One of Qalat Rabad's towers, near Ajlun, Jordan

said there were more antiquities to be seen there. Sure enough, 50 yards from a squad of soldiers sitting on the ground being lectured by an officer, was an underground tomb which I entered through a doorway one of whose stone doors was still on its hinges. An impressive tomb in almost perfect shape. I made sure that I kept my camera pointed towards ruins and never in the direction of soldiers. Nobody bothered me—I must have looked like a crazy archeologist.

After I did one drawing of a sarcophagus with a beautiful road (leading down the side of the Golan Heights to the Israel hot spring of Hammat Gader) in the background, I walked to the road which led down to the valley to the Jordanian spring of El Hama.

The police checked my passport, asked where I learned Arabic, and told me the bus would be by in a few minutes.

I walked right to the edge of the cliffs which led down to the river, and could see an Israeli patrol jeep on the security road above the cliffs on the other side. Being so close to Israel is comforting, exhilarating, and frustrating.

While waiting for the bus back to Irbid and Amman I spoke in Arabic, as usual, with yet another Palestinian who was very suspicious of me. After he asked me if I knew Hebrew and I said, "only 'Shalom,'" he was quiet. After a couple of minutes he asked me, in Hebrew, as he held out a packet of cigarettes, if I wanted to smoke. Hearing a question directed to me, and not expecting Hebrew, I didn't realize until it was too late that he had used Hebrew. I answered "no" in Arabic and then said, "I don't smoke," also in Arabic. He said in Hebrew, "You told me you don't know Hebrew but you answered when I asked you if you smoke—you lied." I said in Arabic, "I don't understand." Then the bus came. On the way up the hill I pulled a letter I'd written in Cyprus to a friend (which spoke of my plan to move to Israel) out of my bag and slowly tore it to bits which I threw out the window. I was worried that he might tell the police that there was an Israeli on the bus, but I guess he didn't. Maybe he believed my act. I doubt it. Phew.

After a night's rest back in the Hotel Bader in Amman I went to the ministry to pick up my permit for the West Bank, and was relieved to find it had been approved. One official at the ministry was particularly helpful and, while I was waiting for the permit to be typed, found me a car rental company which would allow me to pick up a car in Amman and leave it in Aqaba. By eleven I was on the road in my red lemon, rented to me by a short, fat Jordanian who'd spent 26 years in the Jordanian military as a band leader.

I drove east into the desert on a road full of Jordanian military installations, including an air base with concrete camouflaged hangers for fighter jets just before Azraq. In Azraq, at the castle which had been used by Lawrence of Arabia, I was once again the only tourist until a chauffeur-driven car pulled up as I pulled out. I drove along a new highway to a second castle, Qasr Amra, which was guarded by a lone bedouin and contained beautiful frescoes and a 40-meter-deep well. As I sketched the castle, the car with the chauffeur pulled up. Finally, at the third castle, Qasr Kharana, I spoke to the second car's driver. His passengers turned out to be the Brazilian ambassador and his family. I spoke with His Honor in one of the castle's dark, cool, empty rooms. Qasr Kharana is very odd because it stands like a great cube in the middle of a completely empty, flat area, so flat in fact that I could only think of one reason why a concrete helicopter pad had been built on earth which was naturally a perfect spot for helicopter landing. I asked the castle's bedouin if the king had ever visited. He had.

The road back towards Amman was through more empty desert. Twenty kilometers west of Kharana the straight road widened for a mile or so into an emergency landing strip for planes, but there were no buildings to accompany the "airport." I wanted to avoid Amman, so I turned south rather than north when I reached the desert highway. I drove through Madaba stopping only to ask for directions to Mount Nebo. When I reached the mountain the sun was almost on the horizon and the Dead Sea glowed red down below. I didn't have much time to stand and enjoy Moses' view of the promised land (let alone sleep on top of the mountain as I had hoped), because the site's keepers insisted that I leave, and they closed the gate across the road to the peak after I pulled out.

From the mountain top I'd seen a spring (a green spot), in the valley lying slightly to my north and running from the east down to the Dead Sea. I followed a small unmarked road down towards the spring past a few bedouin tents. At the road's end was a walled enclosure with a few huge eucalyptus trees, a couple of buildings, and a dozen cats. The man who came to the gate invited me to have tea, and we sat outside his one-room guard house by the gate, drinking and watching the sky darken. Muhammad Halid ibn Lagnem offered me a white stone from his pocket and popped another one like it in his mouth. I did the same. It was bedouin "candy" of solid sour milk—obviously an acquired taste. I sucked on the rock until I had a chance to fling it into the wadi without offending my host.

Next to where we sat was a spigot running with delicious water from the spring—Ayn Musa. The pumps in the building next to us were silent. They had been broken for the past two years, and remained unrepaired as Madaba had another source of water. When I told Muhammad that I planned to sleep in my car somewhere out in the mountains, he said it would be better if I parked within the pump-station's fence. We ate a meal of thin bread (which Muhammad had made earlier) which we dipped in a delicious tomato stew. I supplied cheese, peach jam, and cookies and followed Muhammad's lead by saying *bismilla* (in God's name) before I ate and *al-hamdulilla* (thanks to God) when we were through. After dinner Muhammad excused himself, removed his shoes, and prayed next to the spigot. The prayers are very simple and sound far more beautiful when they are muttered by one man, at a silent spring in a desert with a view of a million stars, than when they are screeched by a muezzin with a loudspeaker in a noisy city.

Muhammad and I talked for hours as we drank tea, ate, and then drank tea again. He was very patient with my Arabic and explained whenever I stopped him.

A sarcophagus at Um Queis with the Golan and Sea of Galilee in the background   Sept 15, 1984

I wish I remembered what he said word for word. It was fascinating. At first he spoke of how sad it was that there were wars, because we are "all brothers." He asked me if I knew who Adam and Eve were, to explain what he meant. Then he said Isa (Jesus), Musa (Moses), and Muhammad were all brothers, all great. I thought to myself: here is a simple devout Moslem whose Islam makes wars seem wrong. I didn't think that way for long.

It turned out that all men were brothers, but the Jews were "Shaitan." When it struck me that Shaitan might be Satan, I was surprised. He asked me if I knew who Shaitan was. I said, *"Allahu akbar wa'Ash-shaytan mish quayis"* (God is great, and Satan is no good). "Right! Right!" he said, very pleased that I was learning. Then he went on and on about how Israel was only there (he pointed west) because of the United States, which was being taken advantage of by the Jews, who were like the man riding the American donkey. He was completely convinced that if only the U.S. would stop aiding Israel, it would disappear. Israel's origin was equally artificial to him. He told me that before the Balfour Declaration there had been no Jews in Palestine. "What about before Muhammad?" I asked. "What about before the Jews built the temple in Jerusalem?" Always. The Balfour Declaration itself was evidence of the way Jews had bought their way into Arab land.

The whole conversation was rather unreal, moving from the abstract of total brotherhood among all men, to total hatred of a manipulating people who were in fact the devil. All from a very generous, friendly (he was willing to talk with me even though he knew I was an American) hardworking man, who didn't even have the grudge of the Palestinians against Israel, as he was Jordanian. His hatred came from his Islam and from his understanding of the world, which in turn came from Arabic radio. In the morning I drove along the dirt road which led from the spring towards the Dead Sea to get a better view of the valley. Next I went back to Mount Nebo, looked at the church on top with its beautiful mosaics, and went back to Madaba to see The Map. I found it in a small church. The famous section of the church floor was covered during services with carpets and pews, but when I was there the carpets were pulled away and the Cardo of Jerusalem was right there—beautiful and a bit of an anticlimax as I'd seen so many pictures of the map before. I left Madaba down the Kings' Highway for Kerak.

The Kings' Highway was not as spectacular as I thought it would be. The new Desert Highway has replaced it as the main route from the Red Sea to the north.

The reason the new route was built in the desert was to avoid the one thing that made the Kings' Highway interesting: Wadi Mujib. Wadi Mujib is so deep and steep that it took me half an hour to drive down its north side (with the engine off) and another half hour to drive up. At the bottom of this Jordanian Grand Canyon was one building—a post office. I couldn't resist sending a letter from there as a Wadi Mujib postmark is probably truly rare. Before I reached Kerak at noon I made only a couple of stops, at Khirbet Iskander (I had to see a sight named for my namesake) and Er Rabbah, where I sketched a beautiful ruined Roman building.

Kerak was very, very impressive. The ruins of the castle are on the high end of an oblong hill surrounded by deep wadis. The city covers the rest of the hill and is still surrounded by the remains of a wall. The castle is amazing with hundred-foot-high stone walls, and tens if not hundreds of underground vaulted rooms along long dark hallways. There is a hazy but beautiful view from the ramparts of the end of the Dead Sea and the beginning of the Arava.

At the intersection where the road down to the Arava starts, a policeman asked me where I was going, and invited two men into my car when I said Aqaba. One was a policeman and the other was a soldier. I asked them if I need the permit for travelling the Arava road if they were in the car, and they said not to worry. But 23 kilometers later, at a military checkpoint, I was told "even if you had the king hitching with you, you'd need a pass" by an English-speaking paratrooper. I drove with the policeman, one of the stupider people I've ever met, back to Kerak and the office which issues permits, got one after a 20-minute wait, turned around and returned to the checkpoint, where I was invited to have tea by the sympathetic paratrooper who told me, as I drank and his soldiers searched my bags, that all the Jews are "bloodsuckers." I wish I remembered how it came up.

An hour or so later we had a flat tire but, *al-hamdulilla*, the spare, jack, and wrench all worked. If they hadn't we'd have been in trouble. There are almost no cars in the Arava and we were miles from anything. To top it off my permit was only good for one day, and I would have been refused entry into Aqaba if I had had to spend the night in the valley. The ride through the Jordanian side of the Arava was far more dramatic than the ride on the Israeli side. The Jordanian side is emptier and its mountains are higher, sharper and darker. At some point we passed Petra, although I don't know where, as there was no road into it from the valley.

I wish I hadn't had the soldier with me in the car. He was only a bit less suspicious than the man in El Hama. At least when he tried his Hebrew on me I was ready with a good I-wish-I-could-understand-you face. When he asked me if I'd been to Israel (he could tell I had) I admitted that I'd been there in 1973 when I was eleven. He kept pushing me, and said that he knew my father from Tel Aviv (impossible) when he (the soldier) had lived in Israel. When the policeman kept chiming in about how rotten the Israelis were, the soldier, seeing that I wouldn't tell all unless I was convinced that he was all for peace, said that he thought Israel should be Jordan's friend, etc. At times during this interrogation we were only a couple hundred yards from the Israeli border and security fence. I was relieved when they got out in Aqaba.

I wanted to sleep on the beach but after I drove past the ten kilometers of Aqaba port facilites and thousands of trucks waiting to be loaded with food and manufactured goods, or to unload their oil, I found that I needed a permit to sleep there. I drove back to Aqaba, got the permit, returned to the checkpoint, had my bags searched again, and drove along the dark beach until I saw some lights. I drove up and walked over to the circle of people laughing and speaking English around the back of a pickup truck. "Have a beer!" They turned out to be a group of Westerners who work in Aqaba and get together every Monday night on the beach for a party. It was a relief not to hear anymore about being a bloodsucker or Satan. After they left I was alone on the beach. I slept next to the car and watched the lights of Eilat get dimmer as it got later.

In the morning I drove along the beach to a row of palm-thatched roofs put up to shade swimmers. The water was perfect and the coral was beautiful, but I left after 20 minutes to return the car and find the bus to Petra.

Petra, of all the places on my agenda, was where I was ready to be the most disappointed because it was the spot for which I held the highest expectations. From the very beginning I could see that I had no reason to worry. I turned down all of the bedouin trying to offer me a horse for the trip through the "siq" and walked with my camera, canteen, sleeping bag, and small backpack (I left my bigger pack at the resthouse) into Petra. Within minutes the magic began with the huge facades of the Obelisk tomb on the left and mysterious twenty-foot-high cubes carved out of the mountain on the right. From the very beginning (and for the whole time I was in Petra) the torture of not having the slightest idea of why the Nabateans had done what they'd done began. "Why carve a mountain into cubes?"

The trail led me into the next *siq*, which is a very deep wadi with red walls, often only a car's width apart (occasionally a jeep passed me kicking up a cloud of dust from the unpaved wadi floor). After a couple of kilometers of winding the *siq* opened and the Treasury, or *Khaznat Faroun*, appeared to glow in front of me just like the picture on the cover of BAR [*Biblical Archaeology Review*]. I didn't stick around what is supposed to be "Petra's most beautiful monument." The bedouin there were only interested in selling me junk, and I wanted to get far away from the touristed areas before I lay down my sleeping bag for the night. I continued out of the *siq* to the center of Nabatean Petra, past all the famous tombs and onto the trail to the Deir (the "Monastery"). After a half hour of walking up hundreds of stairs carved into the rock, I saw the Deir's urn towering above a final turn in the wadi which housed the steps I was on. I climbed around a rock and there it was, brightly lit by the almost setting sun— a yellowish color rather than the red of the tombs in Petra's center. An unattended Pepsi stand was in a cave opposite the tomb, and sounds from a bedouin tent came from behind a rock into which the Pepsi stand had been carved. In front of me I could see that the Arava was very close and I walked in its direction so as to find a cave with a view to make my home. I found one, ate tuna on pita for dinner, and watched the sunset.

After dinner I walked back to the bedouin tent in search of conversation and tea. I was invited to come in and have tea. I had written down the names of the bedouin mentioned in the BAR article on Petra, and I asked the bedouin I was with if he knew them. "Yes, Mifla and Nawal are in Germany now, I'm Dachl'alla, and my wife is Rachil." Small world.

Dachl'lalla insisted that it would be better for me to stay with them than out in the mountains, so I went back to my cave, brought my things back to the tent, and sat down for tea and talk. Dachl'alla was a good Arabic teacher, and when I called him a donkey by mistake, as I was trying to ask him if he had carried up the canister that provided the gas which lit his tent, he didn't get mad at all. I slept on the rock next to the tent in my sleeping bag on one of the bedouin's mattresses.

I woke up just after first light and set off to climb to the top of the Deir. I can't begin to say how beautiful and impressive the monument is when you sit on the rim of its roof 200 feet off the ground waiting for the sun to rise. I must have spent two hours up there, taking pictures, drawing, and just sitting and looking at the light beginning to hit the red mountains around me. Breathtaking and silent.

By the time I climbed back down, Dachl'alla and his three other Western guests had already eaten. Two of them, an English couple with stomach trouble, left for Amman (I recommended the Bader Hotel to them), leaving Fred (a Dutch biologist

At the top of the Deir at Petra.

and oryx expert) and me to try to keep up with Dachl'alla on his shortcut down the mountain to his work and Petra's center. The route we took was along the side of a steep wadi. Sometimes we had to use our hands to hang on. Dachl'alla pointed to the wadi bed below, which we could then see was very green, and we stopped for a moment to listen to the gurgle from the green of Petra's source of water. When I asked him where he worked, Dachl'alla told me to wait. After the final bit of descent to the wadi bed we turned a corner and he pointed to a stone wall which cut off a tributary of the wadi and said, "That's my work." He had built a field for himself and dug a twenty-five-foot deep well to provide water for irrigation. We had tea next to the wall with the two workers who were helping him, and set off to see more of Petra.

Before we split up (I had promised to bring Dachl'alla a copy of the magazine and a pamphlet written by a friend of his from the resthouse where I'd left them) Fred and I climbed the small mountain topped by Crusader ruins in the center of Petra.

In the afternoon, after retrieving the magazines from the hotel, I hiked alone to the "High Place," a weird altar of sacrifice (with blood gutters) at the top of another of Petra's mountains. At the High Place Bebsi Stand I was the first and last customer of the day and, after having tea with Thanua, the bedouin woman whose stand it was, and after Thanua had locked up the crate where she keeps her ancient coins and shards, and hidden her tea thermos in a crack in the mountain, we walked down together. Thanua is one of three wives and has herself four sons and two daughters. She is also Dachl'alla's first cousin. I gave Thanua half a dinar for guiding me down, and she went to her tent and I continued on my way back to the Deir.

By the time I reached the Deir I was exhausted. I had walked (mostly climbed) at least twenty kilometers since I had left in the morning. Dinner with Dachl'alla of Rachil's potato and yogurt soup with bread and cold yogurt was delicious, and after another Arabic lesson I went to sleep in a cave near their tent whose floor they had covered with mats and which had mattresses and blankets lined up against one wall.

After breakfast with Fred in the morning (Dachl'alla had already left), made from food which I had given Rachil and bread she had made, Fred and I set off to climb the Deir again. After an hour of climbing we reached the top of a wadi and were on a plateau beyond whose edge there was a drop of at least a thousand feet and a view of the entire Arava.... The only point higher than us was a mountain to our south with a small white building on top which was supposed to house Haroun's (Aaron's) tomb. Beautiful.

I wanted to stay in Petra for another few days, but I felt that it was time to return to Jerusalem. I got on the JETT bus to Amman, and was back in the Hotel Bader in the evening.

At 6:15 a.m. I took a service [taxi] to the bus station, found a service to "the bridge" with seven Palestinians and one free seat, and was at the Jordanian side of the bridge an hour later. At the border station I ran into Fallah Bader, who saved me from my lack of dinars (I hadn't known that I would have to pay 1.5 dinars to ride the mile from the station to the bridge) by changing five dollars for me. I had been told that I would laugh at the bridge because it crossed little more than a trickle, and whoever told me that was right. I couldn't help smiling at how little the stream was whose crossing was such a complex affair with permits, armies, bus changes, etc.

The Jordanians had been separated from the Westerners before the crossing, so I felt it was safe on the Israeli side to use Hebrew with the security officer checking my body with a metal detector. "I did a little tourism," I said in Hebrew. "Oh, how was the 'red rock?'" I think every Israeli wants to see Petra. The woman soldier who checked my bags was also surprised to hear Hebrew and her search was very quick.

During the taxi ride to the Old City [in Jerusalem],* I had to continue my Jordan—lying for the last time, and talk of how I was coming to Jerusalem for a week, didn't know Hebrew, and had only been here as a small boy for a visit. I walked from the taxi stand to West Jerusalem along the Old City wall. Crossing into the new city, I finally began to relax completely, and the first thing I did on "our" side was enter our neighbor's art gallery at the end of the Jaffa road. I dropped my bag and said to Said, "I can speak Hebrew again! I can stop lying! It's good to be home."

I really did see a huge portion of Jordan and talked to many of its people. In Jordan I felt completely safe as long it was not known that I was a Jew, but I felt that even the nicest of people could become dangerous if they found out my "true identity." One bedouin whom I met on the bus out of Petra said to me, "I'm like a chameleon—one minute I can be a simple guide in the mountains, the next I can be furious with those who cross me." Jordan is beautiful, its people kind and dangerous.

That's enough gross oversimplification.

Love,

Alex

*The 1948 War of Independence divided Jerusalem into two separate parts: the Old City and the northeastern suburbs were occupied by Jordan; the rest of the city was Israeli. As a result of the 1967 war, Jerusalem was reunified as Israel's capital.

No Doubts About Aliyah

October 9, 1984
[Jerusalem]

Dear Saul,

When I think about my impending aliyah I can't really say I have doubts about wanting to be here. My doubts are over other things—what I'll do here, whether aliyah is the "right" thing to do, whether the fact that I want to live here balances off what I'll miss (future trips to the USSR, other forbidden travel, opportunities in the States). It's better to be like Doobs [Daniel]—to think only about what you can do and not about what you can't.

The Israelis think I'm a spy: When I went to the *aliya* and *klita* [immigration and absorption] office, and they looked me up in the computer, I came up as classified, "no info available." It turns out they're running a check on me because they find it suspicious that a Hebrew-speaker should cross into Israel alone, from Jordan, and ask not to have his passport stamped.

L'hitraot,
Alex

War Stories

October 27, 1984
[Jerusalem]

Dear Dad,

Just came back from a classic evening at the [Shlomo] Baum residence. When I arrived Shlomo was talking to a doctor who had lost his right index finger during *miluim* two months earlier, when a fuse blew up in his hand. The surgeon who fixed his hand cut away the whole side of the hand so that his second finger would be useable as a new index finger.

Shlomo's sister showed up and the conversation moved to tales of their grandfather's heroism in the fight at Port Arthur [China] against the Japanese in 1905.

In walked Talik (who sends warm regards). He brought pictures, and Elana took out some Baum pictures, and I showed Tal my Petra pictures. One of Elana's was of Shlomo in a bathing suit holding a 35-lb. fish in his arms. The fish story goes like this. Shlomo was at the Kinneret [Sea of Galilee] and in the morning, when the others on the beach brought out their fancy rods, Shlomo went for a walk on the beach. A kilometer or so from the camping spot this huge fish washed up for a split second in the very shallow water in front of Shlomo, and before it could swim back, he kicked it in the side, stunning it. Then, before it became undazed, he grabbed it in both his arms and flipped it onto the beach where, in his words, "it was in my territory." Shlomo had offered us anything in the world if we could guess how he caught the fish, so if you'd like to win a nice bet, don't ever let on that I've told you the story.

Next came the war stories, which basically ran along the following lines: Shlomo tells a story about an action with a few men and clever tricks on the other side of a border, and then Tal would say, "That's not very elegant," and proceed to tell of an action as effective as Shlomo's but which involved only one tank shell at just the right moment. (An Israeli tractor driver had been killed by the Syrians, and at 2:55 on the day of the funeral, which was to be at 3:00, Tal ordered another tractor to drive exactly where the first had been hit. He watched the Syrians lift their camouflage net and aim their cannon, and he said "fire." The three Syrians and their gun flew in the air just as Kaddish was being said.)

Best was as Tal left, he said, "You decide whenever you want to go in the army and I'll set it up. You tell Shlomo and he'll tell me." Nice.

Love,

Alex

"God Didn't Finish the Ordering"

Nov. 7, 1984
[Jerusalem]

Dear Mom, Dad, Benj, and Saul,

Last night I started a book called *Why Bad Things Happen to Good People* by Rabbi Harold Kushner. It was so interesting that I finished it by this afternoon. Kushner's son died at age 14 of a weird rapid-aging disease. He deals with the question of why, and of God's relation to bad things happening to good people. He rejects the argument given by some would-be comforters that the pain was somehow deserved, even if we can't see how. He rejects the idea that the pain was justified by some sort of grand plan which we also may not see, which is often used to comfort the mourner. He concludes that God had nothing to do with the genetic mistakes, hurricanes, etc. that take lives which no amount of argument can persuade the survivors deserved to be taken. Creation (which was not the making of something from nothing but the ordering of chaos), he says, was not completed. God didn't finish the ordering, and randomness remains to take its undivine toll. God's role in suffering is as a giver of strength.

One of the good things about Kushner's book was his discussion of the purpose of prayer. He says you can ask God for strength, but not for your baby to be a boy or your biopsy to be negative. There's an Arabic saying, *"Eelee faat maat,"* which means what is past is dead and it only pays to think about the future. The saying applies to prayer as well, for God doesn't change the unchangeable. The strength which God provides comes from the knowledge that you are not alone no matter what happens. And being alone is something which I think about often (but not constantly). I have lonely spurts, which usually last no more than half an hour but are a bit disturbing. I don't think that I, the loner, fear loneliness, but I do think about it now that I'll be moving here. I hope (but don't pray) for the day when I will feel part of a group of people other than my family which is so far away. I have some friends, but no one with whom I am as close as I am to you. I'm not worried about the future, only intrigued.

Love,
Alex

Reactions to Yoni's Letters

November 12, 1984
Kibbutz Ein Tsurim

Dear Family,

On Shabbat at Ein Tsurim I started to reread Yoni's letters—this time in Hebrew. My first reaction to them was one of guilt. Guilt over not investing myself in everything I do as much as I can, guilt over not always utilizing time the best way, guilt over not thinking enough about my family's troubles and thoughts. Now that I've had time to think about my reaction much of the guilt is gone and some is changed. Some of the guilt came from seeing the sensitivity of even the teenage Yoni to the feelings of his parents and brothers. He writes not only of his own loneliness but of theirs; not only of his accomplishments, but of theirs. He praises his family and feels for their problems beautifully. I have always been less sensitive to your (Mom and Dad's) worries than I now see I should have been. This is mostly because I've always seen you two as invulnerable and free from worries. Because you have always put solving your sons' problems and fears above talking about your own.

An equally important thing which Yoni did in his letters was tell his parents and brothers how much he admired them, felt their victories to be important, their accomplishments. I have never been big on praising. In regards to people outside my family that is because I rarely find people who deserve praise, and I can rarely fake undeserved praise. But I have always admired my parents more than anyone else in the world, and have felt all my brothers to be equally impressive. I haven't finished Yoni's letters yet, but what they've done so far, besides what I've written above, is give me a shot in the arm. Finally, the letters have revived my usually healthy optimism about all things working out for the best in the future, based on the way they have worked out in the past.

I would like to send this letter so that it arrives before I do, as it is not the kind of thing which I want to hear read.

I'll try to find a courier so that it arrives before me.

Love,

Alex

Some more of the training devices at Tel Nof   June 30 '86

3.
Pain and Loneliness in Basic Training

....

"At the swearing in I promised to give my life (even) for this country. Saying it really brings into focus what I've done."

"Are You Nervous?"

In January 1985 Alex settled permanently in Israel. The next month he entered the army, four years older than the other recruits, a "lone soldier" with no immediate family except his younger brother in Israel. Alex joined the paratroops because he wanted to be with volunteers in the most "active" service and because his brother Daniel was in the paratroops.

Paratroop basic training ended with a 55-mile masa kumta *or "beret march," mostly at night and with full load, beginning near the Mediterranean, and finishing in Jerusalem at the Western Wall of the Temple Mount. There, the new paratroopers received their red berets.*

From the time he entered the army, Alex kept with him a journal in a small, black-bound artist's sketchbook. On the cover page of the first volume he wrote, "Alex goes to the army..." The journal mixed pencil sketches, watercolors, diagrams, and text.

[Journal]

Jan. 2, 1985

Draft board. *Lishkat Gioos*

Medical test—I shouldn't have responded to doctor's "*Atah mitragesh?* [Are you nervous?]" with "Of course—I've never been drafted before."

Outside doctor's office I felt myself more mature than those around me, not for my extra four years but because some of them were laughing at a Hasid who was there with his father. It wasn't that the sight wasn't amusing—it was. But they were laughing at him *in front* of him—scorning him like a bunch of rednecks at a redneck bar might scorn a city type who walked in. I have other analogies which include the KKK and Germans, but I don't like to apply them to Jews.

Two doctors—a man and a woman—examining the draftees-to-be. The man checked me, but the 17-year-old next to me looked very much like someone had just dropped ice down his shirt when the other doctor said to "drop them" to his knees.

All in all (besides the scornful cowards) I found the first exposure less unpleasant than I expected. I was treated well, people were interested in my coming to the army two days after making aliyah. Not too bureaucratic, and not too impersonal. One soldier there (a man who said he liked what I was doing, especially now that his brothers have moved to the States for the money) even said he thought he remembered Daniel's coming through a year ago!

I go back there on Sunday.

Happiest Person at the Draft Board

January 8, 1985
Kibbutz Ein Tsurim

Dear Family,

Now I don't feel helpless or alone, which leaving [the U.S.A. 12/30/84 and returning to Israel] made me feel at first. In fact, I'm in a good mood and feeling very much at peace finally with my recent decisions.

I finally got a room at the kibbutz (with two volunteers from South Africa and England), which along with getting unpacked and getting to work (in the factory so far) have made Ein Tsurim feel like a home. A group of Americans who showed up from WUJS [World Union of Jewish Students] made me feel both like an old-timer and a native, and I really would prefer to avoid them so I can spend time getting to know those who live in my new home.

I also feel that the army is no longer an "option" for the future but really the future itself. Everyone was surprised to see me grinning delightedly as I told them my draft date: 7:30 a.m. February 5th. Getting the draft date made me happy. So did my profile—97—the highest possible, I think. I'm sure I was the happiest person at the draft board.

L'hitraot,
Alex

Countdown

February 3, 1985
[Kibbutz Ein Tsurim]

Dear Mom and Dad,

I just got off the phone with you—just to show that talking doesn't make me less likely to write. It's Monday now. I'll be a soldier in seven hours. I'm not worried so you shouldn't.

Love,
Alex

Struggling to Get into Paratroops

February 16, 1985
[In the Army]

Dear Harold [Rhode],

On February 5th I arrived at *bakum* [absorption and assignment base] and on the 6th I met with the *kitzin miyun* [assignment officer] whose job it is to fit soldiers to units. I told him I wanted to get to Golani. He said fine. Five minutes later, thinking that if I couldn't pass the paratroop entry test [not required for Golani] I shouldn't serve in infantry, and after being told by others I liked who were waiting to see the assignment officer that they were going to paratroops, I returned to the *kitzin* and said, "Put me on the list for the paratroop test. He said, "fine," and smiled.

After being transferred to the paratroop section, I started the pre-test processing. First came the medical. Next came the interview with a paratroop officer.

I entered the room, saluted as I had been told to salute, was seated, told to relax, and asked to tell about myself. I told them about Cornell, about my book [*Letters from the Diaspora*] (they wanted to know a lot about it) and why I wanted to be a paratrooper. I said that I wanted to serve with people who wouldn't say "Let's work slower so they don't have us do more"; and that I was less likely to find these types in a volunteer unit. The officer pressed me on this point, and asked "What if you have to serve with them; and what if you find those types in the paratroops as well?" To which I responded that I'd be OK.

Anyway, I left the meeting with the impression that the officer thought I was a snob. When I asked others how their interviews had gone, they all said, "Great, it was even fun." This after my meeting was cold as ice. I went into the test feeling good physically, but also that even if I passed I wouldn't go to the paratroops, so unpleasant was my interview and general impression of the attitude there.

The "testees" were divided into groups of 13-14 soldiers each, and each group carried a stretcher (with a 300-350 lb. tent on it), a jerrycan, packs of sand, and other heavy stuff. During the first few hours of the test, I did very well, smiled a lot, and in general stood out as good. But when afternoon came I was tired, I couldn't keep up at the same level and spent more and more energy on thinking how stupid it was to torture myself with going on if in any case I wasn't going to the paratroops. So I dropped out—after five hours with about one and a half hours to two hours to go.

waiting for the JVN 13P on Feb 6, 1985 in BAKUUM.

At the army induction center.

Immediately some sergeants said how stupid I was—that they expected so much from me. I told them how I felt that even if I had finished, I wouldn't have been accepted due to the interview. They said I'd been 100% wrong, and that out of 50 I had scored 48 on the interview! They offered to let me take the test again. I said, "No thanks."

Over the weekend, I realized that my reasons for deciding against the paratroops had disappeared. On Sunday I told them I wanted to do the test again. They said, "Tuesday." But on Monday morning, they suddenly said, "It's this morning."

Now, Harold, you must understand that these tests are the hardest thing I've ever done. So, on Monday morning my reaction to the earlier test date was such total fear that I became physically weak. I had been ready to undergo it again the next day, but not sooner.

Luckily, at the last moment, the test was put off again until Tuesday, which gave me time to get ready for it in my head.

The next morning I was ready and while I wasn't as good as I had been on the previous Thursday morning, I did finish the test. The next evening I found out that I had been accepted for the paratroops and that's where I am now.

So the cost of paranoia and misreading of the meeting was the necessity of going through a whole second test.

All is well. The army is a shock.

> *L'hitraot,*
> Alex

The Far End of Pain

> Feb 23/24, 1985
> [In the Army]

Dear Dad, Mom, Benj and Saul,

Here are some reactions to my first two and a half weeks: My favorite new Hebrew term is one used by the "phys. ed." teachers during our nightly exercise periods. When they want us to stretch, they say "more, more—*ad sof coev*," which means "until the end of pain." I think they mean the far end.

The hardest two things so far about the army have been the cold and the losing of new friends. The cold is no problem when we run or work because the exercise warms us up, but during gun checks and other endless line-ups it shakes my bones. At night I'm warm enough. I find that eating makes me feel cold; I always shiver after meals until I run again, even if I went into the dining hall feeling warm.

The losing of friends will end soon. It's only that during the first weeks of the army, they kept dividing us and redividing us. I used to sleep next to a great English *oleh* [new immigrant] (25 and married), but he was moved and I got depressed. Then they pulled the only other guy from Ein Tsurim out of our barracks. Anyway, that will end tomorrow when we go through our final divisions.

Beautiful first real hike last week: on a cold, foggy cloudy day we climbed Jebel Hureish (758 m [2426 ft]). We climbed the whole thing (450 meters of elevation) in forty minutes! I carried a 10-15 liter jerrycan for about 1/3 of the way to the top. The view is very beautiful and very unlike what I picture Samaria looking like.

> Love,
> Alex

Discipline and Punishment

[Journal]

Sanuur

Sanuur is a beautiful place with much pain. Some of the pain is physical, and some (more) comes from making new friends and then being separated from them, just when you begin to think that being with those people will give you the strength to go through what is to come.

The last week of February was the first week of basic training *(tironute)* at Sanuur. The first few days of basic were a real shock. Discipline became stricter and the punishments more frequent. At the pre-meal lineups the whole *plugah* [company] would be made to run around the square at the center of our base in thirty seconds (as punishment for moving and speaking during, or being late to, attention).

Punished For Laughing

February 25, 1985

Dear Mom, Dad, Saul and Benjy,

I'm on *toranute* now. I'm alone in the company dining hall guarding the guns of the other *toranim* who just left to get food from the central kitchen.

These kinds of moments are depressing because they give time to think. When we don't have time to think, we run around poles (as punishment for little flops). Those punishments are a pain in the neck, for no matter how diligent *you* are, you can still be punished for the slowness of one of the guys in your unit.

What's depressing is thinking what a waste of time all this stupid stuff is, when I should be writing articles or fighting battles.

But for every depressing moment there's a good moment. Last night we had a short (6 km) march to get to know our gear. The whole thing took only one hour (fast pace), and was really enjoyable, even though we soldier's had to run to keep up with our commander's walk. He walked past an Arab village which hugs the round top of a small mountain just like Arab villages are supposed to. Beautiful country.

.... Now it's two days later. After *toranute* I went to sleep, awoke at 4:45 and then ran and shot (quite well) and ran.

Now it's March 2. When you get this I'll have been "in" for over a month. Things are going much better. We've had three beautiful hikes—none of which gave me any trouble. I've been in such a good mood in fact that I've been punished for laughter. Next time I get out I'll send you a copy of a [page from] my journal with a story.

The training is becoming more interesting.

Love,
Alex

A Twinge of Loneliness

March 6, 1985
[In the Army]

Dear Mom and Dad,

This letter is my answer to the first of your letters (of many I hope) to reach me here in the army. I read it to the light of a candle after lights-out.

Dad, your letter lifted my spirits because of the wonders you are always doing. But, *Imma*, it was your letter which made me cry. I'm not sure why. But when I read what you wrote about my "doing great" I got very choked up. Maybe it was because I'm so unused to praise in this pit-of-punishment that I was moved by a long-missed sensation of hearing from someone (other than myself) that I'm okay. You know that I'm not the lonely type. Well, you brought about a twinge of loneliness. Don't get the feeling because it shook me I would have preferred your letter to be newsy and painless—I wouldn't. In fact maybe that was what did it to me. Maybe reading your letter was much more like being with you than I'd expected that I was a bit surprised by it. Newsy is OK because anything from home is OK and news from you folks is more than news. But it is when you move beyond news and into your thoughts that your letters can do more than just put a little smile on my face.

Enough about that. The reason I have time to write a letter is that today is Purim and as I'm fasting I've been given the afternoon off. During the morning I shot and ran with everyone else, but now they're off and I'm alone in the barrack with the only other guy who fasted—Yossi from Kibbutz Shluhot.

Last night we had a mostly painfully boring Purim party, and yesterday was parents day. Yehuda [Chen] came up from the kibbutz with the other two pairs of parents who have kids here. It was a good break and a great charge to see "family" here. Of course, they brought goodies as well (only I can't eat them because I'm fasting).

About the army. It is hard because it is frustrating. You work to be on time, finish your task, only to be screwed over by the sloth of your "hevra" [group of "friends"].

As far as the training and the military stuff goes—I'm not as physically worn as I expected. I have some foot troubles but I hope they're not serious. I've already shot four different types of guns at all sorts of distances. (Another frustration: I shot well one day only to get a zero because my gun clogged, and was still clogged when time ran out after I'd shot only one of the fifteen bullets I was supposed to shoot. The one missed.) I have a whole second letter's worth to talk to you about Jewishness, Alex, and the paratroops, but it will have to wait. Be well and safe.

Love,

Alex

Congratulations, Brother Saul!

March 10, 1985

[In the Army]

Dear Saul,

Congratulations!

I want you to know that your new job* has succeeded in depressing me at times no end. When I'm in "*matzav shtayim*" [second position] (on all fours, as before a pushup) in punishment for nothing, or running around a tree in thirty seconds because someone else in my company was one second late for a lineup, or spoke or moved during attention, I ask myself what I'm doing here and why I'm not with you fighting the bad guys and spreading the word. I'm serious.

Soon we'll be going "into the field" and away from the base, so maybe things will get better for me. I'm less and less pleased with the people in my unit. Many have IQs smaller than their shoe sizes, and I'm finding the age difference to be more felt than I hoped it would be.

I didn't get out this past Shabbat—yesterday. It was my first Shabbat "in the army," and it wasn't bad except that I had no chance to sleep between guard duty, *shul*, meals, *QB7* (by Leon Uris).

Please write to me every week and don't bother sending any but the most

---

*Saul worked as Legislative Assistant to Congressman Dan Burton of Indiana, a member of the House Foreign Relations Committee.

spectacular articles to read—send all of yours—as I don't have the strength for most of that type of reading!

Be well and don't worry about my depression. It will pass as soon as I begin to feel I'm being well used or doing interesting tasks.

Love,
Alex

"My Body Wanted to Cry"

Ides of March + 1, 1985
[Jerusalem]

Dear Family,

I'm in Jerusalem resting after a two-week stretch in the army without a break. The second week was "in the field" and was very hard. We set off Monday on a 6-km hike *pakalim* [unit loads] (jerrycans, two-way radios, stretchers) and *tadalim* [personal loads] (backpacks filled with coats, tents, sleeping bags, clothes...) and, of course, our weapons and battle gear. After the hour-long hike, we trained all day in various skills and also went out running. We went to sleep, awoke before sunrise, and set off on a second hike of 6 km. On the first day, I had a jerrycan and my *tadal* the whole way. On the second day I had the radio for the first half of the hike and only my *tadal* during the second. I used my lightness after I got rid of my radio to run around making sure we walked together, concentrating mostly on Daniel A., who is the baby of the unit. He had been ordered to hike first after the commander, as he had fallen behind before. I pushed him, pulled him, yelled at him, and told him to walk exactly in the commander's footsteps. In the end, he and I were one meter behind the commander and in front of everyone else.

After this second hike, we had a second day of exercises, which were followed by a couple of hours of sleep, and then a 2 a.m. "jump" (7 minutes from sleep to total readiness) and hike to a nearby village. The third day was our sergeant 's hike of 14 km at a fast 8 km/hour pace.

It was very difficult for me to keep up at one point—a steep incline where the gap between me and the sergeant grew from 3 ft to 30 ft. (I find that walking first is far easier than walking "in the pack.")

Just when we thought the whole thing was over, the sergeant said, "Thirty seconds to open the stretchers for the last two kilometers of your hike." At the end of the hike, an odd thing happened. I took off the jerrycan which had been on my back the whole way, and the pain began. The "pillows" of my feet felt like they were about to split, and I suddenly found that all I could do to keep from crying—sobbing—was to close my eyes as hard as I could and clench my fists. I don't know what made my body want to cry. I don't think it was the pain—maybe it was from relief—both from the non-stop effort of the previous 4 hours and 22 minutes, and from the weight of the gear on my back.

Besides a bit of flu, I'm fine. No back trouble at all. No knee trouble. No blisters. Don't worry excessively.*

Love,

Alex

*You like that?

"Promised to Give My Life"

March 22, 1985

[In the Army]

Dear Peter [Kaufman],

I received your letter when my kibbutz "father" [Yehuda Chen] came to see me at my swearing-in ceremony yesterday. The ceremony was very military but moving nonetheless. We were sworn in at the Western Wall of the Temple Mount in Jerusalem—a wall which became a wailing wall 2,000 years ago, but only came under the control of Jews again when it was taken back from the Jordanians by a group of paratroopers on reserve duty.

Army life is a bit different from my world at Cornell. The only reason I have time to write this letter is the fact that I pulled kitchen duty today, and the kitchen is a bit less busy than training. The kitchen is a wood shed which sits on a wind-blown barren hilltop along with a few other buildings and a water tower. There are some armored personnel carriers behind the dishwashing shack, and Jordan would be almost within sight were it not for the wind and dust.

I'm one month into basic training now. It has been as difficult physically as its reputation. And nothing compared to what we'll do, I'm told. Before the swearing in we had a hike which was actually pleasant—25 km with only battle gear and shared jerrycans, etc., from a hilltop on the road to Jerusalem, up to the city, all around the city to the Mount of Olives and views of Jordan, and finally into the Old City itself to the ceremony. At the ceremony I promised to give my life (even) for this country. That was pretty odd, and saying it really brings into focus what I've done.*

I wouldn't say that I have no regrets, because this is a hard place to be. At times I get really down, but when I sit myself down and think rather than just feel, I still know I did the right thing.

Alex

"There's a Good Chance I'll Never See Lebanon"

March 22, 1985
Sanuur

Dear Family,

I'm sitting in the kitchen (I have *toranute* for Shabbat) with a leaky roof (it's raining) on a barren hilltop not far from Beit Shean. I haven't seen Daniel for over a month and I really want a chance to talk to him about how he felt during this part of his service—this lonely, lonely part of basic training.

(Now it's March 25 and I'm back at my first base—near Sebastia.)

The swearing-in ceremony went smoothly, militarily. A poem was read...about the tears of the paratroops at the Wall. Our company commander gave each of us a Bible and our gun (we had handed them in earlier so they could be given to us officially).

Let me tell you a little about what I know or think is coming for me in the future: When Mom comes I'll arrange to get out, because I'm not scheduled to do so as of now. In the longer term:

—My jump course should start in about two months.

—Basic training should end in late July, I think.

—I'll come to the States after basic for one month.

Be well and don't worry. There's even a good chance that I'll never see Lebanon.

Love,

Alex

*This is a translation of the oath Alex took: "I hereby swear, and fully commit myself, to be faithful to the State of Israel, to its constitution and its authorities, and to take upon myself, without reservations or hesitancy, the rules of discipline of the Israel Defense Force, to obey all commands and orders given by authorized commanders, and to devote all my strengths, and even sacrifice my life, to the defense of my country and the freedom of Israel."

A Rare Idealist Zionist

[Journal]
March 23, 1983
Motzei Shabbat
Hamaam [training area]

It has been a long time since I've written in this book. My thoughts have gone into letters but it's probably easier to spill thoughts here than in letters. This past week was probably the hardest I'll go through in my service, even though it was a week free from physical difficulty.

It was a week of deep depression whose causes I would love to know. Part of my problem was that I felt lousy—the continuation of the case of the flu that started sometime during the previous week "in the field."

The flu was not the cause. Loneliness was the cause. I spent too much time thinking about how I not only have no friends in my unit, but also see no chance of finding friends among the 26 of us. At first I spent time thinking how the source of the friendlessness was the lousiness of the people, but now I realize that the people are fine and will work together. The problem of...(writing broken off by my squad leader telling me how I should be working on readiness).

****

Now it's March 26 and it's hard for me to write about my army depression because I'm in such a good mood. Why? Well, much of the reason is that I've started my week of training for the all-Tzahal tug-of-war competition. I left my unit in the Hamaam, and I'm in Sanuur. We have no discipline here; no weapons check, 12 hours of sleep a day the whole place is *rosh tov* [colloquially, "a good thing"]!

The training here is hard and I'm finding that I'm strong in some things (my hands, legs) and weaker in others (arms, stomach). One of the nice things about this training period is that I'm with some people I really like—Paul Curtis, the English *oleh* (married) whom I met in *bakum*, and Leonardo Lederman of Argentina and New Jersey who is in my company.

Leo is truly an impressive guy if only for the one promise he made to himself: A year ago he found that being in Israel on a kibbutz with other volunteers was not teaching him Hebrew, so he swore not to speak English, and hasn't for over a year. When he made his promise he says that he barely knew any Hebrew. Now he's quite fluent. The rest of Leo seems as strong-willed as his promise. He's an idealist Zionist which is nice to see, and surprisingly rare here in this army of Israel.

Confusing Commander

[Journal]
March 27, 1985
Sanuur Training Camp
After two full days of training my body wakes up in the morning with aches it has never felt. We train very hard, rest, eat, then rest and train again.

So, I like it here. I like getting into shape and feeling strength creeping up on me behind the pain. I like being free from discipline, and I like being treated as if we're people with an important task.

My Commanders:

My direct commander, Shai, and I have had a very up and down relationship so far. He has a reputation of being very tough and he works on that reputation through the way he treats us. He says on the one hand, "I'm not your friend," and on the other he jokes with us in the army style.

Until last week we didn't get along because I refused to answer any questions he asked me. This is because I was unable to tell when he was joking and when he was serious—when he wanted me to say "yes sir" and when he wanted my opinion or reaction. When I once jokingly said to him, "Why don't you take the stretcher," he gave me an hour of guard duty. It was after that that I would answer, "I have no answer," and explain myself with, "It's dangerous to answer." (To which he answered "Good.") In fact, it wasn't good.

Along with the problem discussed, I lost respect and affection for Shai when he called me a liar (upon finding a grain of sand in my gun barrel and hearing me say that I'd cleaned the barrel), and when he reversed his opinion of my emplacement when he heard the *mem pey* [company commander] criticize it.

So the tension between us grew and grew, as I refused to speak, and my list of Shai's "*fucks*" grew (the Hebrew, army term for negative marks). But after I told Gai about my problem with Shai, and he said that he thought I should talk to Shai because in fact he (Shai) was a good dude, Shai and I had a talk.

Shai also knew we needed to have a talk and we sat in his guard room and talked. Now we're on fine terms.

This understanding by no means changes the soldier-commander relationship. When Shai found a spot of dust on my Galil I paid for it as anyone might—with my feet, by running around a chin-up bar in 40 seconds until I'd "learned my lesson."

Half Decisions

March 30, 1985
Wingate Sport Institute

Dear Dad,

I'm in the kitchen at the Army's section at the Wingate Sports Institute. I just spoke with y'all on the phone. Sorry about waking you up—I misguessed the time difference. I don't have your articles in front of me but I want to react to them in general. On the Central American* article: I thought the way you organized the article was good. If Americans can learn that decisions must be made wholeheartedly (that half-decisions such as half-supporting the Contras leads to their defeat by convincing the Contras' would-be friends that the Contras can't win), then maybe they will be stronger deciders.

The Israeli example of this weakness is also very clear: When Israel rejected the "big plan" of invading Lebanon in 1982 (which included sending forces by air north in order to block Syria and other troops from moving south), in favor of the smaller plan, of attacking from the south and moving north only to a specific line (even though they knew the "small plan" would snowball into the "big plan," and the IDF would have to continue north), they cost the country hundreds of lives.

I just read the Central America article.* It's better than good. I especially liked what you said about the different audiences in Nicaragua watching the "U.S.-support-for-the-Contras" show. I also liked (as much as horrors can be liked) your scenarios for what would follow Contra failure. They are good for hammering at the consequences of American refusal to be a true friend to those we admit to "our side."

I'll close now to send this with some Americans.

Love,

Alex

*Max Singer testified to Congressional committees and published articles concerning Central America in *Commentary, Reader's Digest, National Interest, National Review* and other publications. The article Alex refers to is "Losing Central America," *Commentary*, July, 1986.

"Saul, Be Driven In Your New Job"

March 31, 1985

Dear Saul,

I got your letter and the collection of articles. What can I say? I'm impressed beyond words. All I can think of is my usual advice—to be driven in your new job [legislative assistant to Congressman Dan Burton], to work at it all hours, and to make of it the strongest weapon you can....

Be well and write about the wondrous battles which you fight.

Love,

Alex

Opening Up to Younger Brother Daniel

April 1, 1985

[In the Army]

Dear Daniel,

I'm glad I got to talk to you this Shabbat but I really want a chance to talk face to face at length about the paratroop business.

I'll try to put down on this small paper a bit of what's been going through my head. As you know I've been away from my platoon for the past week training for the IDF tug-of-war competition. At first the training situation totally reversed my mood and I walked around as I used to, with a big grin on my face.

Now things are less rosy and I'm not grinning. My body is deteriorating again. But more than the physical problems are the problems I have when I have too much time to think.

I tell myself that I'm in the wrong place—that I will never feel a part of my platoon, that I can't picture anyone in my platoon as a good friend, that I don't want to serve in the paratroop battalion, that I'll leave after *tironute* and try to get into intelligence or something...etc., etc., etc.

The irritating thing is that I know that I'll do fine. I have a very good chance to be a machine gunner, I do well on the marches. My commanders like me, etc. In other words: if I get over my minor physical problems I can be a very good soldier (even if I'm not a backslapping member of the *hevra* in the platoon). At least I have friends in the company.

I spoke to a girl named Hadas (whose sister was in your class at Szold) about the problems while I was waiting to use the telephone. We decided that a lot of the indecision comes from the fact that my presence in the army is voluntary, unlike that of the *sabra* [native-born Israeli] soldiers. This means that I spend time thinking about whether I made the right choice (stupid thing to do but I did it anyway). This thinking doesn't go so far as to say that I shouldn't have made aliyah, but it often leads me to think the paratroops was not right for me.

Things like the news of Saul's job (don't get the wrong idea—I was dancing when I heard about it I was so happy for him) are the fuel of my indecision fire. Every letter from Dad and Saul is painful as well as happy for me, because they both write of things which I miss doing and know I could do well.

Love,

Alex

Frustrating Tug-of-War

[Journal]

April 2, 1985

[In the Army]

I was on the final rope-pulling team of ten men, after training for a week and a half with a total of 22 folks (the ten were chosen from the 22). The first team opposing us was that of the officers' school. They beat us 2-0. Our next opponents were the representatives of the Golani Brigade—the traditional rivals of the paratroops. They beat us the first pull but we won on the second of two in a great victory. Sadly, we were lined up for the third competition with MAGAV (short for *mishmar hagvul* [border police]) whose rope team is undefeated (they train constantly and are as close to a professional team as there is—we only trained one week!). They won but we put up an excellent fight, holding out against them for a record 4:47 in the second pull, and a respectable time in the first pull as well. The record of 1:2 meant that we don't "go up" to the semifinals—a situation for which I blame Eliko, our trainer, who did three things to make us lose to the officers (who we could have easily beaten): (1) He put as "caller" a soldier who'd never called for us, rather than the instructor who called for the second and third pulls; (2) he left the fat and inept Peretz (who fell down all the time in training) as our anchor, when he shouldn't have been on the team at all; and (3) he didn't tell us about the strategy to expect or use, which meant that we tired ourselves out and were beaten. It's too bad Eliko didn't invest a bit more effort—at least as much as we did, so that we could have gone on in the tournament.

Wildflowers and Sketching

April 4, 1985
[Sanuur]

Dear Family,

Today we leave the dream world of the training camp and return to the real army of little sleep and many lineups.

The morning sun came up and lit the hills here at Sanuur beautifully. I wish you could see this place. I even had a chance to do a couple of sketches. I did one at night to the light of an almost full moon.

The wildflowers are out now in force. From where I sit, outside the barrack where we slept during training, I see mostly yellow ones, but when we walk in the hills there are no colors we don't see.

Love,
Alex

Passover with Holocaust Survivors

[Journal]
Pesach 5745
North Kedumim, Samaria

I'm sitting in the guard room of the small Orthodox settlement of Kedumim in Samaria. I was sent here with one other soldier (Yuval) and a commander (Yossi) to replace the reserve soldiers who usually help the settlers guard their homes, so they could go home for Passover.

I thought Passover in the army would be at best tolerable but it turned out to be a joy. I went on Friday to *kabbalat Shabbat* in the settlement's synagogue, and was invited by a family to join them for Seder. Yisrael and Tova Michalsky and their little (two-year-old) Eliyahu, and their brother and sister-in-law and kids.

The father of one of the couples was also there. He is a survivor of Dachau, who told me how he was taken the day before the end of the war, with all the other prisoners of Dachau, by cattle train to what they were told would be a sanatorium, but what turned out to be a pit surrounded by machine guns. There they waited, stripped, for a death he said they didn't feel too badly about by then. A woman SS officer arrived with what he expected was the order to fire. Everyone closed their eyes and waited, as the shooting began all around them, for death, each hoping to be killed quickly. But when he found out that he hadn't been killed, he opened his eyes. The soldiers were shooting all the ammunition away from the pit and running. The Allies were on their way.

The family which invited me to join them will remain friends. They were very warm and made me truly enjoy this Passover.

There Is an End

[Journal]
April 14, 1985
[In the Army]
I finally saw Daniel at the kibbutz [Ein Tsurim] this Shabbat. Talking to him helped me somewhat—not by giving me solutions to specific problems...but by reminding me that there's an end to all this shit.

Saved By a Tendon

April 17, 1985
[In the Army]

Dear Dad, Benj and Saul,

This past week has been one in which the commanders have evidently decided to use no carrots and strong sticks to sharpen our discipline. They've been handing out punishments very fast and the soldiers have been run in punishments quite brutally. One "private" punishment was particularly sick. A commander put a radio (like the one Daniel carried) on the back of a soldier who'd done something wrong and for half an hour or more ran him by radio command throughout the base. This is illegal, I'm sure, but I don't think he'll complain. I, on the other hand, have escaped most of the punishments—not by being wonderful or anything, but because I can't run because of my tendon problem. I wish my body would stop giving me trouble. The physical problems (I also have some breathing trouble) make me feel guilty and worn out—guilty because I feel that I should, as a big strong dude, be carrying more. Enough.

Our training is finally beginning to be interesting—learning how to use lots of weapons, including RPGs [rocket-propelled grenades], mortars, grenades, etc.

I can see the end of basic now.

Love,
Alex

Snorting Instead of Drawing

April 17, 1985
[In the Army]

Dear Grandma Jeanne,

The army is hard for me but I think it will get better. It's been hard on my drawing, too, although I have done a few nice ones.

Sometime, not too long ago, after Ellen Epstein wrote that she couldn't picture me running up and down hills since she always pictured me as drawing in the shade of an olive tree—it struck me how incongruous the army is in the hills of Samaria. The hills right around the base are sensual with their curves and crevasses; and everything should move at a pace which is in closer sync with the hills. But whenever we enter the hills we move like marines, and snort and pant and sweat, when we should be lying under an olive tree drawing and sleeping.

Oh well....

Love,
Alex

Grinning and Guarding

[Journal]

April 18, 1985

Hamaam

Two months into basic there is much to report. One of my sergeants has left for officers' school—Yossi Gabbai, who gave me my first personal punishment when I started grinning in an equipment lineup after he said, "I can be a gentle mother or a stern father." You had to be there. I just couldn't see him as either, and when he said, "Singer, wipe that grin off your face!" I cracked up, and he sent me off to guard somewhere.

The past week has been busy and harsh as far as discipline is concerned. We've gone down to exercises and weapons training each day in formation, with time limits, rather than "in song" as we do when "we're good." Yesterday, we were all sent to Yad Vashem to secure the opening ceremony of Yom Hashoah. I wish I could have seen it although being less than 100 meters away meant that strains of the music and speeches made their way through to where I was sitting.

Three Bombs on My Back

May 4, 1985

[In the Army]

Dear Dad, Saul and Benjy,

Dad, I started to write a letter in my journal but didn't get very far with it for lack of time. This past week has been a very full and busy one—"platoon week" it was called, as it was designated for platoon-size training. In fact we started the week with some catching up on squad-size operations. It was also the first week where I had my *pakal*—including my weapon, which I am responsible for carrying and using. I am now an RPGist! I have yet to shoot a live missile but I've done well with dummies—even putting one through a plate-sized hole in a target approx. 100 yards away. The tube, the missile, the scope, everything is made in the USSR, which gives me a little satisfaction, but I don't know if that satisfaction will make up for how heavy and awkward the damn thing is compared with some of the platoon's other tools. I now carry three bombs on my back, my normal battle gear, the RPG tube itself, and my Galil. The biggest problem is that the tube is always bouncing around and getting in the way as I run with it.

Dad, I wanted to send you a copy of what I've put in my journal so far but that will have to wait a few weeks until I'm at the kibbutz Xerox machine. On the last page I began to write you a letter which says, "When I returned from lunch three letters were waiting for me—all from you. Reading that you miss me a lot made me miss you a lot. I don't usually spend much time thinking about missing you because if I did this life would be much harder for me than it already is."

I think that your decision to write lots of short notes is a good one for both of us. I'll try to get back to writing myself but these past three weeks have been hard ones as far as time is concerned. It's also hard for me to send notes so I'll have to pile them up and send them in gobs on my days off.

Did I tell you about the camera crew which came to interview me and Gary (from my platoon) for a symposium on *olim* [new immigrants] in the army? We were chosen because, of the *olim* in the company, two have run away (a Frenchman and an Englishman), one was bitten by a snake (but is otherwise in good shape physically and mentally) and we were left.

One guy (in the tent next to me, from another platoon) shot himself in the foot last week to get out of the paratroops. He was one of the best soldiers in the platoon so it was quite a shock.

Love,
Alex

Lunar Eclipse in Jerusalem

May 4, 1985
[Jerusalem]

Dear Grandma and Grandpa [Fried],

The army continues to be new and at times exciting.

I just found out that there will be a full eclipse of the moon tonight which should be a beautiful sight. The moon in Jerusalem is full and bright against a night sky which is a deep blue. An eclipse of the moon means that we'll see the shadow of the earth pass over the moon. This means that if we go to the edge of the earth and wave we should see our shadow. But, I'd rather not go to the edge of the earth tonight.

Love,
Alex

You Give Me Strength

May 5, 1985
[Sanuur]

Dear Dad,

On the bus back to Sanuur this morning I sat next to a 26-year-old American named Eddy who is in for three years, He's in the other paratroop company which was drafted in February. Talking to him made his grass look greener for two reasons: one is that he's in a platoon with an *oleh* who's a good friend of mine and whose presence is apparently a source of strength which helps through many hard moments. There's an *oleh* in my unit, but while I am a great help to him, our relationship is one-way. (Gary is worth a whole letter, but not this one.) The second reason for the greenness of the 890s grass, in comparison with that of 202, is what Eddy told me about their teaching schedule and the philosophy it implies. His platoon has had eight platoon exercises and two company-size ones so far. We've had only one platoon-size one, and of course none on the company level. We've learned skills one at a time, while they've done exercises and learned the same skill in the context of the exercises. I would bet their exercises are better than ours. They uniformly feel they've come a long way and have done a lot, while I feel that we've proceeded very slowly. Even if I'm wrong and our directly learned skills are greater than their indirectly learned ones, I still prefer their system because it gives soldiers the sense that they do something and makes learning more interesting. The former is especially important to me, and the latter is, I think, universally important.*

As I look around this bus at my sleeping platoon-mates, I see no one who will be the kind of friend who gives me strength. But that's OK (not great) because you give me the strength and I have a lot of my own.

Love,
Alex

---

*The experimental program of Battalion 890 that Alex admired was subsequently adopted as the standard training program.

Pure Fear

May 6, 1985
[Beit Gubrin]

Dear Mom and Dad,

Today has been one of the hardest days of basic so far. Maybe I should say "unpleasant" because it has not had any physical challenges whatsoever. I'm in Beit Gubrin and have had guard duty all day, and all last night away from my company at a central base. I'm here with two others from my platoon—Danny and Ziad.

My head has been torturing me in all sorts of directions: I felt first of all lonelier than I've ever felt, with no one to talk to. When I get like this I lose sight of how short one year and three months is,* and can only see the torture of 86 weeks of Danny and Ziad.

(By the way—I'm writing to you during guard duty [a no no] while sitting [another] without my gun on [another], guarding a three-football-field-sized ammunition dump. It's getting dark, so I'll switch on my flashlight soon.)

The pain which is as great as loneliness comes from fear. Pure fear. I fear failure and I fear challenges—the physical ones ahead. Fear is a carefully chosen word and one I use rarely because it used to be unfamiliar to me. Just as I told you I feared a second *geebush* (or trial) for the paratroops because I knew how hard it would be (fear of the familiar rather than of the unknown), my fear of every march ahead of me is all the greater for those which I have completed. My lack of fitness makes this fear worse because I know it will make the trials ahead more painful.

Remember. This letter was written two weeks before you read it, so by now the problems it discusses are in the past and all is well. Writing what I have written here has helped me immensely—drained the emotion out of me, and given me the peace needed to allow me to rest. I envy Daniel for two things now more than ever—for having what I have in front of me behind him, and for having friends in the army and friends his own age. Don't worry I have the strength to get through all this. I only wish I didn't have to use it all. Be well.

Love,
Alex

*Alex had only an 18-month (not 3-year) obligation to the army because of his age when he became a citizen. When he agreed to go to officers' school, however, he was required to extend his enlistment by one year.

"Infantry Is Not for Me"

[Journal]

May 9, 1985

[In the Army]

Yesterday was catharsis day. I realized what I'd been realizing for weeks—that infantry is not for me. We were on a company-size exercise (our first) and I couldn't keep up. The best thing that happened was being "wounded" and having an "infusion" stuck in my arm by Sharon, our medic. The checker of the exercise saw me standing too high and said "wounded." I was carried out through the burning fields on a stretcher.

Back to catharsis. I'm going to call Talik because only he could get me out.

May 19th

I wrote the above during what must have been the hardest week for me in basic. Now, 10 days later, I'm far more content with my place in the IDF. A large factor in my feeling better is the fact I've participated in, and even done well in, the last two marches: the one two Thursdays ago was a short (11-km) hike with *pakalim*, and stretchers for the second half. The one this past Thursday was 8.2 km with four people to each stretcher! This means that the only time you're out from under the stretcher is when you switch shoulders with the person next to you.

May 21st

My *mem mem* [platoon commander] promised me a few weeks ago (in a one-to-one talk) that I'd be in the APC [armored personnel carrier] driving course. I had asked if there would be a problem with the fact that my only driver's license is American. He said "don't worry." But when we got there I couldn't take the course because I had no Israeli license. Bummer.

In Sanuur I saw Daniel which was great. He's doing well I think, but it's still hard for me to know what he's like as a commander.*

The afternoon was spent at Kibbutz Lochamei Ha Getaot's [ghetto fighters] Holocaust museum, which was interesting as a Holocaust museum, but *very* interesting for the conversations which lead to:

*The Hebrew word for sergeant is often translated as "commander."

121

IDEA FOR TEACHING ABOUT THE DIFFERENCE OF A JEWISH ARMY

Q. What made the Germans able to kill a whole people?

A. Jews were made into a non-people through degradation—beard-cutting, carica-ture, numbers, etc.

Q. How do Arabs train? How are Jews presented to Arab soldiers?

A. Bite heads off snakes—stab dogs—caricatures—*Protocols of the Elders of Zion.* "Jews equal non-people."

Q. What about us—the army?

A. We can go either way!

1: Arabs as *fatmot* [cheap Arab women] and *jukim* [cockroaches]

Disadvantages: incompatible with Judaism

                     wrong

                     will change Israel into fanatic country

Advantages: easier to kill a cockroach than a father of children

2: Arabs as People

Disadvantages: hard to maintain with every terrorist outrage

                     makes it harder to be strong

Advantages: Jewish way

                     keeps us in control of our actions

Israel must take the second path because Israel is a Jewish state, a democratic state, and an *or lagoim* [light unto the nations].

"Being Less Than the Best Is Hard"

May 13, 1985

[Outside Shechem]

Dear Mom, Dad, Saul and Benj,

I'm sitting on the ground just outside my base for this week, just outside Shechem. I have an hour before I have to be back, and rather than throw it away, I prefer to sit here and write to you.

On Saturday night I saw Harold [Rhode]. We went out for a walk, so that we could talk privately. I have trouble knowing what to tell you we talked about, but part of what Harold said was that I have to begin to open up to people, because until I do I won't find the sense of belonging which is needed in hard times. As far as intellectual interaction goes, I've always been great—outgoing, etc., but as soon as things get personal I lock tight.

Another thing we talked about, which I'd thought a lot of before, was my fear of mediocrity, which has made being less than the best so hard for me. I realize that all this sounds maybe a bit like overanalysis, but that's because I can't explain how useful our talk really was. Ask Harold to tell you about it. You'd be interested, and I'm sure he'll keep to himself those things which I don't want him to talk about.

By the time you get this I'll almost be in jump school, and soon after that I'll be done with the first phase of the paratroops. I can't say that I'm looking forward to what will follow, except in comparison to basic, but maybe I'll come to like it.

Love,

Alex

A Few Laughs At Gary's Expense

May 13, 1985

[In the Army]

Dear Mom, Dad, Saul and Benj,

It was good to talk to you last night.

It's amazing how much the mind can exhaust the body. Fear of physical challenge, and the knowledge that my sleep is limited, leave me exhausted before I even start on a march, and tired even on days when we do nothing hard.

May 15

I wrote the above two days ago. Since then and this whole week I've been at an instruction base hanging out. Today I started an RPG course, but I knew what we've done so far. We used computers today to learn how to aim. The Chief of Staff [CoS] was supposed to drop in on the class but went to another. My friend Leo was there, and the CoS talked to him. Leo said everyone else gave "I love the paratroops" fake answers. Leo told the CoS that he found the age difference hard, and that he sometimes felt lonely. I like that. Honesty is better than giving the "answers he wants to hear," especially since they are precisely what he doesn't want to hear.

Gary left today for the three-month medics' course. I'm glad. Even though he was the only other *oleh*, and the only other person over age 18, I think that the benefit of what we had in common was outweighed by the fact that all he talked about was how happy he was to be getting out of the platoon, and about how everyone took advantage of him.

If I miss him it'll be because we spent so much time together (my bed was next to his; we shared a two-man tent for a week). As much as he got on my nerves I've got to admit that Gary gave the platoon some good laughs. (Don't get me wrong—he's a fine person, just a bit slow and a bit of a nudnik.) There was the time, during a company-scale exercise, that the medic yelled, "Gary, do you still want to be a medic?" Gary thought he yelled, "Charge!" So Gary attacked the enemy alone.

A few minutes later in the same exercise, just as he was about to run from one position to another behind our front line (i.e., no shooting so as not to hit our own forces), Gary said, "*Ani yachol l'rot?*" ("Can I shoot?") when he meant "Can I see?" We grabbed him to clarify his plan, before he shot someone.

May 19

Now it's Sunday and another Shabbat in the army is over. My spirits have really been high, despite some irritating behavior on the part of my platoon, and a disgusting episode which I will now relate, which shows how power can make people behave like scum:

The company sergeant (responsible for food, company cleanliness, discipline, etc.) pulled me aside Thursday night after a march and said: "How would you like it if I *kader* (punish in a degrading manner) you in front of your brother?" I smiled and said I wouldn't. He gave me a playful shove, and I thought the episode was over. Next morning, four hours later in fact, Shlomo (the sergeant) has me called out of our barracks. I exit stage left and there's Daniel and Shlomo. Shlomo says, "*Matsav shtayim.*" (This means "position number two" which is a common punishment for small crimes such as talking during a lineup.) I smile (I always smile when I'm mad) and go into a lazy position number two—on a sort of elevated sewage cover. He says, "No, *matsav shtayim.*" I go into a full position number two and immediately get up. He says, "Who released you?" I say, "Daniel." Daniel says, "I did." He says, "*Matsav shtayim.*" Daniel says, "It's not worth messing with these types." I agree and go down again. A moment later he says, "released," and I leave, needless to say, fuming.

Be well.

Love,

Alex

Influencing Soldiers

May 28, 1985

[In the Army]

Dear Mom, Dad, Saul, and Benjy,

I just got the letters you sent. As always they were a joy to read. June is almost here and with it comes jump school. Even though the end is near, these last weeks before jump school look like they'll be tough—not in the sense of endless difficult training—but an increase in pressure.

You asked me to write about people in my platoon. I'm in a tent now with: A.— a *pushtak* [ruffian] who does things like piss next to the tent, steal, lie, smoke, sing obscene and adolescent songs, slip lineups, refuse to guard when it's his turn, hate me, and acts as stupid as he is. Also Itai—who's tall and dark like Benj, and reminds me of him a lot, because he's got a beautiful girlfriend, and he sort of bounces around with a big smile. Also, Ofir—a five foot (or less) Yemenite who turns out to be good for the platoon for his spirit, even though he's personally unreliable. Enough about people I have other things to write about.

Now it's the last day of May. It's Friday, 5:49 p.m., a breeze is blowing through my eight-man tent (all the others are napping); things are good. Just as my letters to you give you a two-week old picture of my state of mind and training, so your letters are usually full of reactions to feelings I've gotten over; but I don't mind, I love them anyway.

While the rest of my platoon is getting over a 45-km stretcher march which ended this morning, I am feeling great. I didn't go on the march because I was sent to another platoon, as a representative of mine, to take part in activities about which I cannot write, but which were far more interesting than a march. I feel quite honored to have been chosen to take part, as I was the only one from the platoon who went.

I have only one more march before the *masa kumta* [beret march]—a 90-km killer next week, for which you needn't pity my pains, as they will have passed by the time you read this.

I don't have much more army news, so I'll respond to your letters.

First: Benj, I would give you all sorts of advice about not lazing around, and hustling, because of how good it feels to work all week (especially if you observe Shabbat), but I don't think I need to give you my advice—your head seems to be in the right place. And Benj, while I know I've already told you your letters are in a different world—so much more free and real—than your letters until two letters ago, I'll say it again, because you should know what a joy it is to read what you write. Saul—what can I say? When I first heard about your job I envied you a lot, but now that things are better with me (especially since my unwritable activities this week), I only envy you sometimes, and can see that as different as our paths are, they will both influence history.

After the "education" I got the feeling that the paratroops was the place to be as far as influencing soldiers—preventing them from becoming like their enemies, and making sure they remain Jews in their soldiery—was concerned. This was a great improvement over the past, when I felt I should have gone into the education corps. Now I'm sure that the best place to educate is in command and not at a lectern. However, now that some time has passed I can see another goal (beside educating) of being in the army—and that is to be a great soldier and do important tasks well. What was it you said about using a shovel in the plumbing world, rather than a tea-spoon, as far as moving mountains of goodness were concerned? Anyway, you can be great anywhere, in the army too, and influence people through your light. But there is still a difference between being a light and fixing leaks, and being a light and fighting terrorism. Is all this coherent?

The sun is about to set and Shabbat is about to start. The light on the hills is beautiful and it's getting chilly. I've got to go now as I've been called to *Kabbalat Shabbat*. (We might even get a *minyan*—but that's hard to do.)

Now Shabbat is over. It was a joy—no less. Friday night one of the *dati* [orthodox] soldiers managed to convince his whole platoon to come to shul—even the super-secular, so there was a *minyan*. At first they joked around, but even though they were uncomfortable, and totally unfamiliar with the tunes of songs in the service, the "*L'cha Dodi*" was beautiful and strange. I wonder whether they'll come back. All day on Shabbat I lazed around the tent, talking with and listening to the guys in my platoon, eating cakes from their homes and kibbutzim, and sleeping. Saturday morning there again was a *minyan* (this time with no leftovers—ten men).

Since I should begin to close this letter I'll ask some questions I've wanted to ask you. Unluckily but typically I've forgotten most of them. One of the questions I haven't forgotten is an odd question for me, because I'd like you to tell me about the relationships (girlfriends/boyfriends) you had before you met. My current situation makes me interested in this, but it is the subject of another letter—a letter I'm not sure I feel like writing just now.

Love,

Alex

First Real Action

[Journal]

May 30, 1985

[In the Army]

I'm writing while sitting waiting in an open truck about to leave with a dozen others to do the first real action (not practice) in my army career. But I can't write about it. One nice thing about this action is that it means I won't have to do a 45-km stretcher march tonight. When you miss a march because of a sickness or a hurt foot you feel guilty, but when you have a reason you don't.

Two weeks ago was the march from Carmiel to the Kinneret. It went very well for me and for the platoon as a whole. The only bummer happened after we'd all laid down to rest. I got up and the platoon commander saw me and asked if there was a guard. I said no. He said there had to be one, so I put on my battle gear and started to guard, thinking that after ten minutes I'd wake somebody to take my place, as I was dead tired and in pain from the march. No one would take my place, so I guarded for over half an hour—boy, was I pissed. But I got even; I was let out at 7:00 a.m. and they all had to stay for a few hours longer (being a "lone soldier"* has its advantages).

---

*"Lone soldier" is the official term for a soldier like Alex who has no parents in Israel. "Lone soldiers" are given special privileges, for example, extra leave time for family-related visits.

Training For Trench Warfare

June 9, 1985

[In the Army]

Dear Mom and Dad,

One of my best days in the army was Wednesday, which was the culmination of a week's training in trench warfare, spent living in two-man tents in the field. The day started with a hike with all our gear for a few kilometers through a wadi to where our platoon-scale exercise was to take place. The hike was strenuous but very pleasant. I hiked second, after the sergeant, Gai. We talked the whole way about all sorts of things, from RPG trajectories to 4,000-year-old loom weights. (I found one, you know, in the training area near the base and brought it back.) Of the whole platoon it turned out that only he and I were hiking well, as at one point he turned around and our closest follower was at least 50 yards back. This is a no-no but it is a no-no which can be, and was easily, repaired by a sergeant with a few simple words: "Thirty seconds and the gap is closed."

We arrived at the open where the exercise was to take place in a tight group, put down our gear, and climbed the hill to our east in order to get a better view of the set of trenches we were to conquer. We arrived in time to see most of the other platoon's exercise. The view from the hill of the live (live ammunition, bombs, etc.) was impressive. Their riflework and choreography was good, but their anti-tank shooting was lousy—their RPG missed and so did their other launched grenade; and most of their mortars fell off target.

Toward the end of their exercise I left my platoon-mates to their watching, and returned to our gear, so as to zero in the telescope on my RPG. When I was satisfied that it was perfect, I tied it to the pack of bombs and was off with the rest of the platoon for the "dry" run-through of the conquest.

When the dry was over we were given the safety rules by the deputy commander. He had to stop, and start all over again, when it turned out that three of our soldiers were missing—they had been left to give cover fire and played dumb—not returning to the platoon when the "dry" was over with the excuse, "No one told us we were through," for which each lost a day of vacation as punishment. We returned to the starting point (near where I found the loom weight), assembled the rocket for my RPG and we were off. The exercise went very well, and best of all my RPG hit just where I thought it would, and blew the turret off the tank-shell which was our target. (I also shot a live RPG the previous day in a squad-size exercise, which also blew its target apart. Each of my hits was followed by a loud whoop of joy, because it's a nice feeling to blow up a target with an RPG.)

After the exercise my officer pulled me and the rifle-grenade launcher aside and paid us the ultimate compliment for our work, saying that if he was ever called to Lebanon we would be the first he would take with him. I went to bed only to wake up in the morning to my most irritating day in the army.

We'd been told that Thursday—before the 60-km march which was to start in the evening—would be devoted to preparing the camp for our departure, never to return, for Jump School. We were also told that Thursday would have free time for us—to rest and work on the gear we were to carry that night.

Our first job was to clear a field the size of a football field of waist-high thorns and thistles. My view is that it is better not to discuss too many strategies for doing simple, mindless work. So I set to work. Unluckily, my platoon-mates felt the need to discuss everything. When the staff sergeant saw that progress was slow, I had to run (in punishment) with the rest of the company.

I kept telling myself that if I worked hard we'd finish earlier and have more time to rest and prepare. I should have saved my strength because there was no way for me to influence the speed with which the company worked.

I got so furious as the orders slowly came and our time disappeared, that at one point I punched what I thought was a plastic window in anger. It turned out to be a glass window which shattered leaving my hand bleeding nicely. Breaking a window...does wonders for releasing pent up anger....

A 60-km hike is a very hard thing to do. Especially with 25+ kg [over 55 lb] on me. The first 30+ were fine. I felt strong and almost free from pain. But somewhere between km 30 and km 40 the company commander started to run, and the run broke me. The last 20 km were a slow agony, and I was in such bad shape (from foot problems to rashes from rubbing between my legs and sides) that I could barely move. I finished last of the whole company, but I finished, and I finished without once giving what I was carrying to someone else. I was very pleased. Some other time I'll write about the march—the breaks, the thoughts, sleepwalking, getting lost, pushing and being pushed and the moon.

But, now I'll close and send this letter off. Be well.

Love,
Alex

A Birthday Letter

June 14, 1985
[Beit Leed]

Dearest Mother,

HAPPY

BIRTHDAY

When I think of the fact that you've now lived for 50 years it strikes me that I've only been part of less than half of your life. This is odd because you've always been such an important part of me. And it's funny to think that for twenty-seven and a half years you lived without me. When I get to be twenty-seven and a half, I'll look back and won't be able to picture having lived without you.

So, as I sit in the Beit Leed army store waiting to go back to the army for Shabbat, I'm thinking of you, and tears are welling up a bit in my eyes, because when I spend time thinking about you I miss you, and now that it's your 50th birthday how can I but think of you?

And what do I think when I think of you? I think three things. I think gratitude (but I won't begin to list the reasons for my gratitude because the list would be endless). I think admiration for how you've raised us, taught us, created a magazine, been able to change and adapt to science, to teaching, to Israel, to archeology, to editing, to Washington, to everything that's crossed our lives as a family. I admire the way you have taken your children for what each of them is, and added to each of them.

Third, I think joy. Joy is maybe what I feel most when I think of you, because you take the world so well and that makes me happy. I love to see you working, talking, writing, everything.

So, this is not a real birthday card with firecrackers and streamers. It is an announcement and declaration of my gratitude and (even more because you've heard enough about my gratitude) my admiration for you.

Now I must go. I wish I could have been with you.

Od meah v'esrim! [May you live to be 120!]

Love,

Alex

Excessive Punishment

[Journal]
June 20, 1985
Tel Nof
The Incident at Jump School

Training had ended at 6. We were already through with dinner when the word came through that we had a battle-gear run in a few minutes. "Eight laps," he said. Commander Tamir led us. At first I kept up with his pace—for the first 1 1/2 mile or so of the slightly less than 1000-meter swings around the base. Then the trouble began: the pain in the lower back and the shortness of breath. I fell back and ran alone. My pace slowed so much that after a few laps, the squad passed me.

Then it happened. I stopped running towards the very end of lap 6. I walked a bit—maybe 50 yards—and started again to plow forward. But just as I stopped heel-toeing in favor of toe-healing, I came upon Tamir and the rest of my "buddies." They had taken off their gear and were releasing the muscles which I still so sharply felt. They'd done seven laps.

Tamir asked, "How many have you done?"

"Six," I panted.

"Do ten!"

"I won't be able to," I said, but I kept going.

After a lap I arrived at my still-stretching squad. I'd by then done the same seven they had, so I stopped, began to take off my gear.

"What the hell are you doing," screeched Tamir.

"I've done seven," I said as I continued to pull my battle gear off.

"You take that off you stay Shabbat."

I was furious. I've never come so close to throwing down my gear and yelling at a commander. But my squad helped me back into my gear, and pushed me off. I walked rather than ran away from the squad. I walked, in fact, the whole lap (my eighth).

As I walked my strength returned, and at the end of the lap I returned to a slow run. My ninth lap went well, but at the end of it I found Commander Tamir.

"You can stop now," he said, as I reached him. But I didn't want to stop. He had given me punishment and I wanted to finish it even if it hurt me. I had something to prove to myself, and I wanted to punish Tamir by showing him how excessive was his punishment. I kept running and his voice grew louder.

"Stop!"

"I have one more to go."

"Stop!"

"I don't want to."

"Stop."

"Make up your mind," I screamed.

"I'll give you one minute to stop and get over here."

It's one thing to argue and something else to disobey a direct order. I stopped. Tamir gave me twenty-five minutes to stretch, shower, put on my "dress" uniform. That night the whole company went to see "Emanuelle." But there's little joy in watching bad people have good sex.

Jump School

[Journal]

June 30, 1985

Tel Nof

Jump school has been sort of bittersweet. On the one hand, we've been on this lush base, with relatively much sleep and interesting training. On the other hand, the grass looks greener when its around you and you can't touch it. We've been allowed to use the pool once—on Shabbat—but for the rest of our two weeks we have passed it, able only to hear the laughter of the swimmers, but unable to feel the coolness of the water.

Training has been mediocre due to the mediocrity of our trainers—Moshe—a formerly Orthodox dude who is now best characterized by his own words, "I used to be a braggart...." He wasted such a large proportion of our training time yelling at us (half in jest), that we didn't get to do as much practice as we could have. We would get onto a training machine just long enough to get over our fear of it, but not enough time to perfect techniques. This was especially true for me on the "big swing" where my first jump pushed my balls up into the center of my chest (or at least it felt that way) due to a strap which went the wrong way. This was irritating as well as painful, because it happened in a jump which followed a check by Moshe of my gear. How can I rely on him if he didn't catch this? Anyway, I wanted to keep jumping to get over the fear which the bad jump caused, but I only had time for one jump. It wasn't too good.

Gliding Whales, Monster Machines

June 24, 1985

[In the Army]

Dear Mom, Dad, Saul, Benj and DANIEL,

Daniel left for the U.S. today. But since he'll be arriving at the address of this letter, I feel a bit funny writing about him in the third person. But I'll get over the awkwardness for long enough to say that, even with all the "problems" which everyone who hears about Daniel and me in the army brings up, I like having him in the army ahead of me. The questions—"What's it like to have your younger brother a commander?" etc.—are the only part I don't like, because they always make me feel I'm on show, and everyone is watching me to see how we are together.

[continued]

June 28

Friday afternoon

I'm in my tent at the base. The company is staying this Shabbat. This is something which I really don't feel too bad about except for the fact that I won't be able to call you during your Shabbat dinner with Daniel there. Thinking about that dinner presses the homesickness button. I usually don't, when I think about you, think of the specific situations you're in and long to be a part of them. But I find myself thinking about being at the dining table with you singing "*Shir Hamaalot*" [the song which begins the prayers of thanks after the Shabbat meal], and missing being there very much. But don't worry. I'm not letting this get me down, and my spirits are very high now as jump training draws to an end, and the five real jumps draw closer, along with the final march—the *masa kumta*.

[continued]

June 31—the 6-month

anniversary of my aliyah

I'm at the edge of an airfield "somewhere in Israel" waiting for the plane which will take me to my first jump. My parachute is on my back and the sun is shining on my face from just above the eucalyptus trees.

I'm not scared, I think. Two planes have already left—immense planes which look like gliding whales which swallow us like Jonah so as to spew us out later. The guys waiting with me are more nervous than I am, but I fear I will join their jumpiness as soon as the plane arrives. They're joking around and the atmosphere is really quite light.

Next to me Leo is sitting with his hands knit behind his neck. His grandparents from Argentina are here and should meet him on the ground after the jump. I FEEL PROUD TO BE JUMPING AS A PARATROOPER IN THE ISRAEL ARMY. MY DREAM HAS COME TO A REALITY!! (in his words)

Now I'm in the plane all buckled in. This thing looks like the bowels of a monster machine, with pipes and pads and straps and nets and cables all around. I feel secure but the tension is building. Now the door is closed and we're moving....

Love,
Alex

A Paratrooper Jumps—And Shouts and Sings

[Journal]

July 2, 1985

Tel Nof

It's late morning now. I've already jumped twice—once this morning, at sunrise, and once yesterday morning. Stepping out of an airplane at 1200 feet is like nothing else in the world. It is preceded by fear which must accompany doing anything as ridiculous as stepping out of a secure place into emptiness. I kept telling myself that I wouldn't jump. Not seriously, because I knew that I would jump, but nonetheless the feeling of wanting to turn around is there.

When my turn came (I jumped second) I guess that I jumped like they taught me, but I remember nothing from the second before I left the plane until I found my chute opening behind me.

Once the fear passes—and the fear passes as soon as you're out of the plane—the jump is so much more pleasant than what I had thought, that I really enjoyed all of its sensations. The opening of the chute occurs with a smooth pull on the shoulders, rather than the jolt which we felt on the machines which simulate the jump. The ride is spectacular, and the landing is also soft as a jump off a milk crate. Today it was a bit faster—like a jump from a truckbed.

It's odd that I also don't remember much of the view from the air. I paid little attention to it, as I was thinking about checking my canopy, releasing the reserve (not opening it, just moving it out of the way), adjusting my flight path so as to land as close as possible to the target, keeping my legs together, and generally being overwhelmed by flying without an airplane.

The kids in my platoon call it "half a fuck." I don't see the connection, but it's pretty great. The second you're in the air you want to shout and sing, so I did.

[continued]

July 2nd

This evening Raful gave a talk about the history of the paratroops. The one interesting part of the talk which I remember was a question about the usefulness of jump training, when p-troops hadn't been used since 1956. Raful said the paratroops still have an operational purpose. Helicopters couldn't bring troops, for example, to the Iraq-Jordan highway in the event of war.

But, more interesting, was the idea that the paratrooper knows the fear of stepping into space—and that knowledge might make him fear battle less.

Tale of Two Companies

July 2, 1985

[Jerusalem]

Dear Dad and Saul especially, but also Mom and Benjy,

Last week, as I think I told you, the company commander of the other company of February draftees told me that Hagai (Michal Milson's boyfriend) was a friend of his, and that if I had any trouble I could talk to him at any time.

Well, today I did. I sat in his tent and we talked for over a half an hour. (You probably don't picture this as a big thing, but to us a company commander is untouchable, unapproachable). Some of the stuff wouldn't interest you much, but I'll tell you some of the things I said to him, because I think they'll interest you as educators.

Yariv asked me about the "feeling" in the company. I told him that while my platoon is pretty healthy, that I think my company is sick. I said that the company commander was unknown to us. What we knew of him was only from the marches which he's led (and we all saw he got lost twice), and from the one time he got us all together to speak to us. The speech was a long-winded threat, which came on the tail of a number of AWOL incidents, saying that he'd hold all of us responsible if anyone else went AWOL.

Another difference which I see between the companies (of 202 and 890) which I'm sure also affects the feeling of the companies (and Yariv sort of agreed although he couldn't out loud due to his position) is this: In Yariv's company every soldier knows that if he isn't good he'll be kicked out. This gives pride to the soldiers who are there, because their very presence implies both continuing good performance and continuing volunteerism (if there's a way out, then being in the company is voluntary). But, in our company, we see that no one is kicked out, and the feeling among the soldiers is that they volunteered once, but their presence long ago ceased to be voluntary. I told Yariv that it seemed to me that soldiers would have more incentive to be good if they felt their efforts were helping to guarantee a privilege.

Now it's Saturday evening. I'm in the apartment [in Baka] in Jerusalem. After I wrote the above, and before our last jump (a night jump with equipment), our company commander spoke to the whole company again. I hoped that Yariv had spoken to him, and that he would use the opportunity of a "talk with the company" to freshen the spirit of February, 202. Well that hope disappeared pretty fast. All he did was tell us about the jump, and threaten anyone who chickened out with stiff jail sentences.

> *L'hitraot*,
> Alex

Alex Has the List

> July 3, 1985
> [In the Army]

Dear Saul,

I just thought you'd be interested in a little army story. It has to do with guard duty. Well, every night we have to have a list of the guards for the night. Every night in my platoon there is a war (in which I have refused to take part) over whose turn it is to guard. The kids in the platoon always try to determine whose turn it is by the setup of the cots, but since we're always moving that never works. Three nights ago this irritating comedy reached a peak when the arguing got to be so loud that it was disturbing our commanders in their tent twenty yards away. Commander Gai came over and solved the problem: he said that the whole platoon had to guard that night.

Now, as you might expect, I was rather unhappy with the prospect of Gai's solution becoming a norm, so I thought up a better one. While on guard duty that night I made out a list of all the people in the platoon, in random order, with spaces next to the names where a record of who guarded when could be kept. The next night I told everyone that I had a system and would do the list. Not one person complained about being told to guard. The ridiculous wars are over. The interesting thing about my system is that everyone is willing to accept it. I didn't ask if they would. I told them that I'd made a list based on a system of record-keeping, and they all began to defend it and say, "Alex has the list." I only wonder why I didn't do it earlier.

Love,

Alex

Masa Kumta—Tears of Joy and Pain

[Journal]

July 12, 1985

Masa Kumta!

Basic training ended Wednesday morning at around 11:30 when we received our red berets. The Western Wall was the end-point of the 87-km, 600-m [55-mile] *masa kumta.*

We left the Paratroops Memorial at Tel Nof at 5:53 p.m. on Tuesday. I started off with a ten-liter jerrycan on my back. The company marched in platoons, with one open stretcher per platoon. At first I carried the stretcher with the jerrycan on my back, but I soon stopped and just carried the jerrycan. After two hours (the hottest two hours of the march) I traded the jerrycan for a place among the stretcher bearers.

At first we stayed under a minute each, and since there were twelve who carried that meant one minute under two out, etc. I found the stretcher work much easier than that under the jerrycan (because of the breaks), even though it was much more painful when the stretcher was on my left shoulder. Our platoon had it good with twelve carriers at almost all times. My friend Leo's platoon was down to six or seven carriers by the end, and the other platoon also was reduced. Sometimes the carrying was hard—when we had to run to catch up or pass another platoon, but the moon was out and mostly the going was good on dirt roads which reflected the moonlight.

From the end of the march I remember only the joy and none of the pain. We entered Jerusalem from Nahal Soreq (Jerusalem's sewer) and came into Ben Zakkai Street below our old apartment. We walked past the Sultan's pool, around Mount Zion, to the Dung Gate where we stopped, caught our breath, and from there we sprinted the final 100 yards to the end of Basic.

The unpleasant part of the march was what it showed me about some of the people in my platoon. In the challenge which I found stimulating, many found no reason to invest more of their own effort in our effort. There was a lot of bickering, cursing, yelling and other junk which showed who really are the "*sotziomatim*" of our platoon.

Among the pleasant bits of memories from that night of carrying were the melon fields we crossed. We kicked melons open and ate them as we went. Delicious. A man from the settlement of the melons brought a whole carload of especially tasty ones to our water point. Generosity is so nice to see, especially when it comes as an appreciation of effort which deserves it.

The views were another joy as they always are when one enters Jerusalem. But on foot, in moonlight, through valleys of pine, the entrance is especially special and moving. At least I was moved. During the *masa*'s harder moments I would think of the end ahead of me—of running the last steps to the Wall—and tears would begin to come to my eyes, and I would have strength. And in the end, when I was about to take those final running steps to the end of basic training, the tears came to my eyes. Tears of joy and pain but mostly of joy.

Adi Natw "breaking" guard duty opposite a UN observer
station on the new road to Gebel Blat

4.
Life
on the
Frontline

*"Patrols are cold, cold
things where the war
is with sleep."*

Guarding on the Golan

July 14, 1985

[The Golan]

Dear Family,

Sunday morning, 6:00 a.m.—at Qala in the Golan. Basic training is over and we've "gone up" to the battalion—"202." From where I'm standing now (guarding) at the edge of my company's tentsite, I can look beyond my still long shadow, across the tents of the battalion's other companies, into the mist which fills the Huleh valley, and to the ridge of mountains beyond (above the town of Qiryat Shmona) which marks our border with Lebanon. If I look in the other direction—towards the sun— I see the silhouette of Mount Hermon above the tents of the other company.

This place looks like a Crusader encampment, with each company's tents accented by the flags of the division and the nation. A cow is here because this is only an encampment (not a base) into which the herds of cattle from the Druze villages of the area can and do walk freely.

All of this sounds very romantic, but in fact Qala is a filthy hole. The wind blows the dust, and the dust sticks to and covers everything. There is no shade, and it is very hot now that my shadow is no longer long. But it is a filthy hole not because of the dust and the wind, but because it is an encampment of my company—and in my company there is enough human filth to ruin beauty.

I spent this Shabbat here rather than in the kibbutz because I pulled a *mispar mavet* (number of death) in the lottery in my platoon which determines who guards and who enjoys the civilian world. The other people here didn't pull "death numbers"—they were here as punishment for misdeeds during the week, and they managed to make miserable our only task here—guard duty.

Now it's (Monday).

I'm in the middle of open territory training. I'm resting. Before me is a deep hole with a few trees in it that used to be a volcano. Above me is a tree which makes very nice shade, and all in all I am not in a mood to continue writing about the bad parts of Shabbat. So here is the nice thing that happened:

Friday night I went to the synagogue at the base next door—an air force base (actually anti-aircraft). We were exactly ten men. After the service we (two others from P-troops and I) were invited to stay for dinner. Dinner was delicious; the air force has it good.

I'm sick of my platoon's refusal to accept responsibility and guard in the sun, but rather than make sure no one guards too long, they only make sure that they don't guard.

The only thing taking my mind off the shmucks in my platoon is this letter. Even from 6000 miles away a one-way conversation with you can turn a torturous tedium into a fast-passing time.

Love,
Alex

The Advantages of Letters

July 17, 1985
[The Golan]

Dear Benj,

In seven weeks I'll be home on leave. I can't wait. Actually, I don't spend much time thinking about or missing home. I only miss it when I write things like, "In seven weeks I'll be home."

One of the best things about keeping in touch, through letters, with you folks, but with Mom and Dad especially, is that I think we can talk in our letters much more than we would if I were at home. I write about my troubles and my joys, and they write about theirs. I even asked them about their relationships before they got married. I don't think I would have asked them about that at home. But even more importantly, in the letters they wrote, they said more than they would have if I asked the same question at home.

The week I just finished was one of the hardest since I was drafted—if not the hardest. We had many exercises and little sleep. Last night we started walking up the heights of Golan in pitch darkness at 12:30. We walked until 3:30 a.m. or so and then did a simulation of taking a certain type of emplacement until past 5! All this after an immense exercise in the same hills for which we got up at 4:00. (And each exercise we do twice—"dry" and only afterwards with shells bursting and guns blazing.) Wednesday night I slept 1 1/2 hours, Tuesday about 2 hours, and about the same Monday and Sunday. Now I'm writing rather than sleeping because I'm too tired to sleep.

Remember when you came to Ithaca and we talked about why not to smoke pot. In the end, only *not* smoking can prevent people who love you from suffering with the knowledge that you're smoking. And whether or not they, and I, are right to suffer with your smoking is irrelevant. I hope you aren't angry with me for preaching, but I care more than I can say about you and about Mom and Dad, and I don't want to see you hurt each other.

Love,
Alex

Low Army Morale

July 29, 1985
[The Golan]

Dear Mom & Dad,

Today's a lousy day. I'm a *toran* in the kitchen, and I want to be out doing the training with the platoon. It's not that I miss the guys in the platoon—not at all. I am really irritated by many of them. That's one of my faults you know—I often have trouble ignoring things which bother me.

While I've always believed in getting the job done as fast as possible so that the quality of my work determines the quantity of free time I have, I've finally learned that working well has no benefits (in my company). Staff sergeant says, "You've got this and this and this to do and that's it." You finish all he's told you and he just gives you more to do. So it pays to work slowly and never to get any job completely done. I hate it.

This part of the letter is being written as the sun sets over the ridge beyond the Huleh valley. I started the letter in the morning, and the day's events proved I was not alone in "down-ness." After lunch Yaron, our officer, called the platoon together for a talk about volunteerism, working as a unit, unit spirit, and all the other nice things we don't have. Everyone sort of committed themselves to try again, if not to push, at least not to complain when we push.

On *Tisha B'Av* I was the only one in my platoon who fasted in the army. The only other fasters stayed home. (I preferred to be in the army and save my special exits.

Alex

On the Edge of the World

[Journal]

July 31, 1985

[The Golan]

Looking north from our encampment towards the Hermon early on a misty morning.

Sometimes, as I sit and watch the sun set beyond the ridge which is separated from us by the Great Rift, when that ridge is hidden by mist, it seems like I'm sitting on the edge of the world.

Curfew in the Casbah

[Journal]

August 12, 1985

Hebron

Our job here is to enforce the curfew which was imposed on the section of this city where two days ago a Jew was stabbed while walking alone by two Arabs. The Jew made aliyah thirteen years ago from the States. I wonder if we know him. He had enough strength after being stabbed to run to the Machpelah cave for help.

So far I've done one shift. It was completely quiet. The area under curfew is dead. No one is allowed to move in, out, or within the area. All of the residents left their shops in such a hurry that mountains of vegetables and fruit are lying out where they were to have been sold. The mountains are slowly eroding—both through ripening into rot and the fact that some soldiers help themselves.

My mood is quite lousy now (a change from the past weeks which have been quite "up"). I'm simply fed up with the immaturity of the kids in my platoon. When, at this very moment, we have time to sleep, they have no sense that if they don't want to sleep they can not do so quietly, so that those who want to can. Until they're ready, there's really no need for silence.

Clever Commander

[Journal]

August 15, 1985

Today, instead of guarding one of the Casbah's gates, I, with Ziad and my platoon commander, Yaron, wandered and climbed the roofs of Hebron's most hectic neighborhood. I've really enjoyed it. The Casbah is as complex a maze as any I've seen....

I wrote the above from a house settled by Jews in the middle of the curfew. The Jews were removed by the army while my company guarded. No force was needed—maybe because the very clever commander of the Hebron district used women soldiers to talk the settlers out.

Not Getting to Fire My RPG

[Journal]

August 26

Last week we had our biggest exercise yet—a battalion exercise. It started with our climbing the Golan Heights on foot at night, attacking emplacements in the morning, mounting APC's and moving in. All in all it was interesting and pretty realistic, but I was pissed at not getting any bombs to shoot with my RPG. Carrying that damn tube is okay if you have the pleasure of shooting to make up for the pain.

One of the things that I've been doing a lot of thinking about recently is what makes a good officer and a good sergeant.

A Mature Conversation

[Journal]

August 31, 1985—Shabbat

Qala

This place is full of cows, and they keep going into the kitchen and eating our food. There's one here now (6:46 a.m.). The base is empty—there are only six of us here, a soldier from each platoon, the administrator and his deputy, and another soldier who's just returned from prison. All four soldiers are members of the "group of six" soldiers who stayed Shabbat at Qala.

This brings me to Saturday night, starting at 6:30 p.m. when I left Qala for

Jerusalem. I got rides to Haifa, then buses to Tel Aviv, and Tel Aviv to Jerusalem. I arrived in Jerusalem just after 11 p.m., walked to the Sonesta Hotel, called Larry [Kelemen] (waking him), and walked over to his place to spend the night.

Larry is a good friend and when I worked at Brandeis [BCI] in California we would talk for hours. The times I spent visiting him and his wife Linda at his parents' place in Mammoth [California] were some of the most idyllic in my life. When I arrived the three of us sat down to talk (and eat).

We talked about the army, we talked about Larry's plans to set up high-quality Jewish schools in America, we talked about the problem with NATO's military strategy (I talked)—which came up when we talked about the relative realism of the military exercises we do.

In the midst of all this—

It happened. Epiphany of sorts. I stopped talking in mid-sentence and just sat there. I said to Larry, "God, this is wonderful. I'm having a mature conversation about something other than guard duty or whose turn it is to work in the kitchen." Far more than during basic training, the age difference is hurting, and I'm left counting the days before I leave for my month-long visit to the States and my family whom I miss. Fifteen days to go.

A Cab Driver's Tale

Alex returned to the States for a visit with his parents. He wrote the following in his journal on the way back to Israel.

[Journal]
October 20, 1985
On the plane back to Israel
I just want to record the conversation I had last night with the driver of the cab which took me from LaGuardia to Grandma's.

The driver looked Israeli to me—dark with a leather jacket and dark hair. He could have been an Arab. When I sat down I looked at his license. His first name was obscured but I could read his last name—Parviz.

I asked Parviz where he was from. Iran.

"When did you get out?"

"'79."

I asked if he had to escape. He told me that he'd been lucky—that he'd been in the Shah's army and that when the Shah was overthrown the officers escaped by hiding their identities by removing their ranks.

Then I asked if he was Jewish, I was sure that he was. Parviz hesitated, looked at me in the rearview mirror, and said, "Yes." When you meet Jews from countries where Judaism is almost a crime, and is something which can bring great suffering, there is a hesitancy in disclosing religion very different from that of the liberal college student who is embarrassed by his belonging to "a religion."

I asked if it wasn't unusual for a Jew to be in the army. Parviz said no, that Jews could rise as high as the rank of (but not including) general. He had been a colonel in the air force—a pilot of Phantom jets. He told me that many Iranian pilots had been trained in Israel, but that he's been trained in the U.S.—in Virginia and Oklahoma. In the U.S., in 1962 (I told him that I was born in 1962—he laughed), he'd fallen in love with an American woman, but they couldn't marry because Iranian law prohibited officers from marrying foreign women. He returned to Iran and married; the woman he had loved also married in the U.S.

He had two children, 14 and 16, at the time of the Shah's fall. On the day that he hid his rank and escaped, the Revolutionary Guard arrived at his home. They killed one of his children, then another, then his wife. In one day he lost all he had—his home, his career, his family—in the name of Allah!

Parviz arrived in the States and called the woman he had loved and she helped him. She must be a wonderful woman. The way he spoke of her showed gratitude and love that was so honest. His love is only exceeded by his hate—his hate for Moslems. He told me that in Iran, his neighbor, a Moslem, had been his closest friend. When the Guard came to Parviz' home his neighbor had an opportunity to warn his wife and two children, but he did nothing. His best friend!

I told Parviz about what I am doing—serving in the IDF, and he liked that. He has much family in Israel.

Actually Defending the Country

October 26, 1985

[Lebanese Border]

Dear Family,

Today is Saturday but it is no Shabbat. Here on the border nothing makes any day holier than the others. The same patrolling needs to be done, the same tasks as any other day.

I can't write about much of what we do here so I'll try just to tell you about what is routine and about the feelings I've had being here.

Our section of the border is patrolled by us in six-hour shifts. Six hours is a long shift, especially when it is cold and rainy, and we're driving fast long the fence.* My company hasn't caught anyone trying to cross yet, but just before I got back from the States my platoon commmander's patrol caught an Israeli Druze smuggler at the fence with eighty kg of hashish which had been thrown over without activating the fence's sensors.

Now it's later. I just took a hot shower which made my day! (There's a diesel-fuel heater outside our corrugated tin shower.) I'm feeling much better now. I found it good to get back to my platoon and company. I've found that frontline life gives something, in knowing that you're actually defending the country, which life during the exercise period lacked. I also have stopped missing you. This is not because I don't miss you, or don't wish I could be with you, rather, it is, because I've gotten completely back into things, and I don't waste time doing useless missing. My only hope or wish about my Stateside family is that you aren't spending time missing me. I'd rather have you happy and supporting when I'm down than to let the distance between us shape our relationship.

Love,

Alex

P.S. I didn't see Daniel when I got to the kibbutz from the airport, but I did run into him at the Jerusalem central bus station, and then again at my battalion headquarters. He is glowingly fine.

*The fence marks the border between Israel and Lebanon and is fitted with electronic devices which sound a warning at a master command post whenever the fence is touched. On the Israeli side, a road of smoothed sand runs adjacent to the fence. Called the "cover-up" road, footprints in the sand reveal whether the fence has been breached. A paved road runs parallel to the fence and sandy path.

Crossing the Border

[Journal]

October 31, 1985

Lebanese Border

I've been back a week and a half. Coming back itself was only tough for a day or two. Within two days in the army I stopped thinking about the States.

Kav, "frontline," is full time with 24-hour-a-day patrols, ambushes and other jobs. I can't put down what we do on the other side of the fence, but I like crossing. Maybe I'd hate Lebanon if I was stationed there, but I'm not, so I don't.

My favorite shift is midnight—6 a.m. with an officer on the command car. When that officer is Yaron—my platoon commander—as it was last night, the chance to talk is a gift which makes the shift a high point.

We can see Haifa, the Hermon, and Tyre [Lebanon] all at once!

Longing to "Go In"

November 7, 1985

[Lebanese Border]

Dear Family,

It's Thursday, before 10 a.m. Last night from 6 p.m. to midnight I was on patrol. I slept until 5:30 or so. Spent an hour in the guard tower looking through my Nikon binoculars at Jebel Blat, Jebel Hrik, Rameca, Yatar, Beit Lif, Tsrubin, Kavsa, Hnin, Ein Ebel, Ait as-Sh'ab, At-tiri, Marun ar-Ras, Yarun, and the Hermon in the distant background. As you see, I spent my time in the tower memorizing the towns and mountains within view of the tower. Except for the Hermon, all the places above are in Lebanon—mostly in the "security belt" but some beyond it.

The patrolling and guarding is basically boring. We go back and forth along the fence 24 hours a day. The rest of the time is spent on our own upkeep—cleaning, cooking, fixing, etc. I end up (I think I'm not alone in this feeling) longing for action; longing to "go in," and feeling crestfallen when a group "goes in" without me. Everyone tells us how lucky we are not to be based inside Lebanon, but that privilege, I feel, is one which can only be appreciated after seeing what we're missing. It's not that I feel reckless, only that, after nine months of training, I'm ready to do something other than guard.

Love, Alex

Changing Moods

November 15, 1985
[Lebanese Border]

Dear Mom,

I'm glad that you loved the portion you read two weeks ago but I can't "relate" to the experience much myself now. I no longer have the time to get enthusiastic about a Torah portion. I hope I will someday soon.

Life here is very busy and the opportunities to write are few. I've only done one drawing so far, even though the views here at sunrise are dreamlike. At sunrise the villages sit on their hilltops. The mist of the cold night settles around them, and they become silent islands in a grey sea with the orange sky.

My mood switched around very fast here—from boredom (busy boredom of guarding and patrolling) to excitement, when we are sent rushing "inside" on APCs in response to some alert or another. I like going "inside." It justifies the boredom and is very interesting, as new faces always are. I wish I could write about it, but I don't know what I can say and what I can't.

The sense that we're defending the country is here, but it isn't strong enough to beat out the fed-up feeling from continued discipline. Patrols are cold, cold things—over six hours long—where the war is with sleep. We feel the border is secure.

Love,
Alex

Intrigued by the Future

November 15, 1985
[Lebanese Border]

Dear Saul,

Congress still sounds great. I had another SPARK yesterday. A SPARK is when suddenly I think for a second about the U.S., about people leading lives different from patrols, ambushes, alerts, and kitchen duty. I happen to have been on *toranute*. I was listening to the radio. A good dancing song came on and I started bopping around a bit as I peeled eggplants. Then wham!—a SPARK. Most people my age—or even more so at the age of the soldiers in my platoon—in the States use the music very differently. It's not that they don't dance, it's that they don't peel eggplants for fifty guys out patrolling a border. You know what I mean.

Soon I'll have a talk with my company commander, and then with the battalion commander about going to *Makim* [squad leaders' training] early.

I am intrigued by the future—my future, about what I'm going to decide to do. Officers' school has many pros, but I might decide to go for civilian life anyway. Also, within the decision to go to officers' school is the decision whether to continue in infantry or to move to intelligence. Who knows? The decision goes differently when peacetime is in my head than the times when I think of the next war. Churchill's *My Early Life*, which was a joy, and which taught me much about war, was about war very different from that which we'll see with chemical warfare, night vision machines, guided missiles, etc. I don't think I'll ever see 2000 soldiers charge on horseback into an enemy armed with a sabre.

Please call Katherine [Baer] for me with warm regards. (Is there a more human way to say that than "warm regards"?) Tell her I'll write soon, but time is very, very short here.

Love,

Alex

"When I Get Out"

November 25, 1985

[Lebanese Border]

Dear Katherine,

Time is going by very quickly. By the time this reaches you I will have only eight months to go in the army (unless I become an officer). There's a good chance that within ten weeks I'll be in sergeants' school. Whenever I do get out of the army, I promised myself one thing: that I won't waste a single day of my time torturing myself over "what I should do with my life." The day I get out I'll start something— some project, whatever it will be, writing, or working, or painting, or travelling (with a purpose), I don't know. We shall see.

Be well and don't miss me.

Love,

Alex

A "Pregnant" Suicide-Bomber

November 29, 1985

[Lebanese Border]

Dear Katherine,

...I'm not stationed in Lebanon but at times we have to go in.

You must never forget to what depths the enemy will stoop to win. Here that means, for example, a Moslem suicide-bomber woman who strapped explosives to her belly so as to look pregnant (she was caught).

Just remember that my being where I am is not a result of my world view, but of the fact that if we (I) weren't here, Israel would live in terror; and because we are here, and what we do, even the settlements on the border are quiet at night.

Be well and vigilant and suspicious and happy.

Love,

Alex

Snow on Mt. Hermon

[Journal]

December 3, 1985

[Lebanese Border]

It has suddenly gotten very cold. We can see snow on the Hermon. Last night I was on patrol from 12 [midnight] to 6 a.m. with Yisrael and Shlomi, and the wind drove through all the layers I was wearing. Today I was out from noon till 6 again with Tamir and Dani, the sharpshooter who almost killed me. Even in the sun it was cold, but I enjoyed the patrol because Tamir is a good dude and I no longer cringe at the thought of being within ten feet of Dani—he's still loud but no longer abrasive.

Anticipating Saul's Visit

December 20, 1985

[Lebanon]

Dear Mom,

Talking to you the other day was wonderful. Before we spoke I had gotten very *lachuts* for a chance to talk. *Lachuts* comes from the root *lachats* or "pressure" and means that I had ants in my pants. One can be *lachuts-bayit* (home) *lachuts-havera* (girlfriend) or *lachuts-felafel* or anything; I hope you get the meaning. In sum, I was *lachuts-mishpacha* [family].

Saul:

I'm looking forward to your visit very very very much. As far as visiting me in the army is concerned—things don't look too good now. I've been moved to the other side of the fence, where no one is allowed to visit, let alone civilians, let alone Americans. What I'll try to do is swap places with someone for a day or two, so you can visit me and get a sense of what this world is like.

Love,

Alex

Beauty Makes Me Sing

January 1, 1986

[Lebanon]

Dear Katherine,

I started to sketch my room when suddenly I decided that I'd rather write to you. I'm not in Israel now. You know. I'm waiting to go guard a tank for a whole night, but our exit from the mountaintop, with its views of Tyre and Haifa and of Mount Hermon, has been postponed until the shelling stops. Don't worry, no one is shelling us. The shells are ours today.

This is my first letter of 1986. Today is a tense day for us because we think the PLO force will make trouble in honor of the anniversary of their founding on January 1, 1960—something. Yesterday was also a landmark—but for me rather than Yasir [Arafat]—it was the one-year anniversary of my becoming an Israeli. I must run now. The shelling is over.

Now it's 5 a.m. I've been up all night. In an hour I have a bit more work to do, but then I'll be free for most of the day. Thank you for the beautiful card and note. I too wish for peace more than I ever have, but I want you to know that where ever I am, I have moments I would like to share with you—when I guard at sunrise and the snow-capped Hermon turns to pink, and the sky to every shade of purple, and the muezzin calls the faithful to prayer in the village below, and I'm warm because the heater is working, and I'm singing to myself because beauty makes me want to sing. Then the moment takes me away from the trials of the army, and I am at peace, and I know you would like to see that.

Love,

Alex

A Sense of Pride

[Journal]

January 4, 1986

Jebel Blat

I like this type of front-line duty more than life along the fence. Being inside Lebanon makes all that goes on closer, even though from here I don't participate in the same types of activities we did at Mt. Amiram (no ambushes).

I also like being with soldiers from other parts of the army—from tanks, intelligence, and artillery—because for the first time we get to see how the others work. My feeling towards their work is at times one of envy, for I like to use sophisticated machines, but also, at times one of pride when I know that we are the ones sent in, in the end, to do the work.

Being with My Brother

January 7, 1986

[Lebanon]

Dear Grandma Jeanne,

I have just bought six sheets of paper that are about 36"x 30". I'm going to do on a big scale what I've done twice already on small scale—a 360-degree panorama of the view from my base. The small ones are beautiful and quite free, and I can't wait to do the big one. I'll use my heavy black magic marker and children's gouache paints.

It is good to have Saul here but not easy. I'm writing to you from the army and he is not with me. I just saw him from Sunday evening until today (Tuesday) and that's not much. I want to see him again before he leaves, but no amount of time they give me can be enough. It's not that we have so much to say. I just like being with my brother. Being alone is hard at times—especially after a taste of family. I miss everyone in the States far less after I've been in the army for a week or two or three with no contact, than I do after a visit or even a phone call.

So, all will be well when I'm alone again. I do OK on my own.

Love,

Alex

Joys, Worries and Sadness

January 7, 1986

[Lebanon]

Dear Mom,

I just read your letter for the second time. It brings tears to my eyes. The news of Inger [Bilde]'s suicide was a shock and very sad. The tears came from your admiration, your support, and your advice.

When I read your words telling me to "continue to draw, to write, to Haiku, to look for opportunities" I think of the distance between us, for such advice is only in a letter because contact between us is so infrequent. Don't think that I miss your advice per se. As much as I like it when I get it, I don't miss it when it is not around. I guess I miss having you around to give advice.

Saul's visit has been very difficult for me. He arrived last Wednesday and was at the kibbutz with Daniel for Shabbat. I was here, and even though Shabbat was one of the best I've had in the army—it was such a beautiful day that I did five drawings even though I don't generally draw on Shabbat—I wish I had been with my brothers. I haven't seen Daniel for a very long time. I think it's been about two months.

To balance my sadness, which I promise is temporary and a result merely of Saul's visit (which I wouldn't trade for anything), I have real joys to report: I love the panorama drawings I'm doing; and I am driven, for the first time, to do something BIG. Tomorrow I hope. I am also pleased with my friends in Israel. I also have joy from the joy of Daniel and Anat.

And, of course, to balance the sadness and the joys, finally are my worries which as usual don't make me sad. I worry, and will continue to worry, about what to do with regard to OCS (officers' school) until I do it. Your words which tell me to "look for opportunities when the time is ready for that" are what I must remind myself at all times, rather than letting failure to plan the unplannable bother me. The unplanned, with patience, either becomes plannable or brings about its own answers.

Enough. I must sleep and stop with this letter, which may give the impression of a tormented second son which is not what you have.

Love,

Alex

Thinking About the Future in the Army

January, 1986

[Marj Ayun, Lebanon]

Dear Dad,

I spend a lot of time thinking about what I'll do after the NCO [non-commissioned officer] course. I've heard I may be asked straight to officers' school, but I don't know about being an infantry officer. I may not have the shape it takes. I may also want to think about other kinds of work as an officer. One interesting conversation I had that might shed light on other officers' jobs was with a lieutenant who's responsible for all the clinics serving the residents of the security belt. He works closely with all sorts of Lebanese, and has a lot to do with the good relations of the Lebanese with our folks. We shall see. I'd love to work on my Arabic and use it. I'll do what is right. I only fear opportunities passing me by.

Love,

Alex

Practicing Arabic at a Christian Hospital

[Journal]

(Martin Luther King's Birthday)

Marj Ayun

On a ridge above the town sits the hospital. From its roof we guard, and from its roof we look through the windows opened by the clouds onto southeast Lebanon. One minute the Mediterranean shines to the west, the next it is gone and all that I see is mist. Then I turn and a new vista, one which hadn't been there a minute before, opens. To the north is a Shiite village. To the east the Hermon, and in the south Israel. Major Hadad's widow lives 100 yards away.

Marj Ayun has a peaceful, happy feeling to it. At least the hospital does. The town is Christian. It is the "capital" of the security belt. When I guard down at the hospital's gate (instead of on the roof alone) with the guards from the South Lebanese Army, I see well-dressed people arrive in their Mercedes. They laugh and smile as we check them. One of the SLA guard's little sons arrives with his school backpack and does his French lessons in the guardroom. I read from his Arabic book and he laughs. He is six or seven and about the size of a five-year-old.

The guards all help me with my Arabic, teaching me words like "hand-grenade," and "God give you strength," and "pistol" and "chestnut." They make tea and coffee on the guard room's small diesel-fuel heater and heat chestnuts on it as well. Guard duty with them goes quickly.

On the roof top, on the other hand, guard duty can go by very slowly. Last night I guarded from 7:30 p.m. to 11:15 p.m. in the rain, with only a piece of tin over my head for a roof—the tin had holes in it so instead of being rained on, water reached me in occasional streams (until the nuns below found a piece of plywood). By the end I was so desperate for songs—for the way to pass time while guarding is to sing—that I sang all of "One Hundred Bottles of Beer on the Wall," only to find that it got me through five more minutes of my shift.

An Arabic Blooper

January 15, 1986
[Marj Ayun, Lebanon]

Dear Saul,

Here's the Arabic mistake I made two nights ago: 2:30 a.m. I'm on the roof of the Marj Ayun hospital. A car arrives at the gate below. I put a bullet in the chamber and approach the two men on the other side of the locked iron gate. One is old, in pajamas, and groaning and holding his left hand. The second is younger, about thirty, and huge and bearded. They want a doctor. I tell them that the old man can come in but not his escort. I let him in and lock the gate, escort him to the emergency room where he is checked by the nurse who tells me to bring his son. I go get him, frisk him, and bring him in. The old man had a rheumatism attack, not a heart attack like we thought at first.

Anyway, after the doctor gave him a shot of some pain killer, I escort the two to the gate and want to wish the sick one well. I say *sahten* which literally means "twice your health" and is used to say *bon appetit* or *b'tei-avon* [good appetite in Hebrew]. His son smiles and tells me that I didn't want to say that. I [then] say *salaamtak* which means "peace to you," and is a bit better than saying ["good appetite"] to someone who has been rushed to the hospital in the middle of the night.

Later, the next day, one of the SLA guards tells me that saying *sahten* to a sick man is like saying that I want him to die of his illness. Oops. At least the old man saw I was speaking from ignorance—which I'll never lack.

Love,

Alex

Drawing in the Round

[Journal]

January 19, 1986

[Marj Ayun, Lebanon]

Still in Marj Ayun. I finished guarding my three-hour day shift at 9 a.m., got out my big sheets of paper, cut them in half, and started to draw from the rooftop all that I could see within 60 degrees of view on each of the six sheets. The first five went well, although along with the clear skies came wind which kept folding the sheet I was drawing on. Then I went to start the last, but the paper was gone. It had blown away. I found it in a wheelbarrow thirty feet below. It had fallen in a puddle and was crumpled. I tenderly carried it to my room, draped it over the heater and waited. So, now I had a 360-degree drawing, 60 degrees of which is more textured than the rest. Then I went down to the dining room, taped it together, and painted it with my elementary gouaches.

Not bad!

With parents in Washington, Spring 1987.

On vacation with sketchbook in the Galilee, 1987.

Sketching in the field as Givati platoon commander.

Writing a letter to send home with Max, September 1987.

The last photo. (from left) Saul, Daniel, Benjy and Alex in Jerusalem, September 4, 1987, 11 days before Alex was killed.

Alex Becomes a Smuggler

January 19, 1986

[Marj Ayun, Lebanon]

Dear Harold,

Writing to you from Marj Ayun hospital in southeast Lebanon. I've been sent here with some others to guard the place. I have three hours of guard duty every night and 4½ more every day, otherwise I'm completely free. I've done a lot of drawing (the view is spectacular—especially to the east where the Hermon towers above us).

What a country Israel is—where else in the world would I worry about being arrested as a "smuggler" for bringing in a $15 radio? I bought the damn thing in the hospital shop (in Israel it would have cost $50). I won't be at peace until I make it across the border.

Your friend,

Alex

No Longer Joking with Abu George

[Journal]

January 22, 1986

Alone at the dining room table of Marj Ayun hospital with a bit of time before the start of my 4 1/2 hours of guard duty.

If I start in this room, I think of Sister Simone who is responsible for the hospital kitchen—a wonderful change from army food. She and the others in the kitchen have been very patient with me. Every meal I ask them in the worst possible Arabic whether the meat (called in Arabic *laham*...) is "from Israel" (I mean kosher) or from Lebanon. Whenever it is local they pull an Israeli army schnitzel from the freezer for me. Then when they give me yogurt with the meat I begin to explain that to the Jew it is prohibited to eat milk with meat. When the cook who's given me the unkosher combo asks why my friends at this table don't bother her as I do—after all they're Jews too—I'm at a loss for language. I don't know the Arabic for "orthodox" and "observant" or "to each his own." They think I'm a bit nuts. But they're patient, and know how to make wonderful tabouli, stuffed grape leaves, rice, and hummos.

Outside, at the hospital's gate, I have gotten to know Lebanese Christians from the South Lebanese Army. They are the official guards of the hospital. They do most of the checking of the visitors and patients who arrive.

They guard in pairs. One pair of SLA guards is Fuad Abu George from Marj Ayun and John Abu George from near Sidon. At first I didn't know John Abu George was a refugee and I would come to the guard room for my shift and joke with him about working for the "Abu George Guarding Company." But now that I know what John has gone through—he left everything behind when he left Sidon with his wife and four children—I joke with him less, and try to learn from him about what his country used to be like. While the other guards are rather simple people, John is bilingual (French, unfortunately) and until seven months ago had a successful business. He tells me that the *muharibin* (one of the many Arabic words for terrorist) have taken everything from his home in Sidon—down to the tiles on the floor.

Once, when I took over from Yossi, a kibbutznik from my platoon at the gate, I got to hear more about the *muharibin*. Yossi asked me to ask Abu George what was the story of a crazy woman who had been shouting at him at the gate. It turns out that she too is a refugee from the Sidon area, and she really has been crazy since just under a year ago, when the "terrorists" came into her home and murdered two of her brothers in front of her eyes. "What had they done?" I asked. "They were Christians," he said. "That's all?" That was all. John said that since the murder she's been crazy, and that her parents and older brother haven't been quite sane either, even though she's the only one who's really crossed the wall.

Today the sun is shining and I look forward to being on the roof. Since it is clear I can see for miles. To the east is the Hermon Mountain range which is covered with snow. And to the west I can see the Mediterranean beyond southwest Lebanon—enemy territory as far as Israel is concerned because it is full of Shiites who dream of loading their Mercedes with explosives and plowing into a nice soft target like this hospital full of civilians. But that's why I'm here. And that's why after tomorrow, when I'm back in warmer, closer-to-home Israel, I'll miss Marj Ayun. It's nice to be a protector.

Decide—Don't Wait

February 11, 1986
[Near Yerucham]

Dear Harold,

Yesterday, I arrived at this training ground near Yerucham for sergeants' school. I can't say that I'm enthusiastic about being here. For the first time since I was drafted, I'm somewhere I don't want to draw at all. (This part of the Negev is ugly desolate, not beautiful desolate.) I also miss my company. Despite all my quarrels with them, I feel very close to them.

I've still got angst in my pangst. No matter how good my intentions are about being an officer here, I still feel that I'll have lots of trouble deciding to stay on. Here are some of the reasons/thoughts on why:

—I care most about doing something important/interesting, but there are many chances to get stuck in something lousy, and its hard to find people who can/will tell me how to get to and what are the "good" jobs.

—I talked recently with a friend of mine who's a Lt. Col. about all this, and he said, "You have to decide what you want to do and work accordingly, because as long as you keep waiting for interesting opportunities to cross your path you won't be able to get into the nitty gritty of anything" (approximately). The problem is I can't make a choice among unknowns. Oy.

—My friend, Zulu (his name, really!), then put his finger on something I thought of about myself. He said it makes sense to go in the direction of my talents (drawing, working with my hands, writing), and that I should realize that failure to do so is a result of fear of closing doors which will be closed if I choose the path of my talents.

On the social scene: While I can't really say that all is rosy in terms of steady girlfriend/feeling at home on the kibbutz, I'm happy enough. I'll soon see what's going to be between Debbi (from Jamaica) and me. Why do all Jewish girls have to be called Debbi or Judy? I wish Debbi had a name like Odetta or Odedda.

Back to Yerucham. This place is horrible not only for the mediocrity of the course and the ugliness of the terrain, but also because at night it is bone-chatteringly cold, and during the day it's shadeless and hot. I guess this is better than summer when it's much hotter.

Now it's Saturday afternoon and I'm still here outside Yerucham. Yesterday

Nada Bakery 3 May, '87   Alex Singer

Alex's favorite bakery in Jerusalem.

morning I put on my "dress" uniform and got ready to leave (as all "lone soldiers" have the right to do), when I was dealt a heavy blow by the lottery which determines who will stay behind (three out of each platoon) to guard. Shit.

Since then I've alternated between guarding and sleeping in equal shares, which has made this my worst Shabbat in the army since I was drafted. Whenever I'm guarding I'm frozen solid by the wind and rain and, just as I thaw out in my sleeping bag, they wake me to guard again. This place is such a hole. On the positive side I've met one good dude here this Shabbat. He's from a unit he won't talk about.

L'hitraot,

Alex

Still Undecided

February 22, 1986
[Jerusalem]

Dear Mom and Dad,

It's Saturday night and I'm sitting with Benj in a cafe near Beit Agron. I'm waiting for ice cream and he's waiting for a shake with Brie.

I'm not in the greatest of moods now. I don't know what to do with myself after sergeants'school. What a bummer. I might want to be an officer, or maybe a civilian, but I think I'll have to wait a bit longer before I can decide. But you know all this already so I won't go through it again.

Sharansky's arrival moved me, and made me very very happy. Hearing on the radio the singing at the airport and at the hotel reminded me of all the other things which bring this country together at times. Entebbe, Osirak, beating the USSR in B-ball.

Love,

Alex

Lost in the Desert at Night

March 12, 1985
[At Sergeant's School]

Dear Grandma and Grandpa [Fried],

I'm out of Lebanon now so I have no stories of adventure. I'll just tell you a bit about navigating at night in the desert—something which I did last week. The goal of a "navigation" exercise is to find five codes in five places, which you must find in any way you think best. The route of my navigation was about seven miles each night—not much compared to what I'm used to walking, but enough to keep me busy for a night.

My second and fourth navigation went very well. We found all the points we needed and in good time too. But there's nothing interesting about knowing I'm in the right place, so I'll tell you a bit about my third navigation.

We (three of us) set off at around 8 p.m. on a dark night to find our first point, a ruin on a small peak. We found our peak, we thought, and started to climb, and climb, and climb until we were far above almost everything else in the area—no "small" peak. Nevertheless we kept climbing until the top, and there was an ancient ruin—but no code. We had climbed the wrong mountain.

Down we went and then found our small peak. As we climbed, a Bedouin approached. I said to him "good evening" in Arabic. "Good evening," he said. "We're looking for a ruin," we told him. "Right over there," he said and pointed us to a spot above us. There it was. So much for the first code of the five for the night. On we walked in the wadi. We passed another trio of navigating soldiers from our company looking for the same peak for which we now searched. They said, "here." We said, "there," and went our separate ways. They were right and we were wrong, and all the azimuths (or angles) we took from our wrong peak led us farther off course. In short we got lost, but we were in a good mood, and I had a transistor radio, so we kept walking back to the truck listening to music and joking around. It helps not to take things too seriously.

Love,
Alex

Dirty Work

March 12, 1986
[At Sergeant's School]

Dear Peter [Kaufman],

It's always a joy to get your letters. Don't envy my action. I'll tell you about this week and you'll see what I mean. Shechem, or Nablus, in the heart of the West Bank. I walk with seven others through the Balata refugee camp southwest of the city center. I carry a rubber grenade which shoots condoms at rowdy crowds—actually rubber pellets. I have a tear-gas grenade in my belt and a wooden club. As we walk we randomly call young men aside and take their IDs, check them, frisk them, yell at them, rough them up a bit.

Maybe this sounds exciting but it's disgusting work. Think of it. We're like Marcos' thugs whose goal it is to create a population which fears us. No more "be nice to the Arabs and they won't turn to the PLO" bullshit. We know that all the Balata Arabs hate us, and our goal is to make them feel too Big-Brothered to move. Two nights ago a patrol from my company—it could have been me—called to two young Arabs who looked to be setting fire to one of our guardposts (empty) to stop. They ran. My friends shot in the air, the Arabs kept running, my friends shot them. One was killed, the other escaped into the maze of the camp. The dead one had a knife on him and the material with which he planned to ignite the post was found too.

I'm not sorry that they killed him. I don't feel any sadness at the "cutting short of the young life of a misguided idealist" crap. The Arab had a knife for stabbing had he had the guts to use it.

I just want you to understand how much dirty work there is—the work I've written about is dirty, but a bit interesting because it is in a new place, with a bit of danger thrown in.

When I was in Lebanon, I could say, "I'm defending Israel" even though my own actions, patrols, guard duty, are dry and routine. Down south, where I'm now in the sergeants' course, I can't say that. I can't really say it in Shechem either. The bottom line is that I've never killed a terrorist.

Shit. This letter is a mess and hasn't come across the way I wanted it to. Be well and don't pay too much attention to this letter.

Your friend,

Alex

Sitting with You from Here

March 15, 1986

Dear Grandma Jeanne,

Hearing of Marion [Brody]'s death made me very sad. I remember her as such a no-nonsense person, who never treated us as cute grandchildren, but as children (when we were younger) to tell stories to—to teach. When I think of your friendship I am a bit in awe, both because of how long it lasted and because of how rare such friendship is. That friendship is something which I hope someday I will be able to have with someone, because I feel that I saw in it your openness and sharing of joy and sorrows which I have yet to find with anyone.

I think of how you will get on now that she is gone. I think of you as a loner—not as lonely—as I think of myself as being a loner. You've always been a model for me—not that being alone became a goal, but that when alone I would (and do) think of you and how, no matter how alone you were, you were always doing things which made a difference to you and others. I always think of you as using your time alone as opportunity to do, to paint, to write, rather than of thinking of it as a burden. I'm having trouble with this letter. I want to comfort you, but I also want to tell you how much faith I have in your strength. I want to share your sorrow a bit, if that would make Marion's absence any easier, but I know it won't. I want to sit with you and hear stories of your adventures with Marion, or just to sit with you.

But, since I'm far away, this letter will have to do instead of a hand to hold. Just know that I am thinking of you and sitting with you from here.

Love and *l'hitraot*,

Alex

A Brutal World

Ides of March 1986

Dear Saul,

Your Africa letter reminded me of my feelings last week in Shechem, and earlier in Lebanon, when I found out that our interrogation methods are more brutal than I would admit to journalists. In Shechem I carried a club, tear gas, a rubber grenade for crowd control and we had very liberal instructions for opening fire. We pulled people over at random to get IDs and roughed them up enough not to forget to hate us and fear us. In Lebanon the Shabakniks [secret service agents] get the info we need from the terrorists we catch.

Both of these more-brutal-than-the-usual-idyllic-picture-of-Israeli-behavior images come to mind when you write of South Africa. This world is brutal, very very brutal, and cruelty is sometimes needed to prevent greater cruelty. The trick is not to let it get out of hand. The reason for unfairness must never be forgotten by those being unfair, or they get carried away.

I wish you were here. I have a lot of things troubling me which I'd like to talk out with you. I dream too much when I sleep, and don't have the self-confidence I know I used to have. I feel very much alone tonight—not when I'm in the army but when I'm out as I am now. Tomorrow are the tests for Officer Candidate School. I'll probably do very well, because I always come across well in tests like these. I need to find a girlfriend who is incredibly beautiful and sexy and doesn't spend too much time thinking of ways to please me.

Write.

Love, Alex

Invited Straight to OCS

April 19, 1986

Dear Saul & Dad,

Well, Mom is going back to the States tonight. We had a good Shabbat together, except that I was in bed for most of it with a fever and a cough. Oh well.

I finished sergeants' course with a high grade—85. My platoon commander asked what I thought about the grade. I told him that I invested nothing in the course and didn't deserve it. The only thing I really learned was navigation, and that I got a lousy grade in, due to the two navigations in which I played the role of "Major Barbara"—from the word *l'hitbaber* or "to get hopelessly lost." Anyway, they're inviting me straight to OCS.

Alex

"Only the Whites Are Falling"

April 20, 1986

[Ein Tsurim]

Note: Don't know whether I wrote this as a letter or to whom.

On Thursday I pinned sergeant's stripes to my uniform for the first time. The ceremony which exposed them, a few hours later, took place in the sun on a plain near one of our training areas. I found the whole business a bit comical, both because I find marching in formation to be amusing, and because my platoon-mates kept passing out. Teddy fell first—flat on his face. After the ceremony I found him with a bandage around his head like a little boy with a toothache. He'd had six stitches in his chin, but was in a good mood. Levinson, the redhead, fell next, like a giant tree struck by lightning. Then Yoram began to totter. I grabbed him and someone else rushed to lead him away. Then, as we marched in place before starting to parade, we saw that as we all lifted our feet high, Shifman's toes were glued to the floor and only his heels were being lifted to the drumbeat. We whispered to him, "Shifman, wake up!" but to no avail. He too had to be led away. A hot day.

As we passed the chief officer of the paratroops on the reviewing stand, one of the guys from my tent, whispered that "only the whites are falling." (Nissim is Sephardic, and all those who had fallen were Ashkenazim of lighter skin.) Just then he passed out.

With the ceremony behind us we returned to our encampment, returned our weapons, and got ready to leave for our own units. That night we celebrated completing the course at a very wild party. I don't like to write about wild parties because, in this case at least, they seem out of character of the soldiers I serve with. I'd rather write about the night before the ceremony.

By eight in the evening or so, all of us were lounging around the tent, some sleeping, some listening to a small radio, eating cakes sent to the kibbutzniks by their ever-loving parents, and some talking. A little bit later the base's few girl soldiers began to drop by for a visit—the education sergeant, the company clerk, the assistant to the camp administrator. Shul, from the next tent, stuck his head through our door and said, "Come on out, let's sing." Others had already brought wood and the fire was burning. Aushalan had a guitar.

Until one or two in the morning we sat around the fire, ten of us and Revital, Orit, Shelly, and a couple of other girls from the base. We sang and laughed and talked and joked and reminisced and warmed our toes by the fire. Some of the songs were Israeli. Others were by Americans, songs that everyone knows well enough to sing to even without knowing the words.

A few days have passed and I'm in the middle of my post-sergeants' course/pre-officers' school vacation. Being invited to go straight to OCS has its pros and cons. While I may find that I miss the experience of having served as a sergeant in my battalion, or training basic trainees, the three months that I am not a sergeant are three months that I will spend as a civilian. Giving my gun back to the sergeants' school armory left me weaponless for my vacation. This is a real problem because I wanted to go for a hike from near Hebron to the Dead Sea, but this is not something safe to do without a weapon.

Discomfort in Synagogue

April 29, 1986
[Negev]

Dear Katherine,

It's just after noon and I'm sitting under a bush in a wadi in the Ramon Crater in the Negev desert. I'm with a group of kids from the kibbutz [Ein Tsurim]. I decided to join them because I'm on vacation and felt like going on a little hike. We've finished hiking and we're waiting under this bush for the two guys who went to get the car.

Today started at 4:15 a.m. when all agreed to meet in the synagogue for the morning service before setting off. I arrived a bit late, probably partially intentionally because I really feel uncomfortable in services. I feel a bit dishonest when I attend because I can't follow everything, and I don't go every day. All those around me find the whole business so natural. On the other hand, along with the discomfort there's a lot I enjoy.

This morning, for example, at 4:15 the only people in the synagogue were the kids going on the hike (the boys, that is, the girls don't go, and if they did they'd be in a separate section of the room) and the three adults leading the trip. The service was the nicest mixture of casual and traditional. One of the boys led the prayers—no rabbi or other leader who's suppose to be closer to God than the congregation. Another read from the Torah scroll. There was no solemnity, but I felt these people don't take life for granted. I like that.

But the discomfort remains, for as much as I like the religious way of life of the kibbutz (for its non-pompousness and what it says about the kibbutzniks), I still feel separated from it.

* * *

Now it is the next day and I'm in Jerusalem. I'm feeling a bit lonely because I'm on vacation, but can't find any of my friends here. It's too bad but not very bad. I like the rest at least. I think I'll go for a long walk in the Old City. A British tourist was murdered there by an Arab yesterday, but I won't be.

* * *

I'm back from my walk. I wasn't murdered and I'm not feeling lonely now—not because I'm not alone, but because walking is good for lonely pangs.

Be well.

Love,
Alex

Summing Up

started May 1, 1986

finished May 15 or later

Dear Saul,

.... I'm on a bus now on my way back to Ein Tsurim from the brigade headquarters where I signed for equipment for the preparation period for OCS. There I ran into my old company on their last day together. Yaron, my platoon commander invited me to sit in on the final talk of the period during which we were all together. The talk consisted of Yaron's very, very frank summing up of what his goals were for us, how we met those goals, and why we did.

He did a beautiful job.... Yaron's favorite part of our fourteen months together, [he said], was Sanuur—basic training. "That is where I first had to turn civilians into *bnei adam* [mature adults; literally, "sons of Adam"] and then into soldiers...."

[unfinished, unsigned]

Independence Day, July 4, 1986   Guarding with Yiftah at Officers School

5.
Becoming
an Officer

"Israeli soldiers spend years learning to kill, but also thinking about the moral side of every step they take."

A Platoon Commander?

Early May, 1986

Dear Dad, Mom, and Saul, but first Dad, whose letter I just received,

All is well with me especially since I got your letter. Edward's [Luttwak] *The Pentagon & the Art of War* is excellent but, except for the few moments when I'm an optimist, I find it hard to believe that unless he becomes Secretary of Defense, his reforms will be implemented. His lessons will continue to be unlearned.

I hope I can be good at OCS. I don't think that I can be *very* good because of my fitness (breathing) problem. This problem is not very serious but it slows me down a bit.

I've written about feeling that I've lost my self-confidence. I feel that the fact that I see this loss, or decline, is good at least. I will do OCS in the best way I can.

In case you don't know, my advance has been very fast. In fact, I'll be a Second Lieutenant after only one year and nine months in the IDF. This has its advantages, but it also may mean that they try to stick me somewhere lousy after the course—saying that I'm not experienced enough to be a platoon commander.

Be well.

Love,

Alex

Angsts and Sub-angsts

May 4, 1986

Dear Saul,

I've written to you before about confidence. It is something very much on my mind—especially in intermediate periods of life—periods of decision. In the past two years I've made the following decisions (the numbers rank difficulty of each decision, with 10 being the most difficult): to make aliyah (8); to go to the army immediately (vs. waiting one year) (2); to go to the paratroops (vs. Golani, tanks, etc.) (7); to try to go to sergeants' school early (3) later (8); to go to officers' school (10+). The difficult decisions in the next two years will be: what to do as an officer (7); what to do as a civilian (10). Note that between this decision [what to do as a civilian] and the previous decision, the decision of "whether to sign on for more time," does *not appear*—I currently can't picture doing that.

Looking back at the decisions I've made, I'm pleased with what I decided, but disturbed (I think that is the right word) about how much angst I've gone through before and (worse) after each choice. The big angsts break down into the following sub-angsts: The "angst of before" is both the angst of feeling the inadequacy of logical weighing of the pros and cons of a choice, and the angst of the fear of making the wrong choice. Next is the "angst between deciding and executing," which is the time of saying to myself, "I've made the wrong decision, I should change my mind." Finally is the "angst of after" a decision's fruit has been harvested and there's no going back—this is less serious than the earlier angsts, but an angst nonetheless.

Maybe all this angst is needed to make good decisions but I doubt it. I feel that it mostly weakens decisions. The other extreme of course is Daniel, who is, at least externally, angst-less.

Back to confidence. When I think about the symptom of my confidence loss, I think I can see its origins. During my LSE [London School of Economics] period, my Russia trip, my travels, my period of being a loner, I had no decision angst. This is partly because I had no major decisions to make. What I had was opportunities to react. At these I was, and probably still am, very good. After reacting decisively, well, and fast to something, I feel wonderful. But even though I thus reacted at LSE, in Jordan, etc. I think the confidence loss was already there, behind the good reactions.

As I said, these were times without major decisions. In fact, they were times when I consciously avoided decisions, because of my discovery at Cornell that studies are better when planned around opportunities (which emerge as one studies), and during my travels when it was clear that itinerary should be spontaneously generated.

Enough on decision, angst, etc.

Tuesday I went over to the other side of the small base where the OCS preparation was—Sanuur—where I did the first part of basic training. A company of new draftees was there whose staff included an officer, a couple of sergeants from Daniel's company whom I know, and two guys, Marcelo and Fernando, who were in NCO school with me.

We joked around, drank coffee, talked. I listened to them talking about the problems they're having with their soldiers; arguments over how harsh the discipline should be (the company commander being in favor of softest discipline, and the sergeants pro "educate through punishment").

Later I sat with Krafo (a platoon commander) and Yoni, an officer who arrived from a different part of the army, who decided to come over to the paratroops, in high grass about 150 yards from the building where Krafo's platoon was bunked. We watched as one of the sergeants punished the platoon for the following "fuck."

The platoon had been given an hour and a half for a morning lineup and inspection. Before the time was up one of the sergeants had gone into the bunkroom to find some soldiers lying around doing nothing. Then, at the lineup, things were dirty. Solution: "All the equipment on you, all the beds, mattresses, duffle bags, everything, out." (This in, say, seven minutes.) "OK, now ten minutes to wash the floor." Etc. etc. etc. In the end, the educational purpose can be seen in the sergeant's words to the soldiers after the lineup rerun: "Look, you just did a spotless morning lineup with all your equipment on, with emptying the building completely, all in forty minutes—less time than you had to do the same task without equipment on, without emptying the building, this morning. So don't tell me, 'We need more time.' Just work like *bnei adam*...."

Alex

My Fever and I

May 8, 1986

[Officer School]

Dear Family (American Branch),

I'm at OCS.

Here's what's gone down in the past week: I went (Sunday a.m.) to Beer Sheva, waited for the bus taking those starting OCS to the school. It came and left without us; it was full. I got there on my own. At the school I waited and waited to talk to those responsible for signing me into the school. In the end they said "no" (no security clearance, that is), and I went to the kibbutz feeling, by that time, lousy. I slept, with gaps, through a feverish night. In the morning I went to the base (luckily very nearby) where I had to find out about my security clearance. (The night before I'd called Talik and he said, "I'll see what I can do.") At the base I waited, my fever and I, from 9:00 a.m. to 4:00 p.m. At 4:00 the major who had to give me my answer finally saw me. He said, "Don't know yet, go back to your brigade." I said, "No go. If I don't go to OCS now, I'll never go." He said, "OK, go home and call me at 5:00." I went back to the kibbutz (this took a long time because the walk from the road to the gate was very hard for me. Fever.) At 4:45 I called. The major had gone home. "Any message for Singer?" "No." "Why don't you look?" "Mmm mmm-ahh! Singer is cleared for OCS." "Thanks." Click....

[letter discontinued]

Natural Leaders Here

[Journal]
May 19, 1986
[Officer School]
After a mixed up week of not being sure whether I was "in" OCS or not, I'm here.

For the past three months I didn't write one word in this or any other journal. I didn't do a single drawing. I'm feeling better about things now, even though my feelings about the decision to go to officers' training are definitely mixed. This will be a good course, but one with the same complaining people I've been with for fourteen months. But there are also people here with enthusiasm (few) and natural leadership in greater numbers than I've yet seen in the IDF.

I want to do well here; I want to learn as much as I can. I'm worried about my health holding up, and what is done with me after the course.

Hoping to Be a Platoon Commander

May 24, 1986
[Officer School]

Dear Mom, Dad, Saul, and (Benj),

Mom. Officers' school is good even though it has yet to start giving me vast amounts of new knowledge. We've done a lot of weapons training, ABC lectures, first aid, and use of artillery, mortars, so far. Most of this has been review for me.

You can't imagine how much I'm looking forward to having a task, a position, in this army. I hope that position will be platoon commander, but who knows. The only thing which worries me is the physical side of the job, but as I get into better shape every day this worries me less and less. I try to tell myself that six months is a long time—plenty of time to get into shape. Indeed everyone who's seen me here after only one week of daily exercise and running and rope-climbing and pull ups has said that I'm looking thinner and in great shape.

So, Mom, don't worry about me thinking of myself as a "sick person." I don't. I know, and am grateful for, how blessed I have been with health.

The others in my course are a mixed bag. I don't really have any friends yet but the folks in my room are good (one is from New Zealand). Some don't want to be at the school, but others think constantly about how to impress the instructors. Some are truly impressive. I've seen guys who do amazingly well in the physical tests, and who seem to have photographic memories for the figures or weights, ranges, calibers, etc. that we're supposed to memorize.

Dad. I read the long Nicaragua piece. I found much in it new to me, and as usual I found the picture it painted of the Central American scene to be some-what depressing. (But when I remember how five years ago we were so sure we were going to lose El Salvador, my hope gets a boost.) I also found many of your ways of illustrating ideas to be very good—especially what you said about sheep not crying for help against the wolf in their midst, and of how that silence helps explain the world's lack of commitment to defeating the wolf.

I'm very eager to hear what you're doing.

I'm going to try to start writing again during the course if I have time. Getting published is very good for my ego, which has suffered from only following orders for over a year. I also have to start to think about my Judaism. I find that I'm not comfortable living with the level of observance that I want for myself and my fam-ily. I've always told myself that "later" I'll wear a *kipah*, observe Shabbat more fully, etc.; but I don't think that later is too close. It's not that I've lost idealism, it's just that I haven't done anything with it in the past year, other than join the Israeli army, which isn't enough.

It's very late. Good night.

Oh, yes. I forgot to write about Benj. I've really enjoyed seeing him during this visit of his here—especially during the past month or so, when I feel we came to be on very good terms. I think his decision to come here is a good one for him, even though I worry that the picture he's gotten of the IDF is too rosy—the result of hearing us go on and on with our stories. Behind them is a lot of crap.

Love, Alex

P.S. Ask Daniel to write to you about his week as deputy battalion commander. He did an excellent job and is proud of it.

Jamming in Knowledge

May 28, 1986

[Officer School]

Dear Mom, Dad, Saul, and Benj,

I'm in bed at OCS. I've been in bed the past two whole days as a result of a killer case of *shilshul* [diarrhea] with a touch of fever. The doc told me not to eat anything so I haven't. He also put me on some beautiful Bordeaux-colored penicillin pills which seem to have cured me. Now I just feel weak. MOM, don't worry—I'm not telling myself "I'm a sick person." I'll be fine again by the time you get this, and trying once again to get into the kind of shape I'll need to be in to pass this course.

People told me not to expect too much from this place, but I've found, even in the first two weeks (which are notoriously dull), that vast amounts of knowledge, skills, leadership are to be jammed into us. Sure, there are those who don't want to be here, but they, too, take all in stride and may change their minds, and don't drag down the others.

Other bonuses have been that I have five good roommates from all over the army, and that my immediate officer is excellent. (He finished the course with Daniel.) So is the commander two levels above him, with the only flaw being the officer in between, who is so boring he could put a *Washington Post* reporter to sleep at Chernobyl (or better, Three Mile Island).

I'm optimistic.

Love,

Alex

A Junction of Futures

June 1, 1986
[Officer School]

Dear Family,

1986 is almost half past us now. In just one month I was supposed to be getting out of the army. But I'm here in the middle of nowhere—only *this* nowhere belongs to the IDF officers' school. I'm at the junction of two dirt roads used by no one, with one other guy. Our job is to make sure no cars enter our training area. But, as I said, there are no cars here—only this junction of two wadis. And the wind, and the rotem and malvah bushes and some rocks. And the darkness coming quickly now that the sun has set over the hill. And the colors of the sunset have dimmed

Guarding a fork in the road of two wadis

and the first star is in the sky.

Today I felt lonely. I've told you that happens sometimes. I feel lonely when I am at a junction—not of wadis but of futures. I want to sit back and look at the junction from the side, and not to analyze it—just to look, to see the perspective which disappears in the dust of turmoil, to let the dust settle and feel at peace.

And so, as it becomes quickly too dark to write, I enjoy the calm of the falling darkness. The calm of the silence but for the wind. The calm of knowing a hard day is behind me and I can rest—maybe even until tomorrow.

And now I don't feel lonely. I feel good. Writing calms me and lets clouds settle—especially writing like this. I must stop now for it's getting too dark to see. So, I'll stop and just sit here and watch the stars fill the sky.

with Janny   June 25, 1986

June 2nd

[Officer School]

All the wonderful things I had to say about OCS in an earlier letter are still true—the chance to manage people, to educate, to create a force which can do things. But when I wrote them I forgot about the other part of the infantry. I forgot the cold, the running in the dark, the lack of sleep; in short, the infantry of the infantry. When I think of myself as a platoon commander I can see myself learning to teach, to discipline, to create a certain spirit, but I don't feel up to the infantry of the job.

Love,

Alex

Running on a Starry Night

June 7, 1986

[Officer School]

Dear Grandma Jeanne,

.... The two guys I'm with are both from the Golani [Brigade]—Daniel an *oleh* from New Zealand, and a Jerusalemite, Eldad. I've already written how little connection there is between being a nice person and a good officer—how I see people here, whom I don't get along with, who will be excellent commanders, and how others who are great to be with are missing that aura of natural command skill. Eldad and Daniel are both excellent people, but if they turn out to be good officers it will be as a result of their training here—not from some sort of natural command skill. I think they'll be OK. I see many who are natural officers. There is such a thing.

I just noticed (I'm sitting with the whole company waiting for a talk to start) that the two guys in front of me have never shaved. This is a very young army.

June 25th

Had a good, short navigation last night with Eldad. We navigated together (that is, we both knew the route rather than one navigating and the other along as a dummy), and were both in a good mood and ran much of the way, and sang as we ran, and found all the codes, and had a good time on a beautiful starry night. Then the moon rose.

Love,

Alex

Creating Humane Soldiers

June 8, 1986

[Officer School]

Dear Katherine,

I was very happy to get your letter today. I have been one of the IDF soldiers on the West Bank and I am still the same Alex you knew before I carried a gun.

It is true that at times people in the refugee camps we patrol might be pulled to the side randomly and checked for documents, and frisked, but *not* beaten up. And I can say with confidence that if an Arab is roughed up by a patrol of my part of the IDF that: (1) he was caught throwing stones, or painting slogans, or with a weapon, and that (2) the case of rough behavior by a patrol on someone who has not met these criterion is very, very rare. And (3) that "roughing up" is nothing like beating up.

What about "due process," innocence until proven guilty, etc.? What gives us the right to rough up a suspect at all? What I'm about to say comes from two perspectives. First, the perspective of a soldier who must patrol and wants to finish the patrol without a knife in my back or a molotov cocktail on my jeep. Secondly, I write from the perspective of a citizen of Israel who wants to be able to travel in my country (*de facto* if not *de jure*) without fear. From both of these perspectives I justify taking off the kid gloves in our work in the patrols, because there is no doubt at all that the only thing that keeps would-be stabbers from stabbing is fear of being caught. Our job is to instill that and only that fear—not a "general fear from the Arabs," rather a feeling that you can't get away with terror.

I think that in this goal the IDF has largely succeeded. I don't think that an Arab family whose children are not involved with the PLO or other terror groups lives in fear, and I believe that the Israeli administration of the West Bank is indeed seen by most residents as a body which can be approached with grievances, and that these approaches lead to changes. The Israeli forces have more eyes looking over their shoulders than any other force in the world. I've even heard of an Arab, caught with a weapon, who has threatened the commander of the forces which caught him with "telling the administration on you if you touch me."

This week I noticed in the paper that one Israeli was shot in Nablus, another was stabbed in Hebron. These were only the cases I noticed—and I don't see the paper more than twice a week.

The common reaction to what I've said is that I'm dealing with symptoms and not the cause of the terror, which is the Israeli presence. The problem is that the PLO was founded before the '67 war, when Israel took the West Bank, and that their goal is the destruction of the Jewish state. Any PLO supporter who said he would be happy with less is not representing the unchanged view of the PLO.

Enough, however, of political philosophizing. There is no end to it. I am not used to doing it anymore either; I don't have time to argue philosophy much. Mostly I do my job with non-philosophizing thoughts on my mind: how I must behave as a human being, and AS A JEW—with the last two thoughts being in the back of my mind—the result of the education in my family and not often expressed.

At officers' school training is two-tracked—towards skills, and towards creating officers who will be Real Men. (Pardon my sexism but my intention is that the officer will be a model to his soldiers.)

You are used to the image of the officer as "part of the military establishment," as craving blood and action. Here the officer craves to create from his group of kids a force which will be mature and humane as much as it will be effective. For they (we) know that as each soldier is, so will be his unit, and as each unit is, so will be the armed forces. And as those forces are, so will be Israel which is our home.

I miss you.

Be very well.

Love,

Alex

Refusing to Return a Criminal to France

June 12, 1986
[Jerusalem]

Dear Mom, Dad, and Benj,

.... Went to a cafe with Saul tonight and ran into my company commander from sergeants' school. He's on a two-year break from the army, during which he's studying economics—at the army's expense—after which he'll return to the brigade. Impressive guy, and good to see that he'll be continuing in the army....

The decision of Minister Sharir not to send the murderer Nakash to France for trial, despite an extradition agreement, is a disgrace, and a horrible precedent, because it means that any Jewish criminal abroad can find safe haven in Israel, if only he says that he "returned *b'tshuva* [with repentance]." Nakash is a criminal, and France, with all its problems, is a civilized state close to Israel. In defending his decision, Sharir apparently said France's prison conditions were substandard. Nakash is a *free man* here. He will not pay at all for his crime.

Did I write to you about the freezing reservists guarding the ammunition store at the base, and what I did for them—bringing news of their conditions to the visiting general in the Question and Answer period, who immediately gave an order to make the change I recommended? Did I tell you about my idea for improving airbase defense? Keep writing.

Love,

Alex

Sleepy Navigation

June 14, 1986

[Officer School]

Dear Saul, Benj, Mom, and Dad,

I'll tell you about a night of navigation. Who knows, maybe I'll produce an epic on the next three pages which can be published to finance my graduate education or the purchase of a fine villa in Abu Tor.

Eldad and I finished Tuesday night's navigations at 4:50 a.m.—ten minutes before the deadline. We had the codes we'd collected approved (all of mine, and three out of Eldad's five were okayed), and I lay down by the truck to sleep until told to move. An hour later I was on the truck, asleep instantly on a bench, bouncing back to our encampment. The encampment had to be taken down because the following night was to be our last in the series of navigations. Everything—tents, kitchen, weapons, vehicles—had to be packed up to return to the officers' school. We had even to take all the stones which had been lined up along the row of tents and put them in a huge pile. An army is an army, and soldiers at some point cease to ask why stones have to be lined up along rows of tents.

Back in the truck to the "Soldiers Home" of Beer Sheva, where we each had received the coordinates of five spots to find, found them on our maps, planned our routes, and began to memorize the azimuths and distances of each section of the night's walk. I was given an electric line post, a junction of a path and a wadi, a well, a "saddle" or low point on a ridge, and a junction of two wadis to find. Because safety rules say that no one is to navigate alone, it works out that each "navigator" spends half the night navigating and half as his partner's dummy. I was lucky and was given the first half to navigate which meant that I would start fresh. Shai was my dummy.

All day we studied our routes, memorizing numbers and the shape of the terrain we would cover. Each of us had over 10 km [about 6 miles] to walk. The problem was that none of us had slept all week beyond the hour or two after each night's navigation which we spent waiting for the trucks to take us back to camp. So, we fell asleep, and got the numbers mixed up, and showered and ate, and before we felt ready the afternoon had come, and we were back in uniform with our battle gear on, waiting for the trucks to be checked before setting out.

Just as it got dark we were on our way to the starting point. I woke up after we'd stopped, shook my head a bit to knock the sleep out of it, got off the truck, found the North Star and was off and running.

Yes, running. The terrain that night was flat relative to the previous nights. This meant that it was easy to move quickly, but harder to find myself because there were no steep hills and valleys to find.

North to the train tracks 500 meters, then on a path which curved to the northeast to the electrical pole—just like I'd seen in the aerial photo. I copied the code, left a slip of paper with my name on it, and was off running amid the Bedouin dogs (not that the Bedouin are dogs—but they have many dogs around their tents), under the electrical line, across Nahal Beer Sheva, north 1000 meters to a junction, 350 meters to my next code—the junction of a path and a wadi. But there was hardly any wadi—just a slightly lower area. No code on the path but I found one on a tree thirty meters from the path. Two down, three to go.

North across a low ridge for 1300 more meters—no longer running but walking, carefully counting my steps so as not to miss the 1300-meter mark which should put me in the next valley. I found it and started to look for my well, next to the dry earthen dams built across the valley, as I had been told I would find it. But it wasn't there. I check all the dams but no well. Finally, I found a well, but no code. I decided to give up on the code and continue to code #4, but as I was leaving the valley I saw a bit of an embankment, which looked like it could hide a well. It did. Three down.

Again off and counting steps at 310 degrees. After about 1000 meters I saw the hilltop which should have been to the left of my "saddle" between two hills—but it was directly in front of me, not to my left. I checked the compass and found that I'd been walking at 295 degrees not 310 degrees. I started moving right, reached the hilltop, and met two other "navigators" looking for the same saddle. I found it thanks to the lights of a jeep which went by. The code was on a single watermelon-sized stone, but was too worn away to read. Next to the stone was an iron stake. Four down.

At the fifth point, in the very wide Beer Sheva Valley, I ran into Yiftah and Alon. We would have walked/jogged to the finish together but Alon, Yiftah's dummy, was feeling lightheaded and weak and couldn't move fast so we split up.

Then 500 meters later, Shai pulled a muscle in his leg and we too had to slow down. We reached the midpoint (the end of my navigation and the beginning of Shai's) at 11:45—165 minutes after starting—not bad, but not great, in terms of time, thanks to the time I'd spent looking for the well. The goal is a five km/hr rate, and I'd done about 3.7 km/hr. At least I had five codes. Finished. A good night's work. But.

Now it was Shai's turn to navigate and mine to be the dummy. I won't go through his whole route. Instead of two hours and 45 minutes, we walked for 4 1/2 hours over 15 or so kilometers, finding only one of his five codes. Oh well, at least I was so tired—asleep on my feet in fact—that I really didn't feel the time or the kilometers. That's the way it is: The minute you stop needing to know where you are, you fall asleep.

All five of my codes were approved. Not a bad night. But best of all, when it was over I was off for the kibbutz and out of the army to sleep enough for a week of navigations.

Love,

Alex

Don't Forget Sharansky

June 21, 1986
[Jerusalem]

Dear Family,

An hour ago Shabbat ended as darkness fell. Now I can settle down to the work which I've left alone for the past 24 hours—the final exercise, or exam, of the past week's classes on military thinking. But, before I go to work, I wanted to take a few minutes and tell you about this Shabbat in Jerusalem.

My company and one other were sent to Jerusalem for an "educational Shabbat" of lectures and walks. We were put up in the Jewish Quarter of the Old City, in an old stone building to which enough rooms had been added to put up thirty soldiers. Friday afternoon we walked together to Mount Zion, and then to the Western Wall before dinner. After the meal (which was delicious—prepared completely from army food by civilians), I went up onto the rooftops of the Moslem Quarter via an iron stairwell I found two years ago. A mist, and the moon, and the lights of the city, and the quiet, made the gold and silver domes to the east more beautiful than I've ever seen them. I went back down to my room, and to sleep on a stone windowsill with a mattress and a view of the sky.

I woke up after my first good night's sleep in a week, and went down to the Western Wall for the Torah service. I found a *minyan* which had just started reading the Torah. (Others had already finished, and others had much to cover before reading the scrolls.) I had on an army T-shirt, jeans, sandals, and an assault rifle, and looked a bit different from the others in the minyan, with their beards and black and white clothes. I was called to the Torah* nevertheless—the ultra-orthodox may hate secularity but they have nothing against Jews stepping into the world in which they live. More than one of those who saw me invited me to their houses for *kiddush*, but I turned them down because I'd run into the father of someone from the kibbutz, who invited me to the house where he has lived since 1967—one of the first ten Jewish families to return to the Old City. I enjoyed being with this family in their house....

An hour or so later I was finally free to walk to the New City, to my room, for

---

*Being "called to the Torah" is an honor. It means being invited to make the blessings before the reading of one of the portions of the Torah.

a quiet place to work and a good meal. I left in a lousy mood because of how the Shabbat had been organized, how a map had been taken from my bag, and because it's possible to be pissed off for no reason at all.

I walked through Liberty Bell Garden, across the empty field to the street which leads to my street. I saw a couple walking along the street in the opposite direction: Natan and Avital Sharansky! "Shabbat Shalom! I've always wanted to meet you," I say to him in Hebrew after shaking hands. He says, "Shabbat Shalom," and asks if I live here. I tell him that I'm in the army (obvious due to the gun on my back), that I've been to Russia, and that I, too, am an *oleh*. That's all, no big talk or deep discussion; but when we parted I had a huge grin on my face. All the tensions of the past week in the army were gone, and I felt wonderful. I wonder if that happens everytime you meet a hero. One thing I'm sure about—it's impossible to be in a lousy mood over a stolen map and other irritations after meeting Natan and Avital. If he could maintain his hope, love, and spirit through his trials, I certainly can't let what had gotten to me bother me.

Be well and don't forget Sharansky. He is a symbol of joy here.

Love,

Alex

A "Heavy Raid"

June 30, 1986

Dear Dad, Mom, Saul, Benj, and Daniel,

I feel like talking to all of you, or just sitting in the living room and reading a book— a book which I don't have to summarize in writing by Sunday—with all of you there. By the time you receive this letter nine weeks of this course will have passed. It is a good course but it has many flaws. There are good times here, but there are also the times when, maybe for one last time before becoming an officer, I'm treated like a soldier.

Tonight we will rehearse a raid which includes six km of walking to the target, and four back from the target. This is nothing, except I've been assigned to carry three heavy imitation land mines—around 40-50 pounds—in addition to my battle gear. I won't have any trouble with this, but I don't like it. I'd prefer to command the operation, and have the weight—of responsibility—on my head rather than on my shoulders and back.

* * *

The raid was so-so. I had no trouble with the weight. (I was the heaviest-loaded person—the only one who came close was the gasoline bomb, but since he blew his burden up, he got to do the four-km return with nothing on his back, while mine were only demos and had to return). The carrying went very well for me—no falls. Enough said.

All's well.

Love,

Alex

A Secret

[Journal]

June 30, 1986

[Officer School]

.... I'm relieved to know the source of my breathing problems—exertion-induced asthma. This would get me kicked out of this place if my commanders found out....

Young Love For Lenin

[Journal]

July 4, 1986

[Officer School]

The whole family is in NYC for the Statue of Liberty's 100th B-Day party, and I'm here guarding the base.

Last week was platoon-sized raids. Last night was one on a two-story house. Leor led the raid. He's easily the most impressive of the people taking the course. He has natural leadership which isn't smug. People just naturally turn to him. He's also the most professional of the soldiers I've met. Good to see that there will be officers in the future with the qualities I associate with heroes of the past.

On a lighter note: here's the ditty which Alex Rosenstock from Russia taught me:

I am a little boy

I don't yet go to school

I haven't yet seen Lenin

But I love him.

This apparently is a ditty which is as common in the USSR as "the mouse ran up the clock" for us. What it means is that the state, which made Pavlik Morosa—and betrayal of family for the state—into models of correct behavior, uses more means than abstract stories. Ditties bouncing around young brains leave echoes. The fact that Alex [Rosenstock] remembers this, even though he left Russia years ago and has even forgotten much of his Russian, means that this must do a lot of bouncing. What a difference between "Hickory Dickory Dock..." and "I Love Lenin."

Decisions: Measured by Blood

July 5, 1986

Dear Katherine,

Happy Independence Day! I got your letter of June 26.

On what you said about the West Bank Arabs' plight: of course, the ideal situation would be one in which they governed themselves. But the Middle East is not the place to look for ideal situations. There are many Arab states and one Jewish one. Arabs who choose to remain in the Jewish one can't have it both ways. The fact that to a certain extent their plight is their choice is important: Israel is not a USSR which cannot be left.

On what you said about my being a thinking person vs. a non-thinking one: don't worry. I will never do without questioning—at least in my mind. You have to understand that the army, however, is not a place which demands its members to cease thinking. To a civilian the idea that orders must be followed is blown out of proportion. I won't go into a discussion now of the "order" vs. its costs—I just want you to know that in my army, and especially where I am now, thinking is encouraged, especially about questions and dilemmas far more difficult than I think civilians see officers as facing. Example: if I am sent on a mission and have the capability to deal with only ten prisoners, and my soldiers capture twenty, and freeing the extra ten will possibly mean the discovery and annihilation of my force, can I decide to kill ten of the prisoners?

You see, the officer must think and do his thinking with a sense of justice far less abstract than that of the law professor or judge. His sense of justice must be combined with his responsibility for the lives of his men, and his duty to complete the mission he has been given, to produce a decision—usually in minutes, rather than in the years which an academic can take to answer (or declare "unanswerable"). The quality of the officer's choice can be measured in terms of blood, while the academic sees his question and answer as largely hypothetical. I know I'm being harsh with academe but I want you to see an army, not as it has been portrayed to you through your whole life by a generation of media men who never served in the armed forces. The young men I'm with are learning to think and make decisions harder than any in the civilian world—and they are not abstract or far away.

I too think there will be a war with Syria. I've heard the arguments of why there won't be one, and I find them unconvincing. The prospect scares me, because the Syrian army is strong and huge and ours is strong and small. [Syria's president] Assad is willing to throw away soldiers far faster than the Israelis—who will go to any length to save a POW or prevent casualties.

But we will win the next war, as we've won every war until now, and Israel will not be pushed into the sea.

I don't want to lecture anymore about Zionism and decision-making, I'd rather tell you about walking through a wadi in the middle of the night with a million stars over my head, and singing as I walk because I'm so content and so enjoying myself, and climbing mountains and looking over the desert, and seeing eagles and a huge waddling porcupine, and the goodness of rest which always comes after a night trekking with so much weight on my shoulders. There are nights which make the weight disappear, and I love those nights.

I'm feeling wonderful and very much at peace with my decision to stay on.

Love,

Alex

Repairing Israel—A Pitch for Aliyah

July 12, 1986
[Officer School]

Dear Dennis [Prager],

I haven't written to you in ages, but this past week has put some thoughts in my head which I'd like to share with you.

The week was spent at the army's education center in the framework of the infantry officers' school. The main topic was "Judea and Samaria: Options and Democracy." The most important point came up in one of the democracy lectures, and while I realized that this point was the most important, I don't think it was noticed as such by most of the listeners. Here it is:

In a democracy the minority must do the will of the majority (unless the majority's will is something which will destroy democracy—such as eliminating elections). This is true not because there is nothing wrong with a situation where up to 49% of the population is forced to do something they oppose, but because the alternatives are worse—dictatorship or anarchy.

This rule can be illustrated by looking at the evacuation of the Yamit settlers. The government (we'll assume the government represents the majority) decided to evacuate the settlers. The settlers finally left (after a long struggle) not because they felt the sacrifice of their homes was justified by the prospect of peace (on the contrary—many believed that leaving the Sinai would bring war to Israel). Their sacrifice was on the altar of Democracy, for they realized that if they were unwilling to do the majority's will, even at the cost of peace (they believed), they, when their turn came, could little expect the majority to do their will. Democracy would have been ruined, because minority refusal to do things the "majority way" means that nothing gets done, because states cannot run on 51% cooperation—with income tax-paying or traffic-law-observing.

Indeed, when the Yamit settlers' side of the political spectrum became the majority, who decided to go to war in Lebanon in 1982, they could carry out their decision only because the army—the people—obeyed their decision. This is something which they could not have been expected to do had Yamit created a precedent of minority refusal to obey majority rule. The result would have been the inability to go to war.

Dennis, the Yamit/[Lebanon] examples are, I think, a brilliant way to illustrate the fact that without popular acceptance of democracy a state cannot survive, because it cannot act. The reason I'm writing to you is because this message is barely understood here.

You are a great explainer. I know that the work you feel you're doing in LA is exposing many more people to the values of absolute morality, etc. than any work you could do here. But there is no one here explaining democracy in a way that brings people to act as if they value democracy and understand the consequence of its disappearance. And, even if there is, there is certainly no one effective at maximizing the spread of this message. You are good at convincing, and an effective people-reacher, and you are desperately needed here.

Enough. I'm finished with my aliyah pitch. I just want you to know that if you decide to stay in the Diaspora for the reason that you "can be more effective *mitaken olam* [repairing the world] in the U.S. than here," you are wrong. Zionism today is not building a new kibbutz or a new hospital ward. Zionism today is turning Israel into an *or lagoim* [light to the nations]—something we cannot be unless we remain an effective, strong democracy. And, democracies can be neither strong nor effective without a population of lovers of democracy. *Tikun olam* must begin with *tikun Israel*. [Repairing the world must begin with repairing Israel.]

I just thought of something else—another reason why you would be a much better spreader of the word than anyone else I've yet heard of: you would never turn democracy into a false god, and would stress the Jewish side of the message as well—something which ACLU-type democracy-preachers forget.

I realize that this letter makes me sound pessimistic and urgent. I am in some ways, but you should know that my spirits are excellent and that all is very well....

Your friend,
Alex

A Kippah Like a Yo-Yo

July 15, 1986
[Officer School]

Dear Larry and Linda [Kelemen],

I was sad, but not very surprised, to hear of the negative reactions among Jews to your religiosity. There's a rule which says that anyone to the "right" of you religiously is a fanatic. For the secular, anyone wearing a *kippah* is a fanatic; for the Ein Tsurim types, who generally don't grow beards and don't wear head-coverings (married women), those who do so are not fanatics, but are seen as "very religious," while the black-coats [Hasidic Jews] are...in the category of "fanatics."

My feeling is that its worthwhile to weigh public reaction to appearance, as well as convictions as to what is "right," in deciding how to look to the outside. I don't feel I've found a satisfactory middle ground myself, with the way the *kippah* goes from my pocket to my head like a yo-yo, but I don't think compromise on appearance has to be compromise on values.

Love,
Alex

Soldiers Attuned to Morality

July 15, 1986
[Officer School]

Dear Katherine,

You can't imagine how letter-hungry I was until this afternoon when your letter came.

Here's a thought I just wrote to a friend: "All around me are guys arguing about moral dilemmas in battle. (Literally arguing! We just had a formal discussion on the subject and they've continued long since the discussion ended.) On the one hand, war appears to be the most immoral of human activity, as the goal of both sides always involves killing. But, I know from my very limited experience, the spectrum of morality in war is very broad, and even the most horrible things can be done immorally or morally. On the other hand, an activity which seems to open little opportunity for immorality—carpentry, let's say, rarely if ever has its moral aspects discussed—and as a result carpenters, who spend their lives doing something as amoral as cutting wood, are likely to be less morally attuned than soldiers (Israeli ones at least), who spend years learning how to kill, but also discussing and thinking about the moral side of every step they take."

Don't worry.

Love,
Alex

Poems

Poems included with the letter of 15 July to Katherine Baer:

NEGEV
The mist sits in the wadis
and the hills rise like islands
and the dawn closes the night
and the stars fade
and the north disappears
and all that is left is desert.
But look!
Closer.
The desert lives.
The wadis are lined with *rotem* bushes.
Snakes and scorpions live under the rocks
and the hawks circle and dive.
And then the night returns
—the night which is the soldiers' day—
and again our work begins
and we forget the wadis
and we don't smell the herbs
and we care only of our footsteps.
Until,
finally,
the conquest over
we can again begin to sense.

The carpenter thinks of wood and nails and pegs and saws.
The soldier thinks of killing and guns and bombs.
But the carpenter need not ask whether each cut is "just."
Only the soldier must judge his every step.
The carpenter goes home attuned to his woods.
The soldier goes home with justice on his mind.
Of course war is full of immorality.
But at least soldiers are forced to think of what is right.

George Bush's Aftershave

[Journal]

August 1, 1986

Since last writing two weeks of the course have passed—two easy weeks. The first was at the Wingate Sports Institute's army section where we did fitness. After that we went to Tel Aviv to train for our new role:...George Bush's honor guard.

I was the only one in the guard who'd voted for the man but George never found out. He didn't stop to ask if any of us were his electors. But he had very nice-smelling aftershave and he has 120 combat flying missions....

Infuriated on the Temple Mount

August 3, 1986

[Jerusalem]

Dear Saul,

I'm sitting in a meeting room in the Knesset. The Speaker of the House, Shlomo Hillel, just spent an hour with us.... This is a most dynamic democracy. There are five parties, twenty-five ministers, lots of committees, and lots of reasons why what appears to mean one thing doesn't. The whole business of the "1% blocking percentage," and how it appears to mean that there will always be lots of parties, hence situations with small parties holding the key to coalitions, is problematic. I think it should rise to 3% or 5%.

I was on the Temple Mount yesterday and was infuriated by something I brought up today in our talk with the Speaker: Moslems enter the Mosque of Omar for free, but all others must pay. Why should Jews and Christians finance the upkeep of the Arab world's third holiest place? Nowhere else I've ever been has money been taken to enter holy places.

As I wandered around the Mount, "Waqfniks" kept yelling at me, "you can't walk there, you can't walk here." What's going on! What chutzpah! Sure the Israelis (Moshe Dayan) handed over authority on the Mount to the Waqf, but that shouldn't mean that they treat the place as private property. It is not, and I have the right to walk it as long as I'm dressed in such a way that I didn't offend Muslim mosque-goers. So...the Speaker said, "Yes, there's a problem, but we don't want to turn a political war between Arabs and Israelis into a religious war between Jews and

Moslems, so we let these little things slip by." I say, "Hell no!" Sure I don't want Jihad [holy war], but I hate to see Israeli fear of Jihad taken advantage of by the Waqf, to finance what Arabs should finance, and to act as if we visit the place out of the goodness of their hearts. They, in short, can go to hell.

Alex

Children as Shields

August 4, 1986
[Officer School]

Dear Mom and Dad and Saul and Benjy,

This is demolitions week. I'm bored, tired, and I miss you. Two *shabbatot* ago I was with the Furstenbergs. Their youngest son, Yair (14), is a very good drawer, so I promised to invite him to draw with me one day. During the week I had time, and we walked to Herod's tomb and drew. (He drew and I water-colored.) As I was walking with him into town, I heard, "Alex!" Amy, who'd called "Alex," was on staff with me at BCI. She'd been in the country for about an hour when she ran into me. I dropped Yair off, and met Amy, her mother, her aunt and uncle at Cafe Atara.

On Friday, when I was back in Jerusalem, Amy and I went for a very long walk through the Christian, Moslem and Jewish quarters, and on the rooftops of the Old City, then down into the City of David, and finally up the Hinnom Valley to the Sultans's Pool. I took my gun, and I'm not sure I was being at all excessive—not that we had trouble, but there have been a few "surprising" terrorist acts recently. (In case you didn't read about it, a soldier was killed last week in Lebanon, when terrorists used children as shields in a run-in with our forces. The IDF officer ordered his men to make sure not to hit the kids. This might have meant that Arieh could have lived had we been more brutal, but who knows. Note: none of the kids were hit.)

The reason I'm writing to you about Amy is that I think she may well make aliyah partly as a result of the Israel I showed her. Jerusalem away from the tour groups is pretty good, and finding that an American can love Israel as I do, and feel it to be home as I do, may have beaten away Amy's fear that no matter how right it is to make aliyah, Israel isn't "home."

August 6th

Between the last paragraph and this one I was supposed to finish my service in the IDF. August 5 was the date of my release. Now I'm on *Keva* [voluntary service rather than draft or obligated service]!

A Few Thrown Stones

August 13, 1986
eve of the Ninth of Av, 5746
[Officer School]

Peter [Kaufman],

Shalom. Writing to you on the back of your letter saves me from getting out of bed to look for paper and eliminates last minute searches for your address. Tomorrow is the Ninth of Av and I'm fasting until it's over, as is the custom. *Tisha b'Av* marks the anniversary of all sorts of horrible things which happened to the Jews—from the destruction of the First and Second Temple to the expulsions from England and Spain. The Book of Job* is read in the synagogue as all sit on the floor as a sign of mourning. The tone is a sad sing-song which puts me to sleep, so that I dropped my copy of Job's woes.

I was tired because I spent the last three nights "navigating." My navigations all went very well. It can be tricky looking for a 20"-square water hole on a moonless night with no map, but it's a good feeling when you find it.

On our first night, navigating through an Arab village, stones were thrown at me and my partner, but by the time I'd turned around and brought my gun to my shoulder to scare the mother, he'd disappeared. No chase—it wouldn't have made any difference.

Alex [signed in Russian]

*Alex made a mistake here. The book he heard read aloud on *Tisha b'Av* was Lamentations.

Life Is Many Things

August 14, 1986
[Officer School]

Dear Katherine,

You've already gotten a couple of letters ahead of me. Sorry.

I see that my letter about "not thinking" bothered you. I don't remember exactly what I wrote, but I certainly didn't mean that the army had put my moral barometer on hold—on the contrary. I find more moral dilemmas here than I can picture anywhere else. I think what I meant is at times, knowing that fighting an order wastes time and is futile makes me accept it without argument, where I might have argued as a civilian. This doesn't mean that *if* the order violated my beliefs I would so behave. I can picture circumstances in which I would definitely refuse orders.

One of the Ten Commandments is "Thou shall not *murder.*" This is what God said to Moses, and what has become the most famous mistranslation in history, when the transcribers of the New Testament said, "Thou shall not *kill.*" The Jew is commanded to give his life if the alternative is doing certain things whose commission is worse than death. One of these things is murder. If I am ever told to "kill this civilian (hostage) or I will kill you," I hope I'll have the strength to accept my fate. But the Jew is also commanded to kill when that killing will prevent murder. There is a difference.

Of course, as you write, men should live in peace—this is better than war. But in the Middle East only being prepared for war allows Israel to live in peace. The day the Syrians believe they can win a limited war with Israel they will attack. There is no alternative of "seeking parties willing to negotiate" as there was with Egypt, and as Israel did. The reality of this area is of dictatorships in which Israel is an island of democracy and of human rights, unique in the region. You talk of "pragmatic alliances and accords" as if there were no Khomeini, no Hafez Assad, no Yasir Arafat, no Saddam Hussein, no George Habash, and no Ahmed Jibral. These men are the power holders in the region, and they want Israel to cease to exist.

Life is many things. It is fragile, beautiful, full of opportunity to create and to improve our world. But it is also short. To kill, in the most extreme cases, can be just. There are things more important than one life.

Love,
Alex

Comforting Grandparents

August 23, 1986

[Ein Tsurim]

Dear Grandma and Grandpa,

I am at the kibbutz. Mom was here until an hour ago.

I am sorry that these are hard times for the two of you. I wish I could be with you to try to help make them a bit easier.

But even though we are far apart I do not feel all of the miles. My mother's visit has brought you closer, and I hope my letters have made you feel that you are always as up to date about what I'm doing and thinking as you would be if I were living in Washington or still studying in New York.

You know that my decision to move to Israel was a hard one for me. You know that my first months in the Israeli army were hard ones for me—that, besides the physical strain, I often asked myself if I was doing the right thing.

I want you to know that now, a month away from the end of officers' school, I have no regrets about any of my three big and hard decisions. I feel glad that I decided to stay the extra year so as to be an officer. I feel no question that joining the army has been a good experience for me—that it has given me the opportunity to play a part in making the one Jewish state in this world, a place where Jews can live without fear as Jews. Finally, I feel that the decision to move here at all was a decision to move *to* my home. Without preaching ideology, or rationalizing, or too many explanations, I can simply say that this new home of mine is my home—that I feel here like an insider not a visitor.

I am telling you all this because I think it will make the miles between us shrink if you know I feel I'm in the right place for me. I also want you to know that I could not feel that way if not for the way you two raised your daughter—my mother. Your strengths became her strengths and your values hers. And she, together with my father, have made me much of what I am today. She is a great model to me of a content, calm, loving, teaching person and I thank you for her.

Shalom.

Love,

Alex

Once in a while.
As I progress towards the course's end.
I feel a pang of fear.

Today I felt such fear.

If the War comes
When the War comes
I will have to lead men to die

But those men were not men a short time ago
Some don't even shave yet
And I will have to have the calm power
to yell to them
or to whisper

Kadima.

And,

I will have to have the calm power
to step forward myself.

"To Step Forward Myself"

[Journal]
after August 17, 1986

Once in a while.
As I progress towards the course's end.
I feel a pang of fear.

Today I felt such fear.

If the war comes
When the war comes
I will have to lead men to die.

But those men were not men a short time ago.
Some don't even shave yet.
And I will have to have the calm power
To yell to them
Or to whisper

Kadima.

And,
I will have to have the calm power
To step forward myself.

Punished by Twerps

[Journal]

September 5, 1986

I've been up on the Golan since Monday setting up camp for the battalion which will come on Sunday. Shabbat will be here which is OK, but I don't know about how my mood will be, because Leor Messinger has said that I deserved to be punished for not telling him I was going to visit my old battalion headquarters yesterday. I thought he knew. I hate being punished by twerps with rank. I'll have a rank soon, and only higher-ranking twerps will be able to punish me. The irritating thing is that the punishment is a report on "violation of discipline," when I'm one of the most disciplined guys I know.

Enough.

Shabbat Shalom.

24th Birthday In Sight of Syria

[Journal]

September 15, 1986

24th birthday

Daniel dropped by to say hello today, but we both forgot it was my birthday. Before that a tour of our emplacement along the Syrian front. This pours cold water on my birthday spirits and makes me quake a little. I saw Syrians below the Hermon.

Nowhere I'd Rather Be

September 22, 1986

Beit Feldman on the

Mediterranean

Dear Saul,

I feel like telling you about some nice moments of the past week or so. The army, as irritating as it can be at times, does have nice moments—moments when, if you thought to step back and think, you would say, "There's nothing I'd rather be doing, and no one and nowhere I'd rather be with and at, than doing this with these guys right here."

Yesterday, after a week of discussion here at this education center, Adi announced that there was a *madas*—a run for the platoon. Everyone complained a bit, but the four of five of us who were about to go out for a run anyway didn't mind. We took off on our own, ran to the beach, stripped and ran into the sea. This was no "political" skinny-dipping, where anyone was thinking of making a statement or anything—we had the beach to ourselves and we wanted a release after a day in a classroom. The water was wonderful and clear and warm and the waves were good ("the waves were good" sounds like Hemingway), and the rest of the platoon was running and we were all having a ball. Then they came by our section of the beach and stole our clothes. This presented a problem because, with swimming not allowed, returning to Beit Feldman, at the top of the cliffs above the beach, with no clothes would not be too cool. Anyway we all got our clothes back except Danny Schneidman from New Zealand, who got his shoes but no shorts, which looked hilarious, but then he too got re-equipped and back we climbed—straight up the cliff to Beit Feldman.

Hitching stories are also good. Maybe I should write about the people I've met on my way to and from the army. Two nights ago I was on my way back from Tel Aviv with Leor, and we were picked up by an amazing BMW with an amazingly beautiful woman in the passenger's seat, and a talkative driver and a good stereo.

I'll close to the sound of the Talking Heads to send this.

Love,

Alex

An Officer At Last

October 5, 1986

[Officer School]

Dear Grandma and Grandpa,

In four days I will be an officer in the Israeli army. Tomorrow Dad will arrive so as to be at the ceremony. I'm very glad he will be here. I haven't seen him in a year—since my last visit to the U.S.

The ceremony, and my receiving the rank of 2nd Lieutenant, will mark a real turning point for me—the end of a period of being a soldier responsible only for myself, and the beginning of a period during which others will be under my command. This should be a challenge, and I look forward to the change.

After the ceremony I should have some time off to do some touring with Dad. There are so many places I've seen since I joined the army that I want to show him. This is a beautiful, beautiful country and the army has allowed me to see more of this beauty than civilians ever see, because I am outside so much.

The army has taught me to love the night. At night we hike and learn to get around as well as during the day. In fact, I feel better oriented at night, with stars to tell me where the north is, than I do during the day. And when there is a moon and I can see almost as well as during the day, and the heat of the day is gone, I truly enjoy walking.

All is very well with me.

I hope that this new year will be one of peace for us all.

Love,

Alex

25 Sept, 1986

Today we had a Tiyul to the Carmel.
Went to Dalyat Al Carmel; the Bahai temple.
The carmelite church, the Kababir (?) neighborhood.
"Little Switzerland," ~~the~~ Good time, good -
spirits, beautiful views, nice education
officer and a Mashakiʔ. -

  Back to Beit Feldman. Run, wonderful swim

    Lecture by אלוף (אלוף)
    Matan Vilnai who
    was Amused about
    Petra.
    ———

    then this guy,

    started a lecture
    - comedy about
    the South
    Pole.

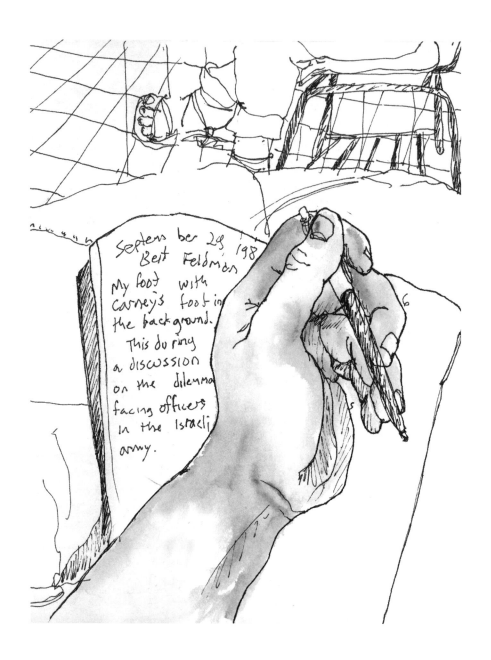

6.
Frustrated in the Air Force

"I didn't sign on to become an officer to eat well and train guards."

Sleeping Under the Moon

October 23, 1986

[Jerusalem]

Dear Mom, Dad, Benj, and Saul,

Yesterday Gai, Dani, Yossi and I met in TA and drove to Qumran where we hiked a few hours in the canyon above the famous caves.

Then we drove to the old Mitspe Shalem—now a rock-climbing school. The others all wanted to sleep at the school for five shekels per person, but I couldn't picture paying to sleep in a room when I'm in the desert. So, we drove a couple of hundred yards west, and slept under the moon.

At sunrise we got up and started to walk. Wadi Darag'eh is known for its pools, which have to be crossed, and little waterfalls (dry) above each pool, which must be descended with ropes. The water smelled a bit, but the walk was beautiful and I love climbing. It's a good wadi.

I hitched back to Jerusalem, came to my garden apartment* and bought tomatoes and onions and garlic. (The guy in the shop said, "You need lemon, oil and parsley too for the salad." He didn't have any to sell but he gave me his salt, and a bag of oil, and some parsley, so that the salad would turn out. Back home I made my first meal, and ate it listening to George Gershwin played by Andre Watts. Mom, you would have loved the scene.

Love,

Alex

P.S. I went to the little Yael Street synagogue for Simchat Torah—very nice. After about the third Hakafa the Torahs flowed into the street and danced with the Torahs of two other synagogues on our block—one Hasidic and one Sephardic. A Sephardic man with a bottle of arak wandered around asking people from our shul whether "any Ashkenazim have been spoiled enough" to have some arak.

---

*Alex was invited by Ruth Zilkha to live in her guest room off the garden of the building where she lived. It is a long, thin room, with a loft on which Alex put a mattress to use as his bed.

A Russian Tale

November 5, 1986

[Jerusalem]

Dear Mom, Dad, and Benj,

I arrived here at my small home after a quick hitch from a base just north of Tel Aviv. My ride into the city was with a retired American couple who moved here two and a half years ago. He had a stroke not long ago but was now almost fully recovered. They used to be '60s radicals and are now *ba'alei tshuvah* [newly orthodox].

They asked me why I'd come, and I told them, "It's home." And I asked them the same question. They said that after their first visit they'd been asked what they liked most about Israel by friends, and they answered, "Three things: the country is much prettier than the desert we expected; and, after three generations in the U.S. and only two weeks in Israel, we suddenly felt that we were not strangers in a strange land, but at home." I forget the third reason.

The man who gave me the ride to where the couple from Monsey had picked me up is on reserve duty for two weeks as the staff sergeant of the course in which I'm one of the three officers. In civilian life Yossi is a lawyer and the head of his law office, but in the army, in theory, I'm his commander. I say "in theory" because I wouldn't dream of giving him an order. We're working together and he's a very good man.

As we walked together through the base today, past a display of Russian tanks and other spoils of war, he showed me the kind of tank he first commanded—a French AMX-13. In '73 he was a reserve tank commander in the Golan Heights.

We stopped at a Russian APC and looked in together. I started to read the signs inside in Russian and he too could read the letters. He was born in 1938 in Bulgaria and moved to Israel in 1948. I asked him if he knew Russian and he said that once he was fluent because, in 1944, after the Russians invaded Bulgaria, a Russian officer and his family rented two rooms from his father in their very large home. On the officer's first night in the Bulgarian family's home, the family had the officer, his wife and six-year-old-daughter for dinner. The officer saw the piano and asked if he could play something. He sat down and played a Czech folk song—"Die Moldau"—named for the large river which flows into the Danube. Yossi's father knew the tune and asked if he knew what he was playing. "I know" was the answer he gave as he looked into the other man's eyes. The tune was also that of "Hatikva" and the officer played it to find out if the family whose household his family had joined were Jews. The officer's name was Yisrael Polodsky. Yossi, who was six years old at the time, learned Russian from the officer's daughter.

When the officer moved in with Yossi's family, his wife was two months pregnant. When her father, back in Russia, heard that she and her husband were living with Jews, he wrote to Yossi's father and asked if he could make sure, in the case that his daughter had a son, that the child would have a *brit* [circumcision celebration]. The woman had a boy and, Yossi says, his father made him the biggest *brit* you could dream of. Two or three years ago, Yossi wrote to the officer in Russia. He knew only his name and the name of his village near Kiev. A few months later a reply arrived. The daughter had become a professor. Tomorrow I'm going to help him write another letter because I can write Russian.

We had walked past the Russian armored vehicle on the way to the building where the soldiers in training live. After a day's shooting I was about to see how

On a cold rainy day in my room in Baka

well they had cleaned their guns. They hadn't cleaned them very well at all, and I told them that sort of work didn't bother me, but should bother their self-respect.

The live-fire exercises I ran today were truly enjoyed by all. The soldiers, who are not from infantry units, enjoyed the chance to charge and shoot, and I enjoyed the chance to teach, shoot and supervise. The exercises were only of three men at a time—the smallest unit into which the army divides itself. But even that can be complex in terms of making sure all three are, as they run, and roll, and charge forward, shooting at the right targets, at the right time, hitting them, and hitting them safely.

When I left the base, one of the guys I'd trained came to me and said, "You were the one spot of light in the preparation." A good feeling: you work hard, show what you know, teach, inspire, and people learn, become enthusiastic, and find quality in the midst of mediocrity.

All is well. Still no word on posting.

L'hitraot,
Alex

Not On the Front Line

November 18, 1986

[In the Air Force]

Dear Katherine,

Have you heard I'm in the Air Force? This change is one that I see as very fattening—Air Force food is excellent. This new posting is an odd one for I am an infantry officer and the Air Force is not infantry. However, the Air Force needs to defend its bases and my role is in training the defenders—a job taken seriously enough by them to warrant their demanding paratroop officers rather than less expert infantry trainers.

Despite the conditions I'm very disappointed with my posting. I signed the additional year demanded by the Army when they put me through infantry officer's school—a position which would mean that I would be on the "front line" of Israel's defense. The sense of accomplishment, and of doing the most important work around, would have made the extra year worthwhile, but I didn't sign on in the army to eat well and do a secondary job like training guards. I still might move [to another posting].

Be well dear Katherine. Remind me that I promised that my next letter would be longer.

Love,

Alex

Death of Gramps

November 23, 1986

[Jerusalem]

Dear Grandma Gerry,

My father called me this morning to tell me that Gramps has died. Saul was with me. Last night we called home and spoke with Benjy and with Dad. This was probably just briefly before Gramps died. They told me Gramps was feeling weaker and I thought of calling. I'm glad now that I did not. I think he preferred to be alone with you at the end, because he never shared his suffering with us. Even when I spoke with him last week he didn't mention his pains, and was interested only in his grandchildren.

Last night I had a dream about Grandpa. Saul and Daniel and I were down in Florida. We had just arrived from the airport and we went right into Grandpa's room. Even in my dreams Grandpa was completely selfless. He was even a bit angry with us for coming, because he thought we were with him because we'd been told to come, and not because we wanted to be there.

But, Grandma, this was only a dream. The phone woke me from my dream with the news Grandpa had died. I hope he knew how much we not only loved him but also liked to be with him.

I'm sure that along with the release which today brings from Grandpa's suffering, which was so hard on you, as well comes great sadness. Please be strong and try not to feel alone because you are not alone.

With all my love,

Alex

Bargaining in the Old City

November 24, 1986

[Jerusalem]

Dear Mom and Dad and Benj,

I've spoken to all of you since Grandpa died. Saul says he heard a lecture about death where the rabbi said that when twins are in the womb, and the first [twin] is born, to the second that birth is a death because his brother has left him alone in the womb. But we know that leaving the womb is not death. Maybe such is passage from this life as well.

Yesterday Saul and I put up my 3.7-meter-long drawing from Lebanon. Saul and I also carried a sixty-shekel table back from the secondhand store I went to with Dad. I still have to sand and stain it. Shlomo gave me a double gas burner of enamel and cast iron which Saul cleaned off, but I haven't gotten a gas balloon yet. What else? We went to the main market street of the Old City to buy another rug. I carried a gun but no uniform. I told the shopkeeper I wanted a 1.5 x 2.5-meter rug, and that I paid thirty shekels for one three months ago. He said that his rug was 100 (had I been a tourist he'd have said 120). This quickly dropped to sixty as he showed me various rugs. I said thirty. Forty, he said, was his final price. "Thirty," I said. He said, "All right, we'll compromise—thirty-five." "Thirty," I said. "Okay," he said, "thirty-three." I said to him that thirty was still what I'd pay. "Thirty," he finally agreed.

Today I also put up two drawings and did the first drawing—of a corner of the room—that I'd done in a while. I started at the right side of the page and worked my way left using only watercolors—no ink. As I got tired of the drawing, I worked faster and faster with less and less detail, but now, when I look at it on the wall, I like the quickest parts far better than the more "worked" sections.

I'll tell you a bit about my work in the Air Force. I'm an infantry officer and my job is to train Air Force people in infantry skills. Last week I had a group of 17 for the whole week. I taught them basic shooting, charging, orders, house-to-house fighting, and some other skills. I enjoyed the week, but when I think of the fact that I'll never progress and carry forward "my" soldiers to more advanced skill, I am angry. What a waste. It also strikes me that I'm not thinking/writing enough about BIG issues. But maybe that will come.

Love,
Alex

Hard to Punish

December 18th
[In the Air Force]

Dear Dad,

We're in the tail end of a week of training of our staffs. The good side of the week was a lot of activity, shooting etc.

Another good thing was how I dealt with a sergeant of mine whose mouth got out of control. He would respond to instructions with arguments, and even called me a derogatory name. I sat with him for almost an hour, heard his complaints, explained why he can't do what he did, why I demand what I demand, and finally told him that even though, after our talk, I saw that he understood what he's done, that what he did deserved punishment and that he should accept it maturely and not as a sign of treating him like a green soldier. He did and I think he'll change.... It's not easy to punish someone.

Love,
Alex

From Ruthi's balcony —view of Rehov Yael   Oct. 8, 1984

Things I Hate About Israel

December 20, 1986
[In the Air Force]

Dear Katherine,

I'm working in the Air Force, but I hope I'll get out soon because not working for something important drives me crazy. At least I like most of the people I'm working with....

This country is my home emotionally, religiously, and in every other way except for the location of my family. When I say that Israel is my home religiously, I mean that as a Jew I should live in the Jewish state, the only Jewish state, the Jewish state which Jews for 2,000 years prayed to return to, and died for, and dreamed of.

You know my family and you know that I was not brought up in an orthodox home. I think that I really could not live anywhere else permanently. I feel more "at home" here than I can describe. This is not an intellectual feeling. It is just the way it is.

My connection to this country is only strengthened as my knowledge of and commitment to Judaism grows.

Don't read any of the above as blind nationalism. It is not. There are many things about this country which I truly hate (others hate them enough to be driven to leave). I hate the economic idiocy; I hate the way the PLO is allowed to determine the anti-Israeli education of Arab children (this may surprise you but it is true); I hate the fact that members of parliament are exempt from all the disgusting taxes they impose on the rest of us; I hate the way talent is wasted. There is a long list. But, because I see this place as my home, I don't pile the cons on one side of the scale, and the pros on the other, and come to a conclusion about whether it was "worth" staying here. Home is home and it will take more than irritations to force me to leave. I want to make this place better.

Love,

Alex

Concrete Accomplishment

December 28, 1986

Mom,

I don't think I've written to you since you wrote the letter about Grandpa.

The letter was a sad one—not so much because in it you spoke of his death—but because you wrote of his disappointments and feeling of failure in his life. Quality is rarely gauged well—tests, grades, evaluations, degrees, etc. all mean less than goodness and level-headedness (both of which he had so much of). When I think about Grandpa, I can't say that I learned from him; I learned *because* of him and his gift. I could have learned from him had I known what to ask, and asked it, but I didn't. All I know is that I liked him, and loved him, and appreciated his stability which you wrote about. I liked being with him.

It's funny, when I look at myself—with my *summa cum laude* degree, my award for my thesis, my paratroop training, and my rank as an officer—I am not short of those things which he felt he missed. But those things don't bring self-esteem. From outside and to Grandpa those thing look greater than they look to me. I find that self-esteem comes from concrete (not paper) accomplishments—whether completing a march or getting up for an Arab woman while in uniform on a bus. It's sad Grandpa didn't see this because he had no shortage of concrete accomplishments.

Love,

Alex

A Path For Benj

December 28, 1986

Dear Benj,

About the army and you. You might be interested in a *garin olim* [a group of new immigrants]. What you would do is: intensive Hebrew course, basic, service on the line, training, and then, in the paratroops, sergeants's school. This is a good path and has the advantage of being in the army with a group of people guaranteed to be more enthusiastic than your average Israeli. Everyone I know who has done this path has felt it to be good.

But you have to decide if you want to go in with other *olim* or not. You might react that, "If I'm already going in, I might as well go all out and not try to stay an *oleh*." That is what I said. I'm not sure that makes sense. The path of the *garin olim* is as serious as anything but the special units, and is definitely real army, with the advantage I told you—of enthusiastic people with you. If you go to Golani or para-troops you'll do OK, but it will be harder and lonelier. Think about it. In any case, there is a *garin olim* in July '87 and Yehuda Chen said there'd be no problem get-ting you in.

I only wrote of infantry because the longer I'm in the army, the more that I'm convinced that infantry is the best thing to do, short of being a frogman or a pilot—almost everyone who does anything else eventually comes to wish he had done the "real thing," and kicks himself for finding the easy way out.

Love,

Alex

Arguing with "Blacks"

January 2, 1987

Dear Larry and Linda [Kelemen],

.... On a bus back from a base near Ashkelon there was no place for me to sit. Then, at one of the small orthodox *moshavim* between the base and Jerusalem a Hasid sitting in the front seat got off. I asked the girl standing next to me if she was planning on sitting down. She said, "No." I said, "Why not?"

"Why not?" was a stupid question. Had I thought for half a second I would have noticed that the girl, whose skirt covered her knees, and who looked generally reli-gious, would not have sat next to the Hasid left on the seat. I sat down.

After a few miles I asked the Hasid—from now on I'll use the term "black man" because "Hasid" is not accurate, and black at least described the man's appear-ance.

I told the black man of the conversation I once had on an airplane with anoth-er black. The flying black had told me three reasons why he (even though he called himself a Zionist) wouldn't serve in the IDF: (1) too much contact with women (2) difficulty observing the 613 commandments (3) the secular "hate us." Note: the black man on the bus, who doesn't want his sons to serve in the army, said that he does not say the blessing for the State of Israel as *"Reisheet Smikhat Ge'ulateinu"* [the first flowering of redemption], but is also not against the state, as the Satmar blacks are. Anyway, I told the flying black that there were orthodox guys in my unit who managed just fine with total observance without any compromise; that there was less contact with women in the paratroops than in Mea Shearim; and that yes, the secular hate him, but that's because he's unwilling to make the single most important contribution demanded by his home. I told him that my orthodox friends' presence in the paratroops made the secular guys see that orthodoxy can go well with Zionism.

The black man sitting next to me on the bus was less impressed with my answers than the one on the plane. He said Jews should spend their time studying. I said that someone had to protect the state or no one would study. He said that if everyone studied then G-d would protect us; I said that the only way to get everyone to study would be to teach them that to study (Judaism) is good, and that they (the blacks) would have a better chance to influence and teach the secular if they served with them than if they helped continue the atmosphere of hate which not serving serves.

This is about where it ended. We arrived in Jerusalem, shook hands, and went our separate ways....

Love,

Alex

No Cut Flowers On Shabbat

February 7, 1987

Dear Saul, Mom and Dad, and Benj,

February fifth was the second anniversary of my being drafted. I spent the day running up and down a hill with a bunch of reservists training them to shoot and hit targets rather than kill each other. I was in the middle of one of their live-fire exercises when I remembered that it was February fifth and I started to laugh. Two years of army leading up to a hill with the 40-year-old father of three under my "command" huffing and puffing and mixing up the command for charging with the command for lying down.

Brought the Kleinhauses flowers for Shabbat. It turns out that this is not wise because they can't be put in water, as irrigating is prohibited. They were nice about it. It reminded me when Saul and I used umbrellas at the kibbutz on Shabbat and couldn't understand why we were the only ones who heard of that great invention. An umbrella is considered building a tent—one of the crafts of the tabernacle—hence prohibited [on Shabbat].

Love,
Alex

Rocca: Act I

February 20, 1987
[Jerusalem]

Dear All,

Friday, 4:25 in the afternoon, sitting outside my room in the garden of 1 Barak as the sun shines on my face and music wanders out of the door.

Hitching home today I was picked up in a Mercedes—a nice Mercedes. The driver moved here from Italy a couple of years ago. He's in the spaghetti business there. He said that he came with millions of dollars, bought a hotel and turned it into an old-age home, is building a yeshiva (he had no *kippah* on, but he said he moved here partly because he wanted his five children to marry Jews). He said (Rocca is his name) he had to wait two years for a building license, and that the income tax people came and threw him in jail for six days, even though all he's done since aliyah was spend and spend, and he'd yet to earn anything, and that he had a criminal case against him for punching a clerk in the nose (I think he turned over his desk too) when the clerk first made him wait until he finished his tea to sign the form Rocca had brought and then, after finishing the tea, told him to come back next week.

We talked about Zionism and agreed with one another (that is, he agreed with me) that Zionism means coming here and succeeding, and that deciding to come here is not the outcome of weighing Israel's pros and cons (which always turn out in *yerida*'s favor) but a decision that this is home which, once made, allows you to view the country's cons as problems with your home, to be ignored or solved or suffered but never leading to divorce.

Wednesday night was the fourth straight night of navigation for the Air Force guys (28 of them) who I was training in preparation for officer's school.

Here's the scene: a scrubby hilltop strewn with boulders and an olive grove not far away. A sky full of stars and two-thirds of the moon. A truck with the driver asleep in the cab and a commander with one of my sergeants always on duty to answer anyone reporting in. Twenty yards northwest of the truck a fire is burning in a small natural pit among a row of boulders. By the fire, boards have been lain on the earth as benches (all brought by us in the command car from a construction site in one of the new settlements nearby). On the board sit my medic—a 22-year-old recruit—another of my sergeants, myself, with another radio strong enough to receive incoming reports but rarely to broadcast, and Buddha.

I called him Buddha. He was the command car driver for the night—a 50-year-old reservist named Reuveni—the Middle Eastern music cassette magnate of TA's central bus station, and concert organizer and promoter. From his ever-smiling lips came an endless flow of wisdom, advice, opinion, and jokes. Buddha, the cassette king and driver, has no car of his own, but in the army he is a command car driver. I decided to try a dirt road I'd seen on the map, so I left my sergeant in charge at the fire and set off with Reuveni at the wheel. The road was passable but he was such a lousy driver that I told him to turn around after a while, and as we drove by some orange and lemon groves we stopped, and out he waddled and crawled over to the headlight-lit trees where he stuffed his pockets with the oranges saying, "Honey! Honey!" (referring to the flavor of the Arab oranges) as he bit into one after another, peel and all. I tried one (peeled) and took one lemon for our tea.

Love,

Alex

Rocca: Act II

Appendix:

Motsei Shabbat

February 28, 1987

[In the Air Force]

Shabbat was spent at the base—first time in about five months. I devoted it to sleep and nothing else.

In the dining room at lunch I got to talking to a reservist who stayed Shabbat for guard duty. I asked him what he does as a civilian and he said, "Research." I asked him to be specific, and it turns out that he works for the income tax police, looking into tax evaders, etc. I said, "Oh, I just met an Italian *oleh* who was in jail for six days and was finally released with a 'we're sorry' from you guys." I told him that the Italian had picked me up hitchhiking in an amazing car, and before I finished describing him, he said, "Rocca."

It turns out that Yossi is the one who was in charge of the raid on Rocca's house. It turns out that Rocca is Mafia—real Italian Mafia. As Yossi was talking with Rocca, one of his men noticed Rocca's seven-year-old son slipping out a back gate. They caught him and found a forged passport. In a hiding place under the floor, they found fifteen other passports and IDs.

Israel is known for "it's-a-small-world" stories, but meeting Rocca hitching and the man who'd been responsible for all the troubles Rocca told me about, here at the base, is amazing.

Love,

Alex

Poems

[Journal]
February 27, 1987

A slow song in Hebrew is playing on the radio.
I lie on my bed and the rain patters on the roof.
The week is over and I am worn out.
Worn out like an old horse.

The song has changed.
The tone is upbeat—more hopeful.
But I am still worn out,
Worn out like an old boot....

Haiku
The rain chills the air
Dark skies dampen the cold stones
Mud makes boots heavy.

Shabbat is coming
I see its restfulness just ahead
Blessed is the God who gave us Shabbat
And made us different from all other nations.

A Place of Endless Opportunity

March 7, 1987

Dear Benj,

I finally got your card and read your letter to Daniel. I don't have either in front of me, but I'm proud to have you as my brother. I see you as a mature, serious, honest, and caring person. I am glad you are coming to make my home and Daniel's home your home as well.

This is a wonderful, wonderful country with more stories and people in it than the rest of the world put together. It is a country full of surprises if you know what stones to turn over. It is a place of endless opportunity if you play your cards right.

But now it's 2:30 a.m. and I must sleep because my eyes are already closing. The step you are about to make is Right, Good and wonderful, and don't let the clouds of dust thrown up by the Bad here ever allow you to lose sight of the ground of the people who love it here.

Love,
Alex

"I Want Only the Chance to Give More"

March 7, 1987
[In the Air Force]

Dear Mom and Dad,

I have a lot on my mind nowadays. Even though it looks like I'll be moved soon, I've just about had it. On Friday when my commander told me his plans for me next week, I said that I've had it—that there's a limit to how long they can dangle a person.

I so want to be doing real work directly involved with defense rather than the difficult and almost purposeless labor I've been doing for the past four months. I hope something comes soon. I'm not drawing now. I'm not writing. I'm unable to argue or care about the kind of arguments in which I see Daniel thrive. I don't have the ability to form opinions quickly about issues nor to defend the opinions I adopt.

I look back and see all my successes and accomplishments as having little meaning. I know I've done well by your standards, but I don't have the peace of mind of which a young soldier who died in Lebanon wrote to his parents—that he could look back and say with confidence and pride that he's accomplished every one of the goals he set for himself. I haven't even been able to concretely define my goals.

I haven't set goals—maybe I should start—I've simply decided and done.

Please don't write and tell me how wonderful I am. I know what you think, and I know the letter you would write. I will get through this period and I will get through it on my own. That is what I want. What's been so hard is the feeling of being manipulated with no ability to affect my future. I've changed that, and I'm only getting out of the Air Force as a result of my own efforts.

I tell myself that I debate sending this letter, but I know I'll send it in the end. Joseph [Telushkin] says that confession is good for one's soul but one must consider the soul of those who hear the confession. You have to promise not to worry about me. I write to you of my trouble with the hope that you can write to me of yours, as well as with your joys, and that you will not try to suggest solutions too much. Your solutions will not understand the situation, and I want to feel I've taken care of myself.

Mostly I love life and I love Israel and Jerusalem and Daniel and my friends and want only the chance to give more.

In the army I finish three-day training session after three-day training session, and each ends with the summary discussion, and always one or two guys say how wonderful I was. After the discussion many always come to me to thank me and shake my hand. My drivers and medics (from the reserve) always say they're impressed at seeing someone who enjoys his work as much as I do. My staff of sergeants all tell me not to leave and respect me.

I am not blind. I feel myself to be a good judge even if not the greatest advocate.

Writing this makes me feel good. I remember writing to you a long time ago during another rough stretch and ending by saying to you, "see, even from 6000 miles away you can give me comfort." Nothing has changed.

Love,

Alex

Another Disappointment

May 1987

Dear Saul,

The seven months since finishing officers' school have been tough because of the string of disappointments of not getting jobs I hoped for. I let this get to me too much. Yesterday, after I spoke with you on the phone and told you I was 90% certain that I'd be starting my new platoon-commander job today, the 10% came through and the job didn't. The officer I was supposed to replace wasn't kicked out in the end. His commander decided to give him a second chance.

At first I felt that was that—I'd find some job for the four and a half months I have left and get out. I called my friend Adam Hocherman (of NJ) who was with me in basic, and who's a great spirit lifter and one who sees the bright side. In this case, the bright side was the alternative I've been offered, which I reacted to negatively, but Adam thought was great. It involves joining a yeshiva-boy company for their final two months (as a platoon commander) and then starting with a new *Hesder* platoon from start to finish including basic (nine months). He said, "This is the chance you were looking for to build a platoon from the start." He's right. It's just that I'm tired. I almost know that if I start a job I'll "get into it" quick.

Love,

Alex

Frustrated

....

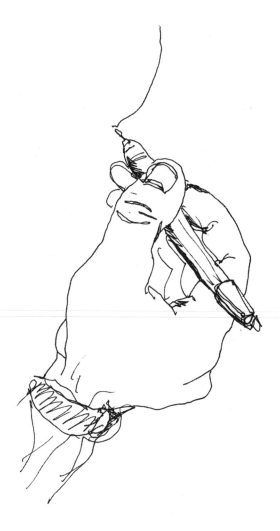

7.
A Platoon Commander in Givati

"I have endless stories to tell of people, problems, mistakes, moonrises, hikes and bombs."

Moving Again in the Army

Since finishing officers' school Alex had been trying every way he could to get an assignment as commander of a regular combat platoon. Finally, when he was paying a shiva (condolence) call at the home of a friend who had died in an accident, Alex met a battalion commander in Givati who was able to put him in touch with another battalion commander who needed a replacement for one of his platoon commanders. So Alex was assigned to Givati, an infantry brigade originally established in the 1948 War of Independence, disbanded, and then reestablished in 1984. When he joined the Brigade, Alex began his third journal and named it Givati.

May 21, 1987

[Jerusalem]

Dear Grandma Gerry and Mu,

It's late Thursday night and I'm sitting in my room in Jerusalem. I have a tape playing and the cool air is coming through my bedroom window.

I took a beautiful walk tonight along the "Haas Promenade"—a stone "boardwalk" along a high ridge linking two parts of Jerusalem and overlooking the entire city. At night the city glows and the air is so clean and cool that you can walk and walk.

All is very well with me. I've moved again in the army—into possibly the hardest job in the whole service—that of an infantry platoon commander. It's quite a challenge.

I hope all is well and that you too have some cool air to make nighttimes pleasant.

Love,

Alex

Patrolling Gaza and Then a New Company in the Golan

[Journal]

May 27, 1987

Jerusalem Day

Segayia Junction, Gaza Strip

It's just gotten dark (8:20 p.m.). Two hours ago I finished a twelve-hour patrol in a command car with two soldiers and a driver....

Earlier in the day I had a nice side-track to a not-so-old ruin which is occupied by an Arab family and had a pump-filled pool of water attached to it. In the ground-floor room was a round ten-foot-diameter dry pool over twenty-five feet deep with a chicken at the bottom. The landlord told me that the chicken had fallen in thirty days ago and had not eaten for twenty days. Now he lowers it food but it can't fly and he has no ladder, so there it will stay for now.

Today's patrol was my first "active duty" in a long time, and the first time out with the soldiers of my new company—of yeshiva students. I joined the company yesterday morning at 7:30 a.m. when we all got on some buses, at the encampment in the Golan where the battalion is based for training, to be jumped to Gaza in reaction to the past week's string of incidents there (two roadside bombs, a couple of terrorists blowing themselves up by mistake, a murder, a stabbing, etc. etc.). Last night a local (Arab) policeman was murdered with a machine gun 1 1/2 km from here. I heard the shots.

My job here has yet to be defined. I might get an existing platoon or one formed of a portion of each of the existing two.

[Journal]

May 29th

Last night was quiet. I slept from 10:30 to 4:30. Yesterday late afternoon command car patrol with Menachem and Eldad. Incidents:

—Bicycle passes us as we wait under bridge in Nahal Aza. When we leave, I see him going the other way. Stop him, check ID, ask him why he turned around after seeing us.

—"*Philastin*" [Palestine in Arabic] written on door. We stop, I call man from house, take ID, tell him he gets ID back when the new graffiti is gone. He calls wife who brings H_2O, washes it.

Before patrolling we did house-to-house search west of main road. Searching every room and closet for five escaped Hiz'bollah terrorists. Search during feast of *id il fitr*—some offer food or candies, some act worn out, some scared. All houses alike: very poor, filthy. Incidents:

—crazy woman shrieks from room to room

—English speaker

—two brothers born in 1927 and 1965

—turkish toilets unflushed.

[Journal]
June 7th
Qala, Golan
I've moved to a new company—this time for good. After leaving Gaza I was in Jerusalem for Shabbat and then back to the Golan to continue training.

June 9th
On my first day in the company I led two (day and night) APC exercises. The day was "eh" or worse, but the night exercise was the best in the company. The next day a company-sized APC exercise with lots of fire and burning fields and two tanks, etc. Visited mother of one of my soldiers because her divorce process is screwing up her son in army.

Yesterday, Monday, we had a company exercise in which I took the beach-head—with two tanks covering. Then I covered as the two tanks and the other two platoons worked on the rest of the target.

Last night on a stretcher run to Wasset and back—there with only battle gear, back with stretchers. Platoon 3 passed us, but I was pleased with our work until the end.

[Journal]
June 11th
Today started badly with my platoon unready to take on platoon-scale trench exercise. After 1 1/2 hours of going over basics we did a fair dry and the best "wet" day exercise in the company—partly because the RPGist blew his target to smithereens. (For which the company commander gave him the rest of the week off.)

The night exercise was good too.

"Just What I Wanted"

June 12, 1987
5 min before Shabbat
[Jerusalem]

Dear Family,

All is very well. In Jerusalem. Have endless stories to tell of people, problems, mistakes, moonrises, hikes, bombs, but no time to write them all. I've been keeping a diary again. I'll copy it for you sometime.

More after Shabbat.

I'm a platoon commander in the August '86 company of a Givati battalion. It's just what I wanted. It's a job that will last until my soldiers go to sergeants' school in November. I have to deal with discipline, training, fitness, and my staff of three—commanding them in exercises above platoon level—and deal with those above me as well. It's late and I've got to go to sleep. I have so much to write about but I'm writing in the journal and not letters. One story for the road:

On trench-warfare day I decided to do some fitness before lunch. Told the soldiers to leave their battle gear behind and open a stretcher for a stretcher run. After about 1 1/2 km we stopped at a lake and I said, "See the ruin on the hill—let's check it out." I got under the stretcher too and of course didn't get out until we got all the way there. At the hilltop I told them to put down the stretcher and for a light soldier to replace the heavy one I'd put up for the return run. Halfway back, at the lake, I got under again. The soldiers of course switched off every 30 seconds to one minute but I wouldn't let them replace me. My machine gunner asked to switch me— I whopped him on the back of the neck and said, "No way." "Why?" he asked. "You'll understand when you're a *mem mem*." Three hundred yards before the trucks he asked again to switch me. I said, "You can come under if you can keep the stretcher running all the way to the trucks—if you can't, don't bother switching me, and if you switch me and *don't* make it, we turn around." He said, "I can do it," and the stretcher ran all the way to the trucks. Good feeling.

Love,

Alex

Clumsy Closedness

June 19, 1987
[On the Golan]

Dear Katherine,

I have mixed feeling about writing this letter—certainly not from anger but from doubts of whether you want to hear from me. Of course, if you don't want to hear from me, you wouldn't have reached this far down the page.

I'm in a tent fifteen minutes from the Syrian border—I'll be here all Shabbat. I'm finally a platoon commander and I couldn't be more pleased. It's not that I haven't made lots of mistakes or that I suddenly am not at odds with anyone. Because I'm so busy, and have so much more to deal with than when I was a training officer (rather than one with soldiers completely under my supervision as I am now). I've made plenty of mistakes. I also have problem soldiers (some in jail!) and tough sergeants to deal with, and a direct commander—the company commander who is sometimes hard to take. But I'm learning about how to deal with people, to improve them, to train them, and much more.

I doubt what I'm learning here would have helped me deal with being with you when I was in the States. My clumsy closedness fell right on you and hurt you and I have the feeling that saying I'm sorry won't help, but if it will—I'm sorry.

I was about to write that I had no intention of hurting you but I realize that while this is true it does not change the fact that our being together was a trial—for me to see if I wanted to continue. I won't go into the reasons I decided "no," because you know most of them and I'm sorry that I didn't say when we first saw each other that "this is a trial period." Maybe I thought it was clear to you, too, that this was to be a trial. Be well, Katherine.

Shalom,
Alex

Pissed

[Journal]
June 22, 1987
Yesterday to Zavra for house-to-house. Pissed off by soldiers who let oil tin spill all over equipment (including mine) and didn't think to turn it right, let alone make

sure it didn't spill.

Turgeman in clinic now because caught fragments in arm during firing into room. I thought it was nothing and did nothing. Ronen told by Pinchas about it. Ronen pissed at me for not notifying him. I'm pissed at Pinchas for not telling me that it turned out to be more than a scratch; pissed at Ronen for not telling me that standard operating procedure with scratch is for doctor to check. Pissed mostly at myself for not being more careful.

Silhouette in the Moonlight

June 26, 1987

[Jerusalem]

Dear Mom, Dad, and Saul,

Returned to Jerusalem after two weeks on the Golan Heights this afternoon. I'll try to give you a picture of this training period by going over these past two weeks and some of their problems, challenges and achievements.

Last Shabbat spent at our encampment after a week which included a battalion-scale complex exercise. After that our company's platoons each had a raid exercise—the "platoon test" it's called. Mine went so-so—the navigation and the hike from the target back to base with open stretcher went very, very well but the work on the target itself could have been better.

I was pleased with the soldiers' work and with all the learning of errors which led to the problems. The problems range from not testing my sergeant's knowledge of his role—which led to his being mixed up on the site—to relying on my radioman to pass a message to the soldiers, rather than breaking "night discipline" and quietly, out loud, giving the message myself. I also got carried away with sticking to my planned arrival at the site (via a crumbled stone wall) rather than changing this route when it became evident that my silhouette would be visible in the moonlight. After Shabbat we went to a built-up area fighting training site for the week. Soldiers slow learners. Problems with all officers not having the same technique. Led to need to re-teach some things....

Dilemmas and problems:

—Soldiers curse and argue under the stretcher—in silence when night discipline in effect, in full volume when not, and when going gets tough. Sad.

—To enforce punishment for lateness (one hour from Shabbat for one minute of lateness) at full price, despite two weeks soldiers not home?

—What to do about sergeant who does not demand of himself as he demands of soldiers?

—How to help soldier used as scapegoat of whole platoon?

—Work with company commander, Ronen—difficult at times. My spirits are high. The problems I have with the soldiers and staff are challenges to be met rather than barriers, like the ones I had to get around before getting to Givati.

Physically the training is tough but I'm in much better shape than my soldiers (who just finished three months of border duty). Healthwise (yechh!) I'm OK too—allergic to something on the Golan Heights. Oh well.

Have done one two-part drawing since moving north. Pretty good.

Love,

Alex

Mock Battle

[Journal]

June 29—July 3, 1987

Got ready to take first ruin of Jebel Mis, which we do as soon as Adi marks extreme left with lights. On the way I get tangled in the wires of a TOW missile fired from far away while artillery was at work—cut little finger.

After taking ruin, told on radio that I have three wounded. We open stretcher. I tell three guys to fall down, and the nine who are left carry them about two hundred yards to the end point. That is, four under stretcher, three staff, plus two soldiers carrying the two "wounded" who are not on stretchers on their backs. They last about one hundred yards, and then I take Basha on my back from Betsalel. After about thirty yards, Alex, my sergeant, runs by with the other wounded soldier— Tal'ker, the featherweight Indian—on his back. Basha is a bit more burdensome. A general is at the end point.

The "wounded" are treated and the trucks arrive (instead of copters) to take us to the final act of the battalion exercise—the "baltam yom" (daytime surprise).

The battleground is Hushniya (ruined Syrian village) and two steep hills. We start spread out to sweep village. Platoon works very well with lots of fire and good movement. At one point Alex's company (to our left) charges in front of us, but we cease fire in time. We go on but are told to put out fire started by tracer bullets, as we are now the last platoon in force. Put out fire with shirts.

After fire out we all wash up in the clean water of the Yehudiya and go to trucks as the exercise is over by now. When all on board we go to Lake Kinneret, and whole battalion goes swimming. (This takes some doing—first payment of one shekel per soldier, and then dealing with problem of orthodox company which won't swim on mixed beach. In the end, they go in too.)

Searching for Tefillin

[Journal]
July 13th
Navigation Week
Shafaran
When we finished our work 2/3 up the tel ("hill" in Arabic), and took defensive positions, I found a metal bucket and filled it with glowing embers from the border marker—a burning tire. Then I had a better idea: heat a rock in embers and put rock under shirt. This I did for all eight of us.

On and off sleep, then down to wait for trucks to take us to Zavra for "dry" of final part of exercise. After sleeping for an hour or so at the waiting point, my radioman, Betsalel, says, "My *tefillin* fell out of the radio during the exercise." Oy. I told Ronen we were off to look for them. We ran and walked over the exercise we'd just finished, and just as I was about to give up, I saw the bag on the ground—right where we'd done the exercise's first charge. Betsalel was pleased and so was I....

Falling in the Dark

[Journal]
July 20th
The "company test" order was given to Ronen the day the exercise ended—Monday. Started at 9:40 p.m. Very hard walking. The platoon does very well in keeping up and working on the hard terrain. I even left them to continue alone, and I went back to mark trail for Adi in rear.

The 5 km of walking took us over seven hours because they were so hard. There was no moon and most of us fell many times—in fact much of the descent into Nahal Sion had to be done on our rear ends and grabbing branches of trees to slow ourselves.

The 300 meters up from the junction of Nahal Sion were also tough because the soldiers spirits were down after little foul-up of passing the junction by 300 meters, and having to retrace our steps. I couldn't understand why Ronen and Baruch kept going past the junction, because to me it was clear that we were off course. The climb was steep to the three big trees, and there was no way to progress without helping each other using branches and rocks for handholds.

We arrived too late, and the darkness raid we were supposed to do ended up being done in daylight. This was too bad and didn't allow us to show what we knew.

After that we did roadside bomb exercise, which was also silly in daylight. More so with no real explosions and no live fire.

Little things:

—Efi, brigade commander, screaming during fire at soldiers to put out flame.

—Amit, my machine gunner, did very well with star-light scope on his Mag [light machine gun] even though this is very awkward.

—Yoni, Arditi, and one other soldier in platoon in front of me opening up gaps, which slowed company's progress.

Enough. We could have taken the test had we left earlier. Too too bad.

Splitting with Katherine

July 24, 1987

Dear Harold,

Harold, you can't understand my problems with Katherine, so your advice about not opening up is not applicable.

I care about Katherine, and even long for her at (lonely) times; K. loves me. I told K. in the States my "conditions"—long-term things on which I can't compromise (Israel, Jewish family). She was hurt but didn't say so at the time. She says, "Don't think so much; do what you feel you want to." I did in the States last time, but I didn't feel the refusal to forget those basics is the same as being inflexible—

it's merely boundaries for the future. Anyway, this isn't the point. The point is that as much as I care about K., she gets on my nerves. I don't have the energy for constant battle. I need someone who understands what I'm going through, and what is hard for me, and with K. I feel the opposite. Not only that she does not understand what is hard for me, but also that what is easy for me she must disagree with, and make into battlegrounds. Less theoretically: when I finally get up whatever it takes to talk out real areas of difficulty between us—Jewish questions—she starts to tell me about visiting Arabs in the West Bank and their problems, and how she saw the article about pogroms in the West Bank. She didn't read it because it was unpleasant (to me it was an important dilemma—to her an ugliness to be Scarlett O'Hara-ed).

This is not coming across clearly at all. Maybe I should give up trying to justify our split. The only reason I feel I have to justify it at all is that you say the source is my unopenness. But you are wrong. And beyond that, I don't feel great pain at the split, because I see the problems of the relationship to be so tiring that the prospect of solving them looks harder to me than the prospect of finding someone easier. This sounds cold, I know, but I find constant struggle to be difficult.

In fact, I'm not troubled, and things are going so well in the army that I can honestly say that all is well (partly because the army has been "all"—I've been very, very busy).

I hope this doesn't sound angry or anything. I'm not. I really am in good spirits.

Alex

Ambush On the Border

[Journal]

July 31, 1987

After company test I went to Jerusalem and saw Katherine. It's too hard to write about Katherine, and I wrote what I could anyway in a letter to Harold Rhode.

Now it's Friday and we're near Kiryat Shimona near the Lebanese border waiting to go into Lebanon. We were told yesterday that something was going on, but now it looks like we won't be going inside because we have no APCs (Company 6 took them). I'm very pissed off—after all our training we, the most experienced in the battalion, sit like *tironim* on the border, while the youngsters go inside for all the interesting work. It also looks like this business will shorten or eliminate the first vacation I've had since I started writing this journal [May 27].

* * *

Now it's Sunday. On Friday I lay in ambush on the border at a spot where there is no fence at the moment. After about an hour I heard footsteps on the other side of the fence, twenty yards from the gap. I put a bullet in the chamber of my gun and looked with the ITT [night-vision device] to find the source of the step-sounds (which continued even after the noise of five soldiers chambering their weapons). My heart was beating fast and we were ready to open fire. I passed on an order left and right *not* to shoot until they heard my shouts of "fire." The tension was unbelievable. After fifteen minutes or so the sounds stopped—they must have been from a wild boar or something. Last night, after a hot, sleepless Shabbat, one day in another ambush, this time on Har Dov—beautiful, beautiful, beautiful. This ambush *inside* (Lebanon) fence.

Funny: we approach ambush spot in line, and I was not pleased with way soldiers are walking, so I stop. They're so "out" and badly (closely) spaced, that they crash into each other like dominoes. I say, "Give yourself a nice hard bang on the helmet, snap out of your stupor, and do what you know"—and they did.

Four Who Fasted

August 5, 1987
[Jerusalem]

Dear Mom and Dad,

I'm at Ruthi's/Grandma's and am amused at the contrast between this past week in the army and sitting at 1 Barak. I have a week off before we start our front-line duty somewhere on the Lebanese border.

When I look back at the training period which has passed, I'm really quite pleased. We covered many subjects and in all of them the summing-up exercise was at a high level. The big exercises—battalion and brigade—were also complex and interesting, and the work of the company in each was always pointed to as very good.

The problems I've had have mostly to do with my soldiers—I think the relationship between my soldiers and me is healthy even if its a bit closer than I would have made it had I been with them from the start. I feel they know what's important to me and that I won't compromise on certain things and that I care enough about their work to work with them on everything.

I have not completely got through to them. I can't rely on them to care about quality on their own.

In a "readiness" lineup Tal'ker, an Indian soldier of mine who we always put on the stretcher because he's as thin as a matchstick, had two bullets missing— this cost him two hours of his time off. But yesterday was *Tisha b'Av* and I fasted and so did two other kipah-wearers in the platoon, and while the rest of the company worked very hard taking down tents for the big move, I worked less hard than I usually do (I ended up drinking water because I felt weak and dried out) and I kept telling the two others who fasted to stop working and go rest in the tent. Only at the end of the day did I find out that Tal'ker, too, had fasted and worked all day without saying a word. The three of them are really good, honest, devoted soldiers.

L'hitraot,

Alex

Advice from the Platoon Commander

August 15, 1987

Jerusalem

Dear Mom,

This letter is only to you because it should arrive when Dad is here. I hope you're not lonely.

With me most is well. Problems in my platoon have passed—some I've dealt with well; others less well.

Three new soldiers in my platoon (orthodox *Hesder* soldiers) are a problem not at all solved. A couple of nights ago, after a company bonfire in which my friend Baruch was given his new rank and a bucket of coronation gook on his head, I called everyone together to talk about the transition we're about to undergo—from training for the past three months to front line for the next few. I told them that while I hoped they would all have the opportunity to do at least one "real" operation that the challenge of the next few months will be dealing with living with each other and with unchanging routine and endless patrols. I said that if they let the issue of home visits become the central topic of their lives, then the next few months would be nonstop battle and bickering and that they should keep in mind how bickering about the unchangeable only lowers morale. It's 2:00 a.m. and I must get to bed.

Love,

Alex

Close Call

[Journal]

August 16, 1987

The tents of the encampment were folded up and sent to brigade headquarters and, in general, the battalion prepared itself for the next two to three months—*kav.*

Today the officers and sergeants are going up and Tuesday the soldiers will join.

[Journal]

August 20

Besides the fort we patrol the border. Last night's shift (1:00 a.m. to 7:30) was my first. Went with three soldiers, Ami and Rotabil in back, and a driver named Gilad. Last of false alarms (but the closest call) was when I wanted to test the squad on one of the other command cars our company had sent out.

Here's the story: I told battalion headquarters that I would be doing an exercise on a secondary radio frequency. I told the sergeant, Ze'ev, that I would be testing him, and not to open fire. I made footprints reaching the fence, and told him that the footprint spot would be where he'd have to show what he knew of reacting to an incursion.

I sent him off to continue his patrol saying that he should be ready. In the meantime, I looked at the footprints I'd left, and they looked like no test for Ze'ev's Bedouin tracker, so I erased them and found a spot a km

Broken off by gunfire above me towards north.
Guard at post heard rocks slide—opened fire.

or so further north and told my medic—Ratsabi—to take off his shoes, walk barefoot (in socks) backwards to fence, and to return on same tracks. I called Ze'ev on the radio and told him there was a "touch" at 407. I waited without lights a few hundred yards north to watch. Just then a real "touch" at 412, and I was off, telling Ze'ev by radio as I went, to continue the exercise on his own.

He called to say he'd found the tracks and did the whole S.O.P., and I told him to return to searching. Five minutes later I hear him say that he'd found tracks at 407 of a man with no shoes, and he started to activate the Real Thing. I had to jump on the radio to tell him that the tracks were mine. It turns out that he did the whole S.O.P. at the tracks I'd erased. Even though I started the exercise by telling him the touch was at 407. Close call.

The Big Thing on My Mind

September 5, 1987
[On the Border]

Dear Mom,

It's been good having Saul and Dad here. About your letter—I remember you asked me to write about something, but I don't remember what, so I'll write in fragments:

1. Musa, one of our Bedouin trackers said he didn't know how to read or write. "What about Arabic?" I asked. No, not Arabic either. He says that he has trouble at public toilets where he doesn't know which is the men's room. He grew up as a shepherd and has been a tracker for eleven years (age 43!). Sometimes, we "open the path" of the border road in the morning and I open with him. Last time he started running and laughing and racing with the soldiers. He's teaching me how to track.

2. Rest stop at 2 a.m. Silence broken by gunfire not far to the north. I call the small outpost above us and ask, "Are you guys making noise?" "Not ours." I call the other patrol: "Is that yours?" "Yes, but it's OK now; it was walking on four," My worst soldier has killed a wild boar with the machine gun he was manning on the side of the command car. He'd hit it with five bullets in a straight line from hip to head.

The big thing on my mind is whether I'll be a company commander—and if yes, when and how.

I keep having inspirations about ways to do all sorts of things. I have to start writing them down. It's late now and I must sleep.

Love, Alex

Last Letter (Unfinished)

Sept. 13, 1987

[On the Border]

Dear Harold,

The day after tomorrow I'll be 25. This is a good age—the "prime of life." It is once again a time of decision for me. I have decided I would like to be a company commander. The problems are how, where, when, under what conditions. The weights on either side of the scale include: feelings of commitment to my current battalion; of anger at the deputy battalion commander who has talked to me in a way one shouldn't talk to officers, even if he is a couple ranks above me; of wanting to start sooner rather than later; of the immensity of the challenge of having a staff of over fifteen! In fact, dealing with staff is the single greatest challenge of the job—more than the marches, the trials of being judge and jury and father to soldiers, and more than the fact of being responsible for my soldiers completely.

So, I don't feel like I'm aging; the fact that I'll finish my next position at age 26 or 27 is not worrisome. I am pleased that....

This letter—unmailed—was found among Alex's personal things and returned to the family after his death.

Afterword

At 7:00 a.m. on September 16, 1987, I was downstairs in our home in Chevy Chase, Maryland, making a phone call when I heard the doorbell and my husband, Max, answer it. A few moments later, Max came down and asked me to come upstairs. I started to explain that I was busy, that my phone call was about to go through. Then—knowing something important brought Max down to me—I asked who was in the house. A delegation, he said, from the Israel embassy.

Mothers and fathers in Israel, who have heard a knock and seen a military officer at their door, fear the words that will follow. I feared and I knew: one of our sons was dead. Every parent, I'm sure, somewhere in the recesses of imagination, has rehearsed this moment, when one learns that a beloved child is gone forever. My heart pounded as I climbed the stairs. Was it Alex or Daniel? Both were officers on active duty in the Israeli army.

Three men sat in our living room: General Amos Yaron, the Israeli defense attache; his deputy; and a physician with his medical kit. General Yaron repeated what he had told Max: Alex had been killed in action near Israel's northern border the night before—on his twenty-fifth birthday. I buried my head in my knees blocking out everything. For that minute life ended. It was an instant of powerless resignation. I felt that Alex and I and all of us were in the hand of a will beyond understanding. I was not angry. I was filled with the extinguished Alex.

The moment of withdrawal ended, replaced by the necessity of telling those who loved Alex that he was gone from us. We woke our sons, Saul and Benjy (then 26 and 20), and asked them to come to the living room. I was the one who told them, I think, that their brother had been killed. Now we joined together, enclosing ourselves in the love and power of Alex. Benjy found words. "God may have wanted Alex now," he said, "maybe Alex's life was complete."

Daniel, 21, and an officer in the IDF's paratroops, had been informed about Alex's death seven hours earlier by an army representative as he was about to return to his army base. He was instructed not to phone before we were told personally by the Embassy delegation. Now we phoned Daniel. We could not speak much of feelings on the phone. We knew that Daniel was living through Alex's death as a brother, but also as a combat soldier who had led the way for Alex in the paratroops, who had experienced what it meant to patrol in Lebanon, and who had learned, as Alex had, what an officer must do under fire.

We spoke about arrangements. Daniel was acting as head of the family, taking responsibility in a characteristic way. He told us that unless we wanted Alex to be buried in the United States he would be interred at the military cemetery on Mount Herzl in Jerusalem. We decided we would leave Washington that night, Wednesday, arriving in Israel on Thursday. We set the funeral for 10:00 a.m. Friday morning. (Jewish law dictates that the dead be buried within twenty-four hours, but the period can be extended to allow the family to gather.) Daniel would speak to the newspapers to announce the funeral and serve as a liaison between the army, which was in charge of all the arrangements, and the family.

Nothing was left for us to do but to communicate the news to our family and friends. We discovered that the only way to tell them that Alex was gone was to say the words straight out and to let them fall on others as they had on us—except for Alex's grandmothers. Older people are experienced with loss, but not with the world turned so violently upside down. Such news denies one of the precious privileges of age—to escape the loss of the beloved young. Max's brother in New York City carried the news to their mother Jeanne, who only two weeks before had left Alex in Jerusalem. Jeanne and Alex recently had lived in the same building in Jerusalem— he in the room off the garden in Baka; she in the apartment upstairs. Both were artists, and they were friends in a way very rarely seen across two generations.

I phoned Alex's Grandma Gerry, my mother, in Tupper Lake, N.Y., when I knew that she and her sister Muriel would be together to support each other.

Close friends began to arrive at the house. They helped with everything, arranging the practical details—from caring for Dune, our Labrador retriever, to planning a memorial program in Washington. The Singer family discovered in those hours that we were part of a community linked by love for Alex and by the devastation his death produced. Shared embraces and tears—for the moment, far better than words—were our support and the beginning of consolation.

From these first hours, I wanted people to know that I was not angry with God or Israel or ourselves; that Alex was a blessing given to us briefly, whom we set free to find his own way. He died doing exactly what he chose to do to make the world a better place.

Late in the afternoon we left Washington for Israel. Daniel met us on the tarmac at Ben Gurion Airport. Together again, the five of us began life without Alex. On the way to our friend's apartment in Baka in Jerusalem, we saw the black-and-white notices posted by the army announcing the funeral and place of mourning.

The next day was bright and cloudless. On Mount Herzl we were surrounded by hundreds of people, some of whom had known Alex, and many others, unknown to us or to Alex, there to honor his commitment to Israel and the Jewish people. We walked among tall, wind-twisted pines behind the slowly moving open army vehicle carrying Alex's wood casket covered by the flag of Israel. A column of weeping faces followed us up the hill and climbed the steps to the newly opened grave.

The army chaplain led the brief service, reading psalms and traditional prayers. Two close friends and two commanders spoke about Alex. Then the casket was lowered into the soil of Jerusalem and, passing the shovel among us, we threw the stone-filled earth into the grave. We buried a son, a brother, a joyous and loving companion, an inspiration, a promise without bounds. We buried someone who had walked with God, whose choices had been measured by the commandment of *tikun olam b'malchut shaddai*—the Hebrew commandment to repair the world under the rule of God—and whose life, while only twenty-five years, had been marvelously full and whole. We left him on an exquisite hilltop in the country and city he loved.

The *shiva* week, the week of mourning, began. Those who knew better than we helped us to mourn in the Jewish way. Sitting on low stools during the day, the men unshaven, we experienced the rhythm of Jewish grieving. Twice each day friends and neighbors would arrive to make the minyan of ten men required to say the mourners' kaddish. Someone came forth to lead, instructions were gently given as needed. A delegation from Kibbutz Ein Tsurim—Daniel's and formerly Alex's kibbutz—made the kitchen kosher, brought dishes and food. The food kept appearing all week; people were always there to serve it at mealtimes and to clean before the end of the day. The family could ignore the matters of daily life—free to think only about Alex, to speak to those who came bearing sorrows or memories, to rest, to be turned within ourselves.

During the mourning week in Jerusalem, grieving friends and soldiers and strangers came to us, reaching out to comfort and be comforted. Alex's army commanders came, including the commander of all Israel's infantry, fulfilling one of the hardest duties of a military commander—consoling the family of a fallen soldier.

Daniel questioned the soldiers who had been with Alex on September 15 to learn every detail about the action. Knowing the army and the terrain, Daniel could ask questions of soldiers and commanders the rest of us did not know how to ask.

We learned that at dusk on the fifteenth, Alex's group of four men from the Givati Brigade were landed by helicopter with eight others onto a boulder-strewn ridge in the rugged foothills of Mount Hermon. The ridge, called the Christofani, is a mile or so from Israel's borders, within the security zone in southern Lebanon. It is patrolled by the IDF to prevent terrorist incursions across the border into Israeli settlements. A few days earlier another Israeli patrol had discovered signs on the Christofani ridge that people had passed that way. The battalion commander decided that on September 15 twelve men would take hidden positions on the ridge to surprise terrorists who might be passing over the ridge on their way to Israel. The first helicopter dropped Alex's company commander Ronen Weissman with three other men. About thirty terrorists were hidden among the rocks. Minutes after the first helicopter landed, Ronen, obscured by boulders from the rest of his men, was shot and killed. Before Alex's helicopter landed, the pilot gave him the option to land or turn back until it became safer. Alex chose to land under fire. Alex learned that Ronen was not answering the radio. Not knowing what had happened to Ronen, Alex, who was deputy commander of the action, took a medic with him and they ran forward to find and help Ronen. As Alex reached Ronen, he too was shot and killed. Now under heavy fire with both their officers dead and two soldiers wounded, the remainder of the small Israeli force held their positions, eventually following commands issued by radio from a helicopter overhead. No one could see Alex or Ronen, and their fate was unknown. The machine gunnist, Sergeant Oren Kamil, went to help them, and he became the third man killed at the same spot. The terrorists continued firing for several hours, but after Israeli reinforcements arrived they eventually retreated, leaving documents behind indicating that their target had been a settlement inside Israel. One terrorist was captured, stuck in a rock crevice. He was a 19-year-old Lebanese who had joined one of the PLO terrorist groups and had been trained by Syrian forces. He was captured with his Russian-made AK-47, perhaps the one that killed Alex, Ronen, and Oren.

In Jerusalem, during the shiva, we passed among us the three journals Alex kept while he was in the army. We looked at the drawings in the journals of places where he had stayed or guarded or rested on maneuvers and of the people he had served with. We read the entries, laughed at Alex's retelling of experiences, felt his physical and emotional pain during the difficult months of basic training, and shared his elation with the challenge of his platoon command.

Max and I, and Saul, Daniel, and Benjy began to think about sharing Alex as he had always shared whatever engaged him. We realized that in addition to his three army journals, there were hundreds of letters in boxes and files that Alex had written to us. Many other letters were written to friends and we hoped that they, too, had saved them. And we had Alex's senior thesis from Cornell, "Letters from the Diaspora," a distillation of Alex's understanding of Jewish history and his responsibility as a Jew, developed during his senior year of study and his travel in England, the Soviet Union, Spain, Italy, and Israel. The decision to exhibit Alex's art and publish his writings was taken in Jerusalem as we mourned.

Three weeks later, on October 18 in Washington, our decision to share Alex through his art and writings was reinforced. Hundreds of people gathered with us at the Israel Embassy on the *shloshim*, the thirtieth day after Alex's burial, to remember Alex and celebrate his life. General Amos Yaron and Benjamin Netanyahu, whose brother Yoni had been killed at Entebbe eleven years before, spoke for Israel. Several of Alex's friends tried to describe what he had meant to them; others read from Alex's letters and journals.

Daniel spoke then, saying that his brother had died doing exactly what an Israeli officer must do. And he spoke of the satisfaction Alex would have felt in the soldiers under his command, men he had trained. Isolated, without their officers, and under fire, they held their positions. Daniel was very proud of him.

Finally, Saul read a letter he wrote to his dead brother:

"I want to explain your life to everyone, to explain your love of life, family, Judaism, and Israel. I will do that. But the message to me of your life is much simpler than the truth and beauty of your thoughts—the thoughts that now the world will have the privilege of sharing. Your message to me is one word. 'Do.' Do as you believe and people will follow you. Do not just *know* what is right, *do* what is right. Only then will other people follow you. Only then will you have the power to affect the world.

"Somehow I believe that I will have the strength to create a tribute to you...by 'fixing the world under God' as I never could before. If I flag I will remember your strength. I will remember the example you were to your soldiers, to your brothers, and to numbers of people you would not believe."

In front of the window in my office hangs a reproduction of a medieval stained glass depicting Noah standing at the window of the ark, hand outstretched, releasing a dove. I think of Alex. Many years ago we released Alex to the world. He had been a gift in trust to us, whom we nurtured and loved and taught, but when the time came, we set him free. Now it is our task, empowered by his energy and joy, to use what he created in order to send him again into the world.

Suzanne Singer

Self-portrait by Alex at age 6.

Suzanne Singer at Alex's grave at Mt. Herzl military cemetery.

Glossary of People, Places and Hebrew Terms

. . . .

ABC Atomic, biological and chemical warfare.

Abu Tor a beautiful residential section of central Jerusalem.

Akedat Yitzhak the story in the book of Genesis of the binding of Abraham's son Isaac (for sacrifice).

Alhambra the palace of the Moorish kings in Granada, Spain.

aliyah immigration to Israel; literally, in Hebrew, the act of "going up."

Almagor a moshav (cooperative settlement) north of the Sea of Galilee.

arak a liquor of the Middle East; traditionally, a Sephardic drink.

Arava the section of desert from the southern end of the Dead Sea south to the Gulf of Eilat.

Ashkenazi the form of Hebrew spoken by Jews of central or eastern Europe and their descendants.

Ashkenazim are Jews who have lived in or are descended from Jews of central and eastern Europe; Sephardim are Jews from the Mediterranean basin as well as Jews who have lived more or less uninterruptedly in the Middle East.

BCI Brandeis-Bardin Collegiate Institute in Simi Valley, California (near Los Angeles).

Baer, Katherine met Alex at Cornell where she was one year ahead of him. Although they were only at Cornell together one year, their friendship continued through letters and occasional periods in Washington and Israel (where she visited Alex).

Balfour Declaration made by the British government in 1917, which became the basis of the League of Nations mandate of Palestine to Great Britain. It was named for one of its leading proponents, Arthur Balfour, the foreign secretary. It stated that, "His Majesty's government view with favour the establishment in Palestine of a national home for the Jewish people...."

Battalion 202 one of the active-duty battalions in the Paratroop Brigade.

Baum, Shlomo a close friend of the Singer family—a retired deputy commander of the famous crack unit from which the Israeli paratroop brigade was formed.

Beaufort a Crusader fortress in Southern Lebanon which had been occupied by the PLO for years, captured by Israeli forces on June 6, 1982.

Bedouin nomadic Arabs and their descendants.

Beit Shean a city in eastern Israel, 15 miles south of the Sea of Galilee.

Bet Sefer Nisui a public experimental high school in Jerusalem that Alex and Saul attended during 1975-76.

Bilde, Inger Johanna and her husband and children, a Danish family, had gone on many hikes with the Singers when both families lived in Jerusalem.

bimah a platform in synagogues from which the Torah is read.

Brody, Marion had been Jeanne Singer's friend since college.

casbah the market in most larger Arab cities.

Chen family, Yehuda and Michal and their four children, had "adopted" each of the Singer brothers as they came to Kibbutz Ein Tsurim; first Daniel, who was there for several months with his high school class, then Alex, and later Benjamin.

Chmielnicki, Bogdan leader of the Cossacks, conducted a brutal pogrom against Jews in the mid-1600s. He offered a choice between conversion to Christianity and death. Many Jews fled; over 100,000 and perhaps as many as 500,000 were murdered.

Druze an Arabic-speaking minority within Israel. Druze are among the few non-Jews conscripted into the IDF. They serve, typically, as border guards and scouts.

Dune the family Labrador retriever.

Epstein, Ellen a friend of the Singer family from Washington, had lived in London as a student.

Fried, Augusta (Gerry) and Maurice, Alex's maternal grandparents.

Fried, Maurice, Alex's maternal grandfather.

Furstenberg, Hillel and Rochelle Americans who had settled in Israel, good friends from when the Singers lived in Jerusalem. Hillel is a mathematician; Rochelle a journalist.

Galil an Israel-produced assault rifle.

Gaza Strip a narrow finger of land extending north a little more than twenty miles into Israel from the Egyptian border of Sinai along the Mediterranean Coast. Since the War of Independence, a large Palestinian Arab population of refugees has been concentrated there.

genizah a storage place for wornout Jewish writings that contain the name of God and, therefore, can't be destroyed. The Cairo genizah in the 11th-12th century Ben Ezra synagogue contained an immense quantity of ancient Jewish manuscripts.

Givati an Israeli infantry brigade in the 1948 War of Independence that had been disbanded and was re-established in 1984.

Golani the name of an infantry brigade in the IDF.

Hadad, Major Sa'ad the first commander of the Southern Lebanese Army. He died of cancer in January 1984.

hakafah a circling dance done with the Torah scrolls as part of the Simchat Torah service celebrating the completion of the annual reading of the Torah in the synagogue.

halachah Jewish law, which is derived from the Torah, from the Talmud (the codified oral tradition) and from rabbinic commentators. Hebrew, literally, "the way."

Hasid a member of the Hassidic movement within Judaism, which began in 18th-century Eastern Europe and whose men are usually distinguished by 18th-century clothing and long earlocks.

havdalah the brief candlelighting service that marks the end of Shabbat (from the Hebrew root meaning "to differentiate").

Herzl, Theodor (1860-1904) as a young man in Vienna, was the paradigm of an assimilated, Europeanized 19th-century Jewish intellectual. Later, facing the reality of anti-Semitism, he became the leading proponent of Zionism, "the restoration of the Jewish State...."

hesder a kind of army service in which a group of Yeshiva students serve together for three years, alternating periods of military service and religious study.

IDF Israel Defense Force. In Hebrew the acronym is *Tzahal.*

Imma and *Abba* Hebrew for mother and father.

jerrycan a narrow, flat-sided container for fuel or water with a capacity of five gallons.

Judea and Samaria the official and traditional names for the districts often referred to as the "West Bank" (of the Jordan River): Samaria is in the north; Judea in the south. These names go back to the Bible and were also used during the British Mandate.

jump school the final part of basic training in the paratroops is parachuting school at Tel Nof airbase.

kabbalat shabbat the service for greeting the Sabbath Friday evening.

kaddish the Aramaic prayer affirming God's greatness that is said at funerals and in memory of the dead.

kadima Hebrew for "go forward."

Kalachnikov a Soviet-made assault rifle, famous for its reliability in battle. The IDF captured large quantities of this weapon over the years.

kashrut the body of dietary laws prescribed for Jews.

Kaufman, Peter a friend of Alex's from Cornell, then studying at Columbia University.

kav meaning "line," refers here to duty on the Lebanese border.

Kelemen, Larry and Linda friends of Alex from BCI.

Kerak the site of Kir Hare-seth mentioned in the Bible, was fortified by the Crusaders against Moslem armies. It fell to Saladin in 1189.

Khomeini, Ruhollah the Shi'ite Muslim cleric who came to power in Iran as a result of the overthrow of the Shah in 1979; Hafez al-Assad in Syria and Saddam Hussein in Iraq came to power through military coups in 1970 and 1979, respectively; George Habash, the head of the Marxist Popular Front for the Liberation of Palestine, was associated with many acts of terror—especially airliner hijackings—in the 1970s and 1980s; Ahmed Jibral, the head of the Popular Front for the Liberation of Palestine—General Command, was associated with the bombing of the Pan Am jet over Lockerbie, Scotland.

kiddush the blessing over wine on the Sabbath or at a festival meal.

kippah skullcap worn by some Jews only when praying, by others also when eating and by some orthodox Jews all the time. (The plural is kippot.)

Kol Nidre the Jewish religious service on the eve of Yom Kippur, called by the name of its opening prayer ("All Vows"), in which Jews ask God to relieve them from promises they make to Him that they cannot keep.

LSE London School of Economics.

L'cha Dodi the traditional song greeting the "Sabbath bride," sung during Friday night service.

Learned Alex's middle name was after the eminent U.S. federal judge, Learned Hand (1872-1961).

Levites descendants of the Tribe of Levi, some of whom—called Kohen (also Cohen) are descendants of the priests who served in the Temple, assisted by the other Levites.

Machpelah cave the traditional burial place of the Biblical patriarchs and matriarchs. The building erected by King Herod on the site in Hebron is now a Jewish and Moslem holy place.

Madaba map a mosaic on the floor of a sixth-century Byzantine church in Jordan, which depicts the Holyland and neighboring regions. The most important aspect of the map is its detailed representation of Jerusalem.

Maimonides (Moses ben Maimon) the great 12th-century philosopher and codifier of Jewish law, born in Spain.

masa kumta a 55-mile march which begins at Paratroops Memorial at Tel Nof airbase and ends at the Western Wall of the Temple Mount in Jerusalem. At its end each soldier receives his red paratroop beret.

Mea Shearim an old neighborhood in Jerusalem populated by orthodox Jews.

Megillat Esther the Book of Esther, which contains the story of Purim, read at Purim.

mem peh acronym for company commander.

mem mem acronym for platoon commander.

miluim a period of active service for reserve soldiers. After completing three years of active service, Israeli men (in 1987) were required to provide up to 7 to 8 weeks a year of reserve service, as needed, until age 55.

minyan a group of at least ten male Jews, age thirteen or older, the minimum necessary for some prayers.

mitzvot the 613 positive and negative religious commandments derived from the Torah (singular is *mitzvah*). Used loosely to mean good deeds.

Morosa, Pavlik a Russian boy whom the Soviets made a martyr after he turned his father over to the authorities who hung him. Pavlik was murdered for this act by his uncle.

Mosque of Omar also known as the Dome of the Rock, stands on the Temple Mount, where Moslems believe Mohammed ascended to heaven. Jewish tradition identifies the site as Mt. Moriah, where Abraham came to sacrifice Isaac.

Motzei Shabbat Saturday, after the *havdalah* ceremony at sundown ends the Sabbath.

Mount Nebo the place from which, according to the Bible, Moses looked down over Israel into the Promised Land he was not allowed to enter.

muezzin the crier who summons Moslems to prayer from a mosque's minaret.

"Mu," Muriel Ginsberg, Alex's great-aunt, Gerry Fried's sister.

Nakash, William a French Jew accused of murdering an Arab in France.

O'Higgins, Dolores a friend from Cornell.

Osirak the nuclear reactor destroyed by the Israeli Air Force in Iraq on June 7, 1981, just before it began to make plutonium for atomic bombs.

Pesach Jewish holiday of Passover, celebrating the exodus of the Jewish people from Egypt.

Petra in Jordan, the ancient capital of the Nabateans, not occupied in recent times. The article Alex mentions is "A Plea for Bedoul Bedouin of Petra," Judith W. Shanks, *Biblical Archaeology Review*, March/April 1981.

Pickett, Neil a student at Oxford who had been a babysitter for the Singer family when they lived in Croton-on-Hudson, N.Y.

plugah an army company.

Podhoretz, Norman the editor of *Commentary* magazine. Alex's letter, about the aftermath of the massacre at the Sabra and Shatilla refugee camps, was printed in the December 1982 *Commentary.*

Prager, Dennis the author (with Joseph Telushkin) of *The Nine Questions People Ask about Judaism.* From 1976 to 1983 he directed the Brandeis-Bardin Institute (BCI).

"Profile," the overall physical and mental rating used to assign soldiers in the IDF.

protectzia the colloquial Hebrew word for influence.

Purim the Jewish festival that commemorates the deliverance of the Jews in Persia from destruction by Haman.

Qumran the site of the caves where the Dead Sea Scrolls were found.

Raful nickname of General Raphael Eitan, a former paratrooper commander and Chief of Staff. On October 29, 1956, then Col. Eitan led the first action of the Sinai Campaign, the combat drop to which Alex refers. Eitan and battalion 202 of the Parachute Brigade secured the eastern side of the Mitla Pass in the Sinai, 150 miles behind Egyptian lines.

Rhode, Harold a friend of Alex's from Washington who is a Middle East expert.

RPG, or rocket-propelled grenade, a Soviet-produced antitank weapon captured from Arabs in sufficiently large quantities by the IDF to become standard issue to paratroop and infantry units.

Salah a'Din a Kurdish fighter who expelled the Crusaders from Palestine and became the sultan of Egypt and Syria in the 12th century (1175-93).

Satmar a large Hasidic sect of ultra-orthodox Jews, which moved from the Hungarian town of Szatzmar to Brooklyn, N.Y. in 1956, and takes an uncompromisingly anti-Zionist position, refusing, on religious grounds, to recognize the State of Israel.

Shamash the beadle, or sexton, of a synagogue.

Sharansky, Natan a Jewish refusenik in the Soviet Union. After requesting an exit visa, he was arrested by the KGB for espionage, found guilty, and sent into the gulag. After nine years of imprisonment, refusing to "confess" to crimes he did not commit, he was finally released and joined his wife Avital in Israel.

Shir Hama'alot "The Song of Going Up [to Jerusalem]" (Psalm 126), is customarily sung before the grace after meals on shabbat and festivals.

shofar the ram's horn blown during Rosh Hashanah (New Year) services and at the conclusion of Yom Kippur, the Day of Atonement, the most solemn of the Jewish High Holy days.

Simon, Melvin, Alex's uncle, Linda Fried's husband.

Singer, Jeanne, Alex's paternal grandmother.

siq a narrow pass between two cliffs.

sotziomat "selfish one," a soldier who cares only for himself and does not help others.

Szold, Henriette an American Zionist, founder of Hadassah, after whom a Jerusalem elementary school was named, which Daniel and Benjy attended in 1973-77.

Talik Gen. Israel Tal, former commander of the IDF Armored Corps, responsible for designing and producing the Merkava, the IDF's main battle tank.

Taub, Daniel from England, a student at Oxford whom Alex had known at BCI.

tironim new recruits.

tironute basic training.

Tisha B'Av literally, the ninth day of the Hebrew month of Av, the day of mourning for the two destructions of the Temple in Jerusalem, and for other catastrophes in Jewish history.

toranute assignment in the army for which soldiers or units take turns—guarding, cooking, staying on base for Shabbat, etc; *toran,* soldier assigned to some kind of toranute, such as guard duty; *toranim,* plural of *toran.*

TOW the acronym for an American-produced wire-guided anti-tank missile.

Two Minutes Over Baghdad, Amos Perlmutter, Michael I. Handel and Uri Bar Joseph (London: Valentine, Mitchell & Co., 1982).

Tzahal Hebrew acronym for Israel Defense Force.

Utevskii, Lev visiting lecturer at Cornell University; senior chemist at Ben Gurion University in Beersheva, Israel; formerly underground teacher of Jewish history and religion in the Soviet Union.

VOA Voice of America, U.S. government radio station broadcasting to other countries.

wadi a bed or valley of a stream, usually dry except for brief periods during winter rains.

Waqf in Moslem law, a committee with jurisdiction over a Moslem religious site or charity.

Weiss, David visiting scholar at BCI in the summer of 1983, the head of the Department of Immunology at Hebrew University Medical School and at Hadassah Hospital in Jerusalem.

Weissman, Ronen Alex's company commander in Givati.

Wilburn, Deborah a friend from Cornell.

Wingate, Orde captain in the British Army stationed in Palestine from 1936-39, who organized Jewish auxiliary guards against Arab terrorism. He created Jewish Special Night Squads— exploiting mobility, darkness, and surprise—to render Arab raids ineffective, in the process refining the doctrine of "active defense." He became a general and was killed in World War II.

Yad Vashem the Holocaust memorial museum in Jerusalem.

Yamit a town in Northern Sinai near the border of Israel. Yamit was built by Israelis after the 1967 war with Egypt. In the 1979 peace treaty between Egypt and Israel, Israel agreed to return all of the Sinai and was, therefore, required to move out of Yamit.

yerida emigration from Israel, literally in Hebrew "going down" (the opposite of *aliyah*)

Yom Hashoah Holocaust Remembrance Day.

Yoni Yonatan Netanyahu, one of Israel's most famous soldiers. He was killed while commanding the force that rescued Jewish hostages from the Entebbe (Uganda) airport on July 4, 1976. His letters were published in *Self-Portrait of a Hero* (Random House, 1980).

Volloch, Anat Daniel's girlfriend from kibbutz Ein Tsurim, whom he married in 1988.

Alex's Family

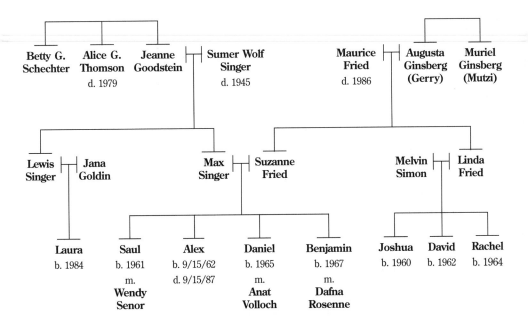

Betty G. Schechter | Alice G. Thomson d. 1979 | Jeanne Goodstein | Sumer Wolf Singer d. 1945 | Maurice Fried d. 1986 | Augusta Ginsberg (Gerry) | Muriel Ginsberg (Mutzi)

Lewis Singer | Jana Goldin | Max Singer | Suzanne Fried | Melvin Simon | Linda Fried

Laura b. 1984

Saul b. 1961 m. Wendy Senor

Alex b. 9/15/62 d. 9/15/87

Daniel b. 1965 m. Anat Volloch

Benjamin b. 1967 m. Dafna Rosenne

Joshua b. 1960

David b. 1962

Rachel b. 1964

Index